INTERNATIONAL COURTS AND TRIBUNALS SERIES

General Editors: Philippe Sands, Ruth Mackenzie, and Cesare Romano

PROVISIONAL MEASURES IN INTERNATIONAL LAW

INTERNATIONAL COURTS AND TRIBUNALS SERIES

A distinctive feature of modern international society is the increase in the number of international judicial bodies and dispute settlement and implementation control bodies; in their case-loads; and in the range and importance of the issues that they are called upon to address. These factors reflect a new stage in the delivery of international justice. The International Courts and Tribunals series has been established to encourage the publication of independent and scholarly works which address, in critical and analytical fashion, the legal and policy aspects of the functioning of international courts and tribunals, including their institutional, substantive and procedural aspects.

PROVISIONAL MEASURES IN INTERNATIONAL LAW

The International Court of Justice and the International Tribunal for the Law of the Sea

SHABTAI ROSENNE

THE PROJECT ON PICT
INTERNATIONAL COURTS AND TRIBUNALS

This series has been developed in co-operation with the Project on International Courts and Tribunals

OXFORD
UNIVERSITY PRESS

OXFORD
UNIVERSITY PRESS

Great Clarendon Street, Oxford OX2 6DP

Oxford University Press is a department of the University of Oxford.
If furthers the University's objective of excellence in research, scholarship,
and education by publishing worldwide in

Oxford New York

Auckland Cape Town Dar es Salaam Hong Kong Karachi Kuala Lumpur
Madrid Melbourne Mexico City Nairobi New Delhi Shanghai Taipei Toronto

With offices in

Argentina Austria Brazil Chile Czech Republic France Greece
Guatemala Hungary Italy Japan Poland Portugal
Singapore South Korea Switzerland Thailand Turkey Ukraine Vietnam

Published in the United States
by Oxford University Press Inc., New York

First published 2005

British Library Cataloguing in Publication Data
Data available

Library of Congress Cataloging in Publication Data

Rosenne, Shabtai.
Provisional measures in international law : the International Court of Justice
and the International Tribunal for the Law of the Sea / Shabtai Rosenne.
p. cm. – (International courts and tribunals series)
"This series has been developed in cooperation with the
Project on International Courts and Tribunals."
Includes bibliographical references and index.
ISBN 0-19-926806-1 (hard cover : alk. paper)
1. International Court of Justice. 2. International Tribunal for the Law of the Sea.
3. Provisional remedies. I. Title. II. Series.
KZ6275.R673 2005
341.5′52–dc22 2004023567

ISBN 0-19-926806-1

1 3 5 7 9 10 8 6 4 2

Typeset by Kolam Information Services Pvt. Ltd., Pondicherry, India
Printed in Great Britain on acid-free paper by Biddles Ltd., King's Lynn

To the memory of my Mentors—
Hersch Lauterpacht and Jacob Robinson

Peace be upon them

Preface

Since the establishment of the Permanent Court of International Justice in 1921, Article 41 of its Statute, on provisional or interim measures of protection, has been the subject of prolonged controversy. The language of that provision gave rise to the question of whether orders of that Court indicating provisional measures of protection created any legal obligation of compliance on the parties to whom they were addressed. It seems, on good authority, that most writers of that period were of the view that those indications were in the nature of recommendations, to be considered by their addressees in good faith, but not creating binding obligations. This controversy among the writers has continued after the establishment of the International Court of Justice as a principal organ of the United Nations. It was finally put to rest by the clear decision of the present Court in the *LaGrand* case in 2001 (ICJ Rep. 2001, 466), that an Order indicating provisional measures of protection creates binding obligations on the parties, and that non-compliance with such an Order could give rise to an instance of international responsibility.

Diplomatic practice showed some impatience with the idea that orders indicating provisional measures of protection could not be binding on the parties, and a number of treaties, both bilateral and multilateral, were concluded, even during the days of the League of Nations, providing for compliance with such orders. That diplomatic position was finally consolidated in the complicated settlement of dispute provisions of the UN Convention on the Law of the Sea of 10 December 1982 and the establishment of the International Tribunal for the Law of the Sea, with compulsory jurisdiction over requests for provisional measures in certain cases. That Convention contained a specific provision obliging its parties to comply with any provisional measures of protection prescribed by any court or tribunal having jurisdiction in accordance with that Convention.

In addition to this, both the International Court of Justice and the International Tribunal for the Law of the Sea have been faced with entirely new types of requests for provisional measures. These are bringing the whole machinery of the judicial settlement of international disputes more closely into the broader regime for the peaceful settlement of international disputes and the maintenance of international peace and security, the prime purpose of the United Nations, of which the International Court of Justice is not only a principal organ but also the principal judicial organ, and through which the international community established the International Tribunal for the Law of the Sea, itself brought into a co-operative working arrangement with the United Nations.

These are a series of radical and far-reaching changes in the standing of international tribunals, especially the two standing tribunals mentioned here, and in the mechanisms available to diplomatic processes for the settlement of disputes. In that context, judicial decisions on provisional measures of protection are beginning to assume a new position and a new importance.

This has led me to re-examine in greater detail the present position of provisional measures of protection in the context of the judicial settlement of international disputes. The former controversies of whether such measures are binding and whether they are an example of a general principle of law recognized by the nations of the world within the meaning of Article 38, paragraph 1 (c), of the Statute of the International Court of Justice have lost much if not all of their importance (except perhaps as a matter of legal theory). While this book concentrates on the present position, the historical evolution, especially between the *Alabama* arbitration of 1872 and the establishment of the League of Nations in 1919, cannot be ignored, as it is there that the germs of the institution of provisional measures are to be found.

I wish to thank the Center for Oceans Law and Policy of the University of Virginia and Martinus Nijhoff Publishers for permission to include extracts from their *United Nations Convention on the Law of the Sea: A Commentary* (1989–2002); Martinus Nijhoff Publishers for permission to include extracts from my articles originally published in their journal *Law and Practice of International Courts and Tribunals* and in different collections of essays which that House has published; and Oxford University Press for permission to use extracts from my article in *State, Sovereignty and International Governance*, edited by Gerard Kreijen (2000).

I owe a special debt of gratitude to the Registrars of the International Court of Justice and of the International Tribunal for the Law of the Sea for helping to keep me supplied with relevant materials. Professor Myron Nordquist of the University of Virginia assisted me in obtaining some obscure documents of the United States Senate relating to the Bryan Treaties. Dr Cesare Romano of New York University and one of the managers of the Project on International Courts and Tribunals gave me valuable assistance regarding the activities of the short-lived and controversial Central American Court of Justice, the first international tribunal to exercise its power to order provisional measures. Dr Chester Brown of St John's College, Cambridge, unearthed for me the details of the discussions in the Institute of International Law in 1871, when the first code of international arbitration procedure was drawn up. I have also had the advantage of being able to use the manuscript of Dr Silvina S. González Napolitano of the University of Buenos Aires, *Las Medidas provisionales en derecho internacional ante las Cortes y Tribunales internacionales* (2002), a work crowned with the Rolin–Jaequemyns Prize of the Institute of International Law in 2003. Finally, I wish to thank John Louth and all his colleagues at Oxford University Press for seeing this book through the press.

This manuscript was completed on 30 April 2004.

Sh. R.
Jerusalem 2004

Contents

Abbreviations and Note on Documentation

adv. op.	advisory opinion
AJIL	American Journal of International Law
BYIL	British Year Book of International Law
CTS	Consolidated Treaty Series
GAOR	General Assembly Official Records
ICSID	International Centre for the Settlement of Investment Disputes
ILR	International Law Reports
Law and Practice	Sh. Rosenne, *Law and Practice of the International Court, 1920–1996* (The Hague: Martinus Nijhoff, 1997)
LNTS	League of Nations Treaty Series
Recueil	Academy of International Law, *Recueil des Cours/ Collected Courses*
SCOR	Security Council Official Records
UNCIO	United Nations Conference on International Organization (The San Francisco Conference, 1945)
UNRIAA	United Nations *Reports of International Arbitral Awards*
UNTS	United Nations Treaty Series
YBILC	Yearbook of the International Law Commission

As far as possible documents of international organizations, of the International Court of Justice, and the International Tribunal for the Law of the Sea, are taken from their official publications. However, many documents and cases are not yet available in printed form. These have been taken from their respective websites and are indicated in this book by their dates and, if relevant, their case numbers. Published arbitral awards are taken from the United Nations *Reports of International Arbitral Awards* or from the International Law Reports. Some unpublished awards have been taken from the website of the Permanent Court of Arbitration. The most commonly used websites are as follows:

United Nations: www.un.org (in all the official languages of the UN)
International Court of Justice (including all the publications of the Permanent Court of International Justice): www.icj-cij.org, also available through the UN website
International Tribunal for the Law of the Sea: www.itlos.org (English), www.tidm.org (French), also available through the UN website
Permanent Court of Arbitration: www.pca-cpa.org

The International Seabed Authority has published in three CD-ROM discs all the records of the Law of the Sea Conferences 1968–94 as follows: Disc 1: Peaceful Uses of the Seabed and the Ocean Floor beyond the Limits of National Jurisdiction (1968–73); Disc 2: Third United Nations Conference on the Law of the Sea (1973–82); Disc 3: Preparatory Commission for the International Seabed Authority and for the International Tribunal for the Law of the Sea (1983–94).

Table of Cases

(All cases are from the PCIJ or the ICJ except where otherwise indicated)

Part I

Origins: Basic Texts

1

Introducing the Topic

1.1. WHAT ARE PROVISIONAL MEASURES OF PROTECTION?

It is a commonplace that when a dispute is submitted to a court or tribunal for judicial decision, the rights and duties of the parties to that dispute are in principle determined by reference to the situation that existed at the date on which the proceedings were instituted.[1] As the Permanent Court of International Justice has stated, there is a principle universally accepted by international tribunals and also laid down in many conventions to the effect that the parties to a case must abstain from any measure capable of exercising a prejudicial effect in regard to the execution of the decision to be given, and in general not allow any step of any kind to be taken which might aggravate or extend the dispute.[2] Normally nothing that occurs after that date will be considered, except where subsequent events render the case moot, deprived of practical significance.[3] The International Court has put it in the following way in the *Passage through the Great Belt* case: 'no action taken *pendente lite* by a State engaged in litigation before the Court with another State "can have any effect whatsoever as regards the legal situation which the Court is called upon to define".'[4] From that it follows that technically, nothing that either party might do while the judicial proceedings are in progress would bring that party advantage or adversely affect the rights of the other party in relation to the object of the dispute, but it might make it difficult if not impossible for the court or tribunal to render an effective decision. In that respect, the institution of proceedings is itself a 'measure of protection' which preserves the rights of each party vis-à-vis the other, pending the settlement of the dispute, that is pending the definitive decision in the case. The premise

[1] The expression 'court or tribunal' is taken from Part XV of the UN Convention on the Law of the Sea of 1982 (1833 UNTS 3), the two terms being used indiscriminately in the statutes of present-day international judicial organs. There are other standing courts or tribunals under specific treaties for limited purposes. We are not concerned with those courts and tribunals in this book. For a broad conspectus, *see* Y. Shany, *The Competing Jurisdictions of International Courts and Tribunals* (Oxford: Oxford University Press, 2003).

[2] *Electricity Company of Sofia and Bulgaria* (Interim Measures) case, PCIJ Ser. A/B 79 (1939) at 199.

[3] For examples, *see* the *Nuclear Tests* cases, ICJ Rep. 1974, 253, 457.

[4] *Passage through the Great Belt* (Provisional Measures) case, ICJ Rep. 1991, 12, 19 (para. 32), citing and adapting a passage from the Judgment of the Permanent Court in the *Legal Status of the South-Eastern Territory of Greenland* (Provisional Measures) case, PCIJ Ser. A/B 48 (1932) at 287.

is that the object of the litigation will be protected and maintained in its state as it existed on the initiation of the proceedings, and that neither party will wilfully either destroy it or tamper with any relevant evidence pending the determination of the case.

The law-applying organ may also have an interest in having the possibility of requiring provisional measure available to it in the performance of its functions. This has been expressed in the following terms:

> In modern law the primary function of provisional and protective measures is to preserve the integrity of the final judgment, but there are historical grounds for seeing their origin in the desire of those administering the law to prevent violent self-help, as in some of the interdicts of Roman law, and the sequestration of the Middle Ages . . . [5]

That succinctly summarizes the nature and the purpose of the concept of provisional measures of protection in the modern law of international judicial proceedings, whether before a standing court or tribunal or before an ad hoc arbitration tribunal. It is an essential instrument to enable any international court or tribunal to perform its functions.

Experience in domestic litigation shows that the position of principle arising from the institution and persistence of legal proceedings is not always adequate to protect the principle, and that circumstances can occur making it necessary for the court or tribunal seised of the dispute to take action to ensure the conservation of the object of the dispute, whether that object is something concrete or something less precise such as a 'right' that is being claimed, and sometimes the protection of the evidence, if that court or tribunal is to render a meaningful decision that can be implemented. The internal courts of many States have faced this problem and have developed interlocutory procedures for dealing with it, the most notable being the interim injunction, explained as 'to preserve the *status quo* until the relevant facts can be ascertained'.[6] However, here, as in many other respects, the analogy of internal litigation within the States, which is compulsory in that the respondent, whether a natural or a juridical person, has no choice but to accept the institution of the proceedings against that person and comply with the decision, cannot be carried too far in international litigation where that compulsory element does not exist and all contentious international litigation is based on the consent of the parties to the dispute. The most that domestic experience and precedents can do is to point to the existence of the problem, and perhaps suggest the direction in which possible solutions might be found.

It is equally a matter of common knowledge and is not contested that under current international law the jurisdiction of every international court or tribunal empowered to decide a dispute between States is based on the

[5] L. Collins, 'Provisional and Protective Measures in International Litigation', 234 *Recueil* 9, 23 (1992–II) (footnote omitted).

[6] D.M. Walker, *The Oxford Companion to Law* 618 (Oxford: Clarendon Press, 1989).

consent *ad litem* of the States that are parties to that dispute and which should be parties to the litigation, in whatever capacity they are parties to that case (with the exception of what is known as the 'non-party intervener'). At the same time, the constituent instrument of all existing standing courts and tribunals gives the competent court or tribunal power to take necessary decisions for the conduct of the case. In the present state of the organization of the international judicial system that refers to the following courts and tribunals: (1) International Court of Justice (ICJ), a principal organ of the United Nations (Charter, Articles 7 and 92) and its principal judicial organ; (2) the International Tribunal for the Law of the Sea (ITLOS) established by Article 297 and Annex VI of the United Nations Convention on the Law of the Sea of 10 December 1982, and (3) the Seabed Disputes Chamber (of ITLOS) established by Article 190 and Annex VI, Article 14, of that Convention with limited jurisdiction in connection with activities in the international seabed Area instituted by that Convention, and the other courts or tribunals having jurisdiction under Article 297.

The practice of the International Court of Justice, followed in this respect by the International Tribunal for the Law of the Sea, is to enunciate its decision on provisional measures in the form of an order. Article 48 of the Statute of the ICJ and Annex VI, Article 27, of the Convention on the Law of the Sea empower each to make orders for the conduct of the case. In both those judicial organs, orders regarding provisional measures (like all their other orders) are composed in the French style. That consists in a series of introductory paragraphs usually commencing in English with a word such as *Considering*, to indicate the nature of the proceedings and the provisions of the Statute and of the Rules of Court or Tribunal, as necessary, relied on as the basis for the action taken, and ending with semicolons. That is followed by a series of preambles, usually commencing with the word *Whereas*, used to introduce a recital of facts (including a summary of the parties' contentions in fact and in law and the conclusions on those arguments of the court or tribunal), and ending with the operative clause (*dispositif*) introduced by the verb *indicates* (in the ICJ) and *prescribes* (in ITLOS), followed by the action required of the parties formulated in executory terms or dismissing the request. However, it is not essential that an order should be composed in this way, which is inclined to be elliptical and not always easy to follow, and arbitral tribunals sometimes couch their orders in a narrative form, similar to the formulation of an international judgment or arbitral award. In both the ICJ and ITLOS, and probably in most arbitral tribunals, a judge or arbitrator who does not agree in whole or in part with the interlocutory decision may append a separate or dissenting opinion, but of course the decision is binding on that judge or arbitrator for the future phases of the case.

This book concentrates on the law, practice, and procedure of the International Court of Justice and the International Tribunal for the Law of the

Sea (including the Seabed Disputes Chamber). These are the only standing judicial bodies existing at present with virtually universal jurisdiction, although in the case of the Tribunal that jurisdiction is in principle limited to States parties to the United Nations Convention on the Law of the Sea of 1982 and for the Seabed Disputes Chamber is extended to private persons engaged in activities in the international seabed Area with some connection with the International Seabed Authority and the Enterprise under Annexes III and IV of the Convention. There are other standing courts and tribunals empowered to order provisional measures for cases coming within the scope of their limited jurisdiction. These are courts and tribunals operating within the framework of a regional organization of economic integration, and regional human rights courts. The setting in which those courts and tribunals function is different from that of the universal courts and tribunals, and it would unduly complicate this book, and divert it from its primary purpose, to discuss them in any detail, although the practising international lawyer will certainly be aware of their existence and activities and refer to them when necessary.

The leading example today of a standing court operating within the framework of a regional organization of economic integration is the European Court of Justice (the Luxembourg Court). Article 203 (formerly 186) of the Treaty on the European Economic Union provides shortly and pithily: 'The Court of Justice may in any case before it prescribe any necessary interim measures.'[7] Other courts and tribunals falling into this category include the new Central American Court of Justice of the Central American Integration System.[8] Article 31 of its Statute provides:

> The Court shall be authorized to prescribe pretrial or protective measures which it considers advisable to safeguard the rights of the parties from the moment that a claim is made against one or more states, organs or organisms of the Central American Integration System until a definitive verdict is issued. This authority shall permit the Court to stabilize the situation in which the contending parties are to remain, so as not to aggravate the harm and so as to maintain matters in the same state pending resolution.

In the MERCOSUR (common market between Argentina, Brazil, and Uruguay), the Protocol of Brasilia for the settlement of disputes prefers a system of arbitration.[9] Article 18 of that Protocol provides:

[7] For the consolidated version of the Treaty, *see* the *Official Journal of the European Union*, No. C 325, 24 December 2002.

[8] 552 UNTS 15; K. Oellers-Frahm and A. Zimmerman (eds.), *Dispute Settlement in Public International Law*, 2nd edn, vol. I, 242 (Berlin: Springer, 2001). Website: www.cij.org.ni[.] That Court prescribed protective measures on 12 January 2000 in the case of *Honduras* v *Nicaragua*. Nicaragua brought part of that dispute before the International Court of Justice as the *Maritime Delimitation between Nicaragua and Honduras in the Caribbean Sea* case, filed on 8 December 1999 and now ready for hearing.

[9] Oellers-Frahm and Zimmerman, op. cit. in n. 8, vol. I, 956.

1) Upon request of the party concerned, and if there is good cause to believe that a continuation of the existing situation will produce serious and irreparable damage to one of the parties, the Arbitral Tribunal may order such interim measures as it deems necessary or desirable, to prevent an aggravation of the situation.
2) The parties shall comply immediately, or within the delay established by the Arbitral Tribunal, with all interim measures, until an Award is entered...

Likewise, of the principal human rights courts, Rule 39 of the Rules of Court of the European Court of Human Rights provides:[10]

1. The Chamber or, where appropriate, its President may, at the request of a party or of any other person concerned, or of its own motion, indicate to the parties any interim measure which it considers should be adopted in the interests of the parties or of the proper conduct of the proceedings before it.
2. Notice of these measures shall be given to the Committee of Ministers.
3. The Chamber may request information from the parties on any matter connected with the implementation of any interim measure it has indicated.

Similarly, Article 63, paragraph 2, of the American Convention on Human Rights[11] empowers the American Court of Human Rights

in cases of extreme gravity and urgency, and when necessary to avoid irreparable damage to persons, the Court shall adopt such provisional measures as it deems pertinent in matters it has under consideration. With respect to a case not yet submitted to the Court, it may act at the request of the [Inter-American] Commission [on Human Rights].

However, both the dispute settlement procedures in regional organs of economic integration and the regional human rights courts are *sui generis* and their actions are heavily influenced by their regional *ambiance*. They require separate treatment of their practices and procedures, and caution is required before adopting their precedents for universalist courts and tribunals.[12] They illustrate how every international court or tribunal requires a specific provision in its constituent instrument to empower it to order provisional measures.

International disputes that are submitted to judicial settlement or arbitration can be said to fall into two principal categories. One includes a dispute arising out of a single incident, usually a case of State responsibility originating in the actions of one or both of the States concerned. The dispute is over its consequences in terms of a duty, if any, on either of the States concerned

[10] Ibid. 456, 468.
[11] Ibid. 522, 531, 567.
[12] The decisions of the International Court of Justice on the capital punishment cases (*see* § 8.5) furnish interesting examples of this. The issue of the interpretation of the relevant provision of the Vienna Convention on Consular Relations had arisen in the same context in an advisory opinion delivered by the Inter-American Court of Human Rights. The International Court of Justice made no mention of that advisory opinion in any of its orders or judgments in the parallel cases brought before it. For criticism of that advisory opinion, *see* Sh. Rosenne, *The Perplexities of Modern International Law* 103 (Leiden: Martinus Nijhoff, 2004).

to make appropriate reparation for the internationally wrongful act. The second category is more complex. It relates to a dispute which has continued for a period of time, sometimes even a long period of time, accompanied with incidents, including the use of armed force by one or both parties and intended to influence the future development of the dispute. It was in connection with that type of dispute, especially in Central America around the turn of the nineteenth century, that the question of provisional measures first came into prominence. In those cases the immediate tension was relieved (but not completely negatived) by the agreement of the parties concerned to submit the dispute to arbitration—indeed the former Central American Court of Justice (*see* § 1.4) was established with this type of dispute in mind.

Provisional measures might be required in both types of case, for instance to ensure the preservation of the object of the dispute or the protection of relevant evidence if there is a risk that it may be damaged or destroyed or if the court or tribunal should feel that its ability to render a meaningful decision is otherwise hampered. But it is in the second category of case—which today may also simultaneously be on the agenda of a political organ such as the General Assembly or the Security Council of the United Nations if it should constitute or come to constitute a threat to the maintenance of international peace and security—that the need for provisional measures of protection is the greater. What is involved is not only the preservation of the object of the dispute or of the relevant evidence, but also the prevention of the use of force in violation of the Charter of the United Nations or of any aggravation or extension of the dispute and of risk to human life. This broader approach to the requirement for provisional measures of protection is on the whole the outcome of the Charter and of the establishment of the International Court of Justice as a principal organ of the United Nations, and as such impelled by the principles and purposes of the United Nations alongside its function set out in Article 38 of the Statute (an addition made in 1945), to decide in accordance with international law such disputes as are submitted to it. However, it is impossible, and would be unwise, to attempt to lay down any hard and fast principles about this. The cases entered in the List of the International Court of Justice as the *Questions of Interpretation and Application of the 1971 Montreal Convention arising from the Aerial Incident at Lockerbie* cases furnish a striking example.[13]

[13] Those two cases were instituted by Libya in 1992 against the United Kingdom and the United States of America. They led to the following judicial pronouncements: Orders on provisional measures, ICJ Rep. 1992, 3, 114; Judgments on preliminary objections, ICJ Rep. 1998, 9, 115; Orders on discontinuance with prejudice, ICJ Rep. 2003, 149, 152. For the 1971 Montreal Convention for the Suppression of Unlawful Acts against the Safety of Civil Aviation *see* 974 UNTS 177.

1.2. PROVISIONAL MEASURES AS A FEATURE OF INCIDENTAL JURISDICTION

The power of an international court or tribunal to order provisional measures of protection is commonly understood as coming within the scope of its 'incidental jurisdiction'.[14] 'Incidental jurisdiction' is a term with no precise legal meaning in international law. It implies that a court or tribunal regularly seised of a case, and provided that it has prima facie jurisdiction over the merits, can take all necessary decisions for the conduct of the proceedings or the conduct of the parties in relation to the subject-matter of the dispute pending the final decision, provided that it remains within its jurisdiction both *ratione personae* and *ratione materiae*. A Chamber of the ICJ has put it in the following positive and negative terms:

> Incidental proceedings by definition must be those which are incidental to a case which is already before the Court or Chamber. An incidental proceeding cannot be one which transforms the case into a different case with different parties.[15]

The main characteristic of incidental proceedings is that, except where the decision is in the form of a judgment deciding with the force of *res judicata* whatever issue is decided in that phase, the decisions are usually rendered in the form of an order (except decisions on preliminary objections to the jurisdiction or to the admissibility which are usually in the form of a judgment). Such a decision, howsoever it may be formulated or expressed, is in principle compelling at least for the duration of the case, both for the parties and for the court or tribunal (including members who did not agree with it), but it does not constitute the final disposal of the principal case: it is simply a decision on the procedural or incidental issue that gave rise to the incidental proceedings, expressed in formal terms, and without prejudice to either side's position on the merits of the case or to the final position to be adopted by the court or tribunal. The exercise of this incidental jurisdiction is not dependent on the specific consent of the parties. A State's consent to the existence and functioning of the court or tribunal and to the exercise by that court or tribunal of the principal jurisdiction to decide the particular dispute carries with it its consent to the exercise of any incidental jurisdiction for which the constituent instrument of the court or tribunal makes provision, should this

[14] Hudson suggests that incidental jurisdiction includes a request for interpretation as well as proceedings in revision. M.O. Hudson, *The Permanent Court of International Justice 1920–1942: A Treatise* 408 (New York: MacMillan, 1943). When that was written there was no experience of either procedure in the Permanent Court. The practice of the present Court is to treat those proceedings as new cases, even when the request for revision refers to an interlocutory judgment. *Request for the Interpretation of the Judgment of 11 June 1998 in the Case concerning the* Land and Maritime Boundary between Cameroon and Nigeria, Preliminary Objections, ICJ Rep. 1999 (I), 31.

[15] *Land, Island and Maritime Frontier Dispute* (Application to Intervene), Judgment, ICJ Rep. 1990, 92, 134 (para. 98).

become necessary for the conduct of the case, provided that the State can produce an acceptable argument for the jurisdiction or competence of that court or tribunal over the merits of its claim.

The implication of the term *incidental* is firstly that the court of tribunal must have been duly seised of the case that is still pending, and secondly that there must be a connection between the subject-matter for which provisional measures are requested and the claims in the principal proceedings. The existence of a 'case' before the court or tribunal is established by the fact that a valid document has been filed instituting the proceedings. The Statute and the Rules of the ICJ together with accumulated judicial experience establish the connection that has to exist between the subject-matter of that claim and the specific conduct that is being requested as a provisional measure, and that has been taken over into the relevant provisions of the Convention on the Law of the Sea. Whatever is being claimed by the parties with their own interests in mind, the Court has to be careful to protect the rights of both parties, the nature of those rights being identified by the original claim and the subsequent pleadings in the case to the date of the decision on the request for provisional measures.

Although there may be differences of opinion over what is included within the scope of this incidental jurisdiction, which nowadays is frequently addressed in the constituent instrument of the court or tribunal, there is no controversy over the inclusion within the concept of decisions on provisional or interim measures to protect the rights of the parties *pendente lite* if the constituent instrument empowers the judicial or arbitral organ to make such a decision.[16] Any such decision is without prejudice to the final decision of the court or tribunal, including a decision on its jurisdiction or on the admissibility of the case. It is sometimes suggested that this jurisdiction is inherent in the nature of a court or tribunal.[17] However, it is not necessary to pursue that aspect here, since the constituent instruments of all the courts and tribunals to be considered in this book empower the judicial organ to make such decisions.

The existence of incidental jurisdiction to indicate or prescribe provisional measures in this sense is now a firmly established feature of the modern law of the judicial settlement of international disputes through a competent organ,

[16] As a matter of English terminology, early usage referred to *interim measures of protection*. Current usage seems to prefer *provisional measures of protection*. French terminology is stable—*mesures conservatoires*. The current French dictionary of international law gives the following definition: '*Disposition à caractère obligatoire* ordonnée par une autorité avant qu'elle ne rende sa décision sur le fond et qui, sans préjuger de cette dernière, a pour but d'éviter que la décision au fond soit privée de son efficacité. Le plus souvent il s'agit de régler momentanément une situation urgente en attendant une décision définitive.' J. Salmon (ed.), *Dictionnaire de droit international public* 701 (Brussels: Bruylant, 2001).

[17] Sir Gerald Fitzmaurice, individual opinion in the *Northern Cameroons* case, ICJ Rep. 1963, 3, 103.

the Statute of the Permanent Court of International Justice and now of the International Court of Justice setting the lead. It follows from this that the failure of a party to bring its conduct into line with what the court or tribunal requires as an interim measure is an internationally wrongful act within current concepts of international responsibility. The International Law Commission has defined an internationally wrongful act as conduct consisting of an action or omission (*a*) attributable to State under international law; and (*b*) constituting a breach of an international obligation of the State.[18] A binding decision of a court or tribunal ordering provisional measures of protection now comes within that definition (*see* § 2.5).

That was not always so. The idea that an international tribunal could in any way order provisional measures of protection in any form was not found in the arbitration proceedings common in the nineteenth century. In fact, like much else that is generally accepted in modern international litigation procedure, the full integration of this concept in the procedures for the judicial settlement of international disputes was really only made possible through the institution of a permanent international court in the Permanent Court of International Justice, established in 1920 and active in the inter-war period. Its early experience was hesitant, and in fact it is only with the lengthy and quite variative experience of the current International Court of Justice, coupled with an important political innovation confirming the binding nature of such an order introduced by the Third United Nations Conference on the Law of the Sea, that it has become possible to perceive the far-reaching implications that this procedure may come to have, not merely for the judicial settlement of international disputes but for their peaceful settlement more generally.

A judicial decision, whether in a judgment or in an order, directing either or both of the parties to observe a certain line of conduct pending final determination of the case is in a special position. If the decision is binding on the parties, meaning that they are under a legal obligation to conduct themselves in accordance with its terms so long as the case is pending and the decision requiring such conduct is outstanding, it may have an effect that goes beyond the time that the case is pending before the court or tribunal, or it may by implication have an effect while it is in

[18] International Law Commission, Draft Articles on the Responsibility of States for Internationally Wrongful Acts, Art. 2, Report of the International Law Commission on the work of its fifty-third session, UN, GAOR 56th session, Sup. No. 10 (A/56/10), chapter IV (2001); reproduced in J. Crawford, *The International Law Commission's Articles on State Responsibility: Introduction, Text and Commentaries* (Cambridge: Cambridge University Press, 2002). Crawford was the last of the Special Rapporteurs of the International Law Commission on the topic of State Responsibility. Nevertheless, if that non-performance comes within current concepts of the international responsibility of States, it would seem to follow that what those draft articles designate as 'circumstances precluding wrongfulness' (Arts. 20 to 27) would also be applicable in appropriate circumstances.

force extending beyond the parties to the case. As we shall see (Chapter 6 note 19 below), there is at least one instance of this. This is not to say that a decision calling for provisional measures is the equivalent of an interim judgment, something not encountered in international litigation unless the constituent instrument of the court or tribunal or the agreement to submit a dispute to litigation provides for it. It is not the equivalent of a final judgment if only for the reason that it is not final and without appeal, but as will be seen is subject to a built-in *rebus sic stantibus* condition, which is not the case for a final decision, nor does it come within the scope of Article 94, paragraph 2, of the Charter providing for recourse to the Security Council in the event of non-compliance with a judgment. But it does set this type of decision apart from most interlocutory and incidental decisions that an *international* court or tribunal can make, since it is now clear that it refers in terms of binding obligation to the State's conduct vis-à-vis the other parties in the litigation, and not merely to the conduct of the case. For this reason it may require the court or tribunal to take a closer look at the relation between the provisional measures requested and the claim of the party making the request, its jurisdiction to deal with that request, and the anticipated decision on the merits of the case, than has hitherto been the practice.

1.3. THE BEGINNINGS

One of the features of the development of international law in the nineteenth century has been the increasing use of arbitration procedures, culminating in the *Alabama* arbitration of 1881–82 between the United Kingdom and the United States.[19] That led the Institute of International Law, founded in 1873, to examine the topic of arbitral procedure as one of its first projects. Professor L. Goldschmidt of Leipzig was appointed rapporteur.[20] In the subsequent discussion the Dutch jurist T. M. C. Asser proposed adding a sentence reading: 'Le tribunal arbitral peut rendre des jugements interlocutoires ou préparatoires.' But Asser did not explain on the record what he had in mind or what those interlocutory or preparatory judgments could encompass, and there is no account of any discussion of that proposal. Nevertheless the

[19] For that arbitration, *see* J.B. Moore, I *History and Digest of the International Arbitrations to which the United States Has Been a Party* 653 (Washington DC: Government Printing Office, 1898); 61 *British and Foreign State Papers* 40 (1871); A.M. Stuyt, *Survey of International Arbitrations 1794–1989* 96 (Dordrecht: Martinus Nijhoff, 1972).

[20] 'Projet de règlement pour tribunaux arbitraux internationaux présenté à l'Institut de Droit international (Session de Genève, 1874)' 6 *Revue de Droit international et de Législation comparée* 421 (1874).

proposal was accepted and is included in the final text of Article 19 of the *Projet de règlement pour la procédure arbitrale internationale* adopted by the Institute on 28 August 1875.[21]

An authoritative commentary on that paragraph explains that thanks to the last sentence of Article 19, the arbitral tribunal will have the right to lay down a provisional measure, such as the sequestration of contested territory or of captured ships or goods when difficulties have arisen over their capture.[22] This suggests that in academic circles at least there was interest in introducing the concept of provisional measures to protect the rights of the parties. It is also believed that the first use of the verb *prescrire* to describe the nature of an interlocutory decision on provisional measures was in that passage of Mérignac's book.

1.4. ARBITRATION: THE HAGUE CONFERENCES OF 1899 AND 1907 AND LATER ARBITRATIONS

Asser was a prominent member of the Dutch delegation at the Hague Peace Conference of 1899. He was active in the work of the Third Commission, which was responsible for the preparation of the Convention for the Pacific Settlement of International Disputes, containing the first internationally agreed code of arbitral procedure. However, on the record there is no direct mention of provisional measures. Article 21 of the Russian draft of an arbitral code proposed: 'Every decision, whether final or interlocutory, is taken by a majority of the members present.' There is no explanation on the record of what was intended by the words 'whether final or interlocutory'. The Committee of Examination proposed deleting them, but again there is no explanation for this on the record.[23] Accordingly, Article 51 of the Convention of 1899 read simply: that 'Every decision is taken by a majority of members of the Tribunal.' There were no comments on Article 51 at the 1907 Conference when it was adopted as Article 78 of the Convention of 1907 in the same

[21] For text of the final resolution, *see* 1 *Annuaire de l'Institut de Droit international* 126 (1877), reproduced in H. Wehberg (ed.), *Tableau général des Résolutions de l'Institut de Droit international* 147 (Basel: Editions juridiques et sociologiques, 1952). For Asser's amendment, *see* 'Procès-verbal de la session de Genève: Procès-verbal No. 1, Séance du 31 août 1874', previous note, 583, 588.

[22] A. Mérignac, *Traité théorique et pratique de l'arbitrage international: Le rôle du droit dans le fonctionnement actuel de l'institution et dans ses destinées futures* 275 (Paris: Larose, 1895). In the original: 'Il aura également le droit de prescrire une mesure provisoire, telle que la mise sous séquestre d'un territoire litigieux, ou de navires et marchandises capturés et sur la saisie desquels une difficulté s'élève' (footnote omitted).

[23] The Proceedings of the Hague Peace Conferences, Translation of the Official Texts under the supervision of J.B. Scott, *The Conference of 1899*, 803 (New York: Oxford University Press, 1920).

form.[24] There is no known case heard under the provisions of either of those Conventions in which a question of provisional measures was raised.

In 1949 the newly formed International Law Commission selected arbitral procedure as one of the topics for codification, and appointed the French Professor Georges Scelle as special rapporteur. In the draft convention submitted by the Commission in 1953, Article 17 used the word *prescribe* in this context, and a Comment explained that the word implied an obligation on the parties to take the measures prescribed.[25] In 1958, after its draft convention on the topic had not been accepted by the General Assembly, the Commission prepared a set of model rules on arbitral procedure. That led the General Assembly to adopt resolution 1262 (XIII), 14 November 1958, bringing those draft rules to the attention of Governments for their consideration and use. Article 20 of those Model Rules followed Article 41 of the Statute of the ICJ, and provided that any arbitral tribunal or, in case of urgency its president subject to confirmation by the tribunal, shall have the power to indicate, if it considers that the circumstances so require, any provisional measures which ought to be taken to preserve the respective rights of the parties. There is no reported use of those model rules.

The Optional Rules for Arbitrating Disputes between two States, adopted by the Administrative Council of the Permanent Court of Arbitration in 1992 as part of its process of modernizing the arbitration provisions of the 1907 Convention, clarified the position.[26] By Article 26:

Interim Measures of Protection	Mesures provisoires ou conservatoires
1. Unless the parties otherwise agree, the arbitral tribunal may, at the request of either party, take any interim measures it deems necessary to preserve the respective rights of either party.	1. A moins que les parties n'en conviennent autrement, le tribunal arbitral, à la demande de l'une ou de l'autre partie, peut prendre toutes mesures provisoires qu'il juge nécessaires pour la protection des droits de chacune des parties.

[24] The Proceedings of the Hague Peace Conferences, Translation of the Official Texts under the supervision of J.B. Scott, *The Conference of 1907*, vol. II, 588 (New York: Oxford University Press, 1921).

[25] Report of the Commission on the work of its fourth session (A/2163), Comment on Art. 17. *See* YBILC 1953, vol. II (A/2456), Ch. II, 200. This was changed to 'indicate' in the model rules of 1958 (next note), without comment. These draft articles are conveniently reproduced in A. Watts, *The International Law Commission 1949–1998*, vol. III, 1778 (Oxford: Oxford University Press, 1999). A Commentary prepared by the Secretariat on Art. 17 of the earlier draft convention is purely historical and avoids all controversy of the nature of the measures prescribed. *Commentary on the Draft Convention on Arbitral Procedure adopted by the International Law Commission at its Fifth Session, prepared by the Secretariat* (A/CN.4/92) 72 (New York: United Nations, 1955).

[26] Permanent Court of Arbitration, *Basic Documents: Conventions, Rules, Model Clauses and Guidelines* 41, 58 (The Hague, 1998)/Cour permanente d'Arbitrage, *Documents de base; Conventions, Règlements, Clauses Types et Directives* 41, 58 (The Hague, 1988) (separate editions in English and French). An equivalent provision is found in the other sets of Optional Rules adopted around the same time.

2. Such interim measures may be established in the form of an interim award. The arbitral tribunal shall be entitled to require security for the costs of such measures.

3. A request for interim measures addressed by any party to a judicial authority shall not be deemed incompatible with the agreement to arbitrate, or as a waiver of that agreement.

2. Ces mesures provisoires peuvent être prises sous la forme d'une sentence provisoire. Le tribunal arbitral peut exiger un cautionnement au titre des frais occasionnés par ces mesures.

3. Une demande de mesures provisoires adressée par l'une ou l'autre partie à une autorité judiciaire ne doit pas être considérée comme incompatible avec la convention d'arbitrage ni comme une renonciation au droit de se prévaloir de ladite convention.

The relevant set of optional rules, now frequently adopted in arbitration proceedings with or without modification, supplies a ready-made set of rules that can be used if necessary before an arbitral tribunal has finally settled its rules of procedure. Likewise, Article 26 of the popular United Nations Commission on International Trade Law Arbitration Rules (designed primarily for commercial arbitrations) permits an arbitral tribunal to take any interim measures it deems necessary in respect of the subject-matter of the dispute.[27] That provision also formulates the principle that a request for interim measures shall not be deemed incompatible with the agreement to arbitrate, or as a waiver of that agreement. It would depend on the constituent instrument of the arbitral tribunal or commission whether it is empowered to issue such decisions, and to what extent the parties would be bound by them.

The 1907 Conference also adopted a draft convention for a court of arbitral justice, but was unable to complete this work primarily because of difficulties in the composition of the court and its constitution. By Article 22, the court was to follow the rules of procedure laid down in the Convention of 1899, except in so far as the procedure was laid down in the present Convention.[28] In addition the Conference adopted Conventions on the Limitation of Force for the Recovery of Contract Debts[29] and on the International Prize Court.[30] However, neither of those dealt specifically with provisional measures.

In the nature of things, it is exceptional to find provisional measures being required in arbitration proceedings, especially as these normally take place with the consent of both parties. With the modern expansion of the concept

[27] These optional rules are reproduced in Permanent Court of Arbitration, op. cit. 241.

[28] Above n. 23, vol. II, 341; Sh. Rosenne (ed.), *The Hague Peace Conferences of 1899 and 1907 and International Arbitration: Reports and Documents* 109 (The Hague: Asser Press, 2001).

[29] Above n. 23, vol. I, 616.

[30] Ibid. 660.

of compulsory recourse to arbitration, initiated by the UN Convention on the Law of the Sea of 1982, it may be assumed that more frequent use of provisional measures will become a feature of arbitration proceedings under that Convention and more generally. What is possibly the first direct instance of this procedure taking place not in the context of the Law of the Sea Convention occurred in the course of the complicated delimitation and demarcation proceedings conducted by the Eritrea–Ethiopia Boundary Commission.[31] That was a form of arbitration conducted after proceedings in the Security Council and administered by the Permanent Court of Arbitration. The Commission delivered a reasoned delimitation decision on 13 April 2002, on the basis of which the demarcation process was put in hand. In June Eritrea asserted that Ethiopia was settling its nationals in territory that had been determined to fall within Eritrean sovereignty, and it requested the Boundary Commission to adopt an interim order instructing Ethiopia immediately to cease this practice. After an exchange of correspondence the Commission sent a Team to determine on the ground and from the air the exact location of the places mentioned in the exchange between the parties and, so far as possible, the extent to which there had been movements of population in or around them since the delimitation decision. After the Team had reported its findings which were communicated to the parties, the Commission held a hearing at which the parties addressed those findings and presented oral arguments on the question. In its Order of 17 July 2002 the Commission stated:

> 18. The Commission finds it appropriate to observe that it would not be in accordance with the obligations of the Parties for either of them to take, or permit to be taken, any actions that prejudice, or might prejudice, the fulfilment of the Commission's Decision of 13 April 2002. By a letter addressed to both Parties on 21 June 2002, the Commission has already reminded them that it would not be in accordance with the obligations of either of them to take, or permit to be taken, any actions that prejudice, or might prejudice, the fulfilment of the Commission's Decision of 13 April 2002. It followed that both Parties should assist the Commission in the performance of its task and that neither Party should do anything to prevent or hinder the demarcation process or act in a manner contrary to the rights of the other. The Commission was also mindful of the duty of the Parties to do nothing that would aggravate the dispute. Neither Party should do anything to prevent or hinder the demarcation process or act in a manner contrary to the rights of the other, or otherwise aggravate the dispute.

The Commission formally rejected Eritrea's request for the prescription of interim measures. However, it went on to decide that any Ethiopian Government-sponsored resettlement of Ethiopian nationals in a prescribed area

[31] This and all other decisions of this Boundary Commission are available on the website of the Permanent Court of Arbitration. Sir Elihu Lauterpacht is president of this Commission and his reports are included in the reports of the Secretary-General to the Security Council.

should not have taken place, and it required Ethiopia forthwith to arrange for the return to Ethiopian territory of those persons who had gone to the territory in question from Ethiopia pursuant to an Ethiopian resettlement programme, and to report to the Commission on the implementation of that decision. Each party was to ensure that no further population resettlement should take place across the delimitation line established by the Decision of 13 April 2002. This is an important illustration of the invocation of provisional measures—with no specified time-limitation—to enable a boundary commission which had already determined the delimitation of the boundary to proceed unhindered with the second phase of its work, the demarcation of the boundary. This is not the first instance of an arbitration being divided into two phases, the second being dependent on the decision in the first. The introduction of the concept of provisional measures to protect the decision in the first phase, so as to enable the arbitration to proceed to the second, is thus an important addition to modern arbitral procedure.

The agreement to refer the dispute to arbitration may expressly prohibit the arbitral tribunal from ordering provisional measures. For example, the agreement between Egypt and Israel referring the *Boundary Markers at Taba* dispute to arbitration included Article XI, paragraph 2, stating that the Tribunal 'shall have no authority to issue provisional measures concerning the Taba area'.[32] By implication it may thereby have had authority to issue provisional measures in other areas. However, that question did not arise.

1.5. THE CENTRAL AMERICAN EXPERIENCE

The first standing international court of modern times was the Central American Court of Justice, created by the Convention for the Establishment of a Central American Court of Justice of 20 December 1907.[33] It was certainly inspired by the proceedings of the 1907 Peace Conference, but it was centred in a politically unstable area and the major inter-State cases that were brought before it were all fraught with difficult political issues which could not be overcome by treating the disputes as legal disputes. It also is not to be overlooked that this Court was active during the First World War,

[32] For that Agreement, *see* 20 UNRIAA 1, 107, 112.

[33] 206 CTS 79. For the proceedings of that short-lived court, *see Anales de la Corte de Justicia Centroamericana* (San José de Costa Rica: 7 vols. 1911–17) (*Anales*). I am indebted to Dr Cesare Romano and the Project on International Courts and Tribunals for making this material available to me. *See* also Stuyt, op. cit. in. n. 19, 614. For a modern reappraisal, *see* J. Allain, *A Century of International Adjudication: The Rule of Law and its Limits* 67 (The Hague: Asser Press, 2000). In 2000, in the context of a regional organization of economic integration, a new Central American Court of Justice (La Corte Centro-Americana de Justicia) was established by the Protocol of Tegacigalpa, referring to the Charter of the Organization of Central American States constituting the Central American Integration System, of 13 November 1991 (see n. 8). This must be kept distinct from the previous Central American Court of Justice of 1907.

although before the United States, the dominant political power in the area, had entered that war. The time was not propitious for what was a new and untried venture in international organization for the maintenance of international peace.

Article XVIII of that Convention provided that

> From the moment in which any suit is instituted against any one or more governments up to that in which a final decision has been pronounced, the court may at the solicitation of any one of the parties fix the situation in which the contending parties must remain, to the end that the difficulty shall not be aggravated and that things shall be conserved *in statu quo* pending a final decision.[34]

Article XXIII required that every final or interlocutory decision of the Court should be rendered with the concurrence of at least three members of the Court, and by Article XXIV the decisions must be in writing and be signed by all the judges. However, by Article XXV only the judgments of the Court are expressly mentioned as binding on the parties, leaving decisions under Article XXIII in an unclear status.

The first contentious case between States before this Court was *Honduras* v *El Salvador and Guatemala*. Disturbances in Honduras were seen to constitute a threat to international peace, and were believed to have been instigated by Guatemala and El Salvador. On 10 July 1908 Honduras instituted proceedings against those two countries. On 13 July the Court, apparently acting *proprio motu*, issued two interlocutory decrees in which it ordered Guatemala and El Salvador to halt all military action and related matters.[35] The parties concerned did not comply with those orders, but the Court attached no blame to either of the respondents. In its Final Conclusions and Award of 19 December 1908, the Court gave the following interpretation of Article XVIII:[36]

> 4. [T]he function assigned to this court by article XVIII . . . of arresting . . . the course of an armed conflict by determining, from the very moment a claim is filed, the situation in which the contending governments are to remain pending the rendition of an award, presupposes the right to have recourse to the court without delay in matters of urgency, as occurred in the case under consideration, and if we accepted the above-mentioned view of the matter, the humanitarian and unquestionably utilitarian purpose for which this important article was inserted would be essentially frustrated, the article being reserved perhaps for emergencies of minor risk and significance or converted perhaps into a simple expression of wish.

[34] Conferencia de paz centroamericana, Washington, noviembre y diciembre 1907, *Actas y Documentos: Minutes of the Preliminary Central American Peace Conference, September 1907* 65 (Washington DC: Government Printing Office, 1907). The record is woefully inadequate and simply states that after a long debate the proposal was adopted. The Convention is reproduced in English in Oellers-Frahm and Zimmerman, op. cit. in n. 8, vol. I, 209.

[35] 2 AJIL 838 (1908).

[36] Ibid. 729, 730. There was a question of the validity of this Judgment as it was not signed by two of the five judges, but that is of no relevance here.

5. [T]his error becomes obvious, moreover, if we observe that it would often shut off the nations from the path of judicial controversy, compelling them to accept war or humiliation as the only alternative.
6. [T]he object of the reservation contained in the article under discussion is to hold intact the right of the nations to settle their controversies by amicable agreement notwithstanding their pledge to submit them to the court, but its purpose is not to lay down an inviolable rule that negotiations to this end must be made and exhausted, and if we construe its text in this manner there are no grounds upon which the plea in question can be sustained [a plea by Guatemala of inadmissibility].

The last two cases before that Court concerned the so-called Bryan–Chamorro Treaty between Nicaragua and the United States. That Treaty envisaged the construction of a canal between the Atlantic and Pacific Oceans parallel to the Panama Canal. In *Costa Rica* v *Nicaragua*, filed on 24 March 1916, Costa Rica alleged that the Treaty violated a boundary treaty of 1838 and asked the Court to declare that Nicaragua lacked capacity to enter into the Treaty with the United States. Here the Court first issued an interlocutory order on 1 May 1916 upholding its jurisdiction and requiring the parties to maintain the *status quo* pending the final decision.[37] The final decision was rendered on 30 September 1916.[38] The Court confirmed its jurisdiction and declared that Nicaragua had violated Costa Rica's rights under the 1858 Treaty. Nicaragua refused to accept that decision.

The Bryan–Chamorro Treaty was again the subject of litigation in a case filed by El Salvador against Nicaragua on 28 August 1916. This case concerned El Salvador's rights in the Gulf of Fonseca said to be violated by the Treaty. In its Judgment of 9 March 1917 the Court largely found in favour of El Salvador.[39] Nicaragua rejected that Judgment and shortly afterwards withdrew from the Convention. That brought this Court to an end.[40]

In the development of international judicial organs, this Court is important as its proceedings brought out the distinction between legal disputes and political disputes, and the unsuitability of attempting to dress political disputes as legal disputes and applying legal procedures, including provisional measures, to their solution. The Court's insistence on issuing orders on provisional measures, apparently on its own initiative, contributed to this.

[37] V *Anales* 87 (1916). For Nicaragua's *Contestación see* p. 122.

[38] Ibid. 130.

[39] VI *Anales* 96 (1917). The status of the Gulf of Fonseca was later to become the subject of a dispute between El Salvador and Honduras, in which Nicaragua was admitted as a non-party intervener, in the *Land, Island and Maritime Frontier Dispute,* determined by a Chamber of the International Court of Justice, ICJ Rep. 1992, 351, 580 (paras. 369 ff.). The Chamber was careful not to criticize or upset the findings of the 1917 Judgment as to the status of the Gulf, and concentrated its attention more on its consequences. In 2002 El Salvador instituted proceedings for the revision of that Judgment. The Chamber formed to hear that case decided that the application for revision of the earlier Judgment was inadmissible. ICJ Rep. 2003, 18 December.

[40] For Nicaragua's rejection of that Judgment, *see* VII *Anales* 18 (1917).

1.6. THE BRYAN TREATIES

On 23 April 1913 the United States Secretary of State W.J. Bryan laid before the Senate Committee on Foreign Relations a proposition to create commissions of enquiry for the advancement of international peace. The Committee gave a favourable response, and the next day Bryan delivered his plan to the foreign diplomatic representatives in Washington.[41] This proposal, with the First World War looming, was connected with naval and military disarmament. A number of treaties were concluded: they provided for recourse to a Permanent International Commission when ordinary diplomatic proceedings had failed and the parties did not have recourse to arbitration. Each of the treaties with China,[42] France,[43] and Sweden[44] contained a clause regarding provisional measures, reading:

> In case the cause of the dispute should consist of certain acts already committed or about to be committed, the Commission shall as soon as possible indicate what measures to preserve the rights of each party ought in its opinion to be taken provisionally and pending the delivery of its report. (Agreement with France, Article 4)

Those indications were not binding, since by Article 5 the parties reserved full liberty as to the action to be taken on the report of the Commission. The comments mentioned above in note 41 do not offer any further information about these clauses.[45] Nevertheless, they appeared only in those three treaties and not in any of the others. Nevertheless, as will be seen in Chapter 2, they had an influence on the drafting of the Statute of the Permanent Court of International Justice.

In the opinion of the Swiss jurist Guggenheim, those treaties were attempts to rectify the unsatisfactory consequences of the Central American Court's

[41] For a series of unsigned 'Editorial Comments' on these treaties, *see* 7 AJIL 566, 823 (1913);. 8 AJIL 565, 853 (1914); and for a fuller survey by G.A. Finch, 'The Bryan Peace Treaties', 10 AJIL 882 (1916).

[42] Treaty looking to the advancement of the cause of general peace, signed at Washington 15 September 1914, entered into force 22 September 1914, Charles I. Bevans, 6 *Treaties and other International Agreements of the United States of America 1776–1949* 711 (hereafter *Bevans*). For the submission of this Treaty to the Senate, *see* 63d Congress 2d Session, Executive GG. The Committee on Foreign Relations reported these treaties out with a recommendation for ratification without any comment on any of their provisions. *And see* G.H. Hackworth, VI *Digest of International Law* 5 (Washington DC: Government Printing Office, 1943). According to State Department publication *Treaties in Force* this treaty is in force as between the United States and Taiwan.

[43] Treaty for the pacific settlement of disputes, signed at Washington 5 September 1914, entered into force 22 January 1915, 7 *Bevans* 883. For the submission of this Treaty to the Senate, *see* 63d Congress 2d Session, Executive HH.

[44] Treaty for the advancement of peace, signed at Washington 13 October 1914, entered into force 11 January 1915, 11 *Bevans* 741. For the submission of this Treaty to the Senate, *see* 63d Congress, 2d Session, Executive PP.

[45] It is not clear today why this clause appears only in these three treaties.

experience, which he thought showed that in political disputes to attribute binding effect to provisional orders might be going too far, at least having regard to international organization of that period. Accordingly, the treaties aimed at providing an alternative to arbitration in political disputes.[46] However, it appears that only one of these treaties, that with Chile, has been invoked, and that was in 1990.[47]

1.7. PREPARING FOR THE PERMANENT COURT OF INTERNATIONAL JUSTICE (1919–20)

With the end of the First World War following the Armistice of 11 November 1918, preparations for the peace conference included proposals for an international organization for maintaining international peace, and with them the idea that to be complete, such an organization should contain a court.[48] That, in turn, led to a revival of the efforts to establish a permanent international court, efforts which had failed at the 1907 Conference for the reasons stated in § 1.4. Several plans for such a court were drawn up, some before the signing of the Treaty of Versailles (28 June 1919), when it was thought that the court would be part of the new League of Nations, and some after that date, when it had been decided that a new court would be created apart from the League.

Most of those plans addressed the major issues left open in the 1907 Conference. Others went further and contained detailed proposals for the working of the court. The Peace Conference accepted the principle of the establishment of such a court, but left the details for future action. Article 14 of the Covenant of the League of Nations required the Council of the League to formulate and submit to the members of the League for adoption plans for the establishment of a Permanent Court of International Justice, which would be empowered to hear and determine any dispute of an international character which the parties thereto submit to it, and might also give an advisory opinion upon any dispute or question referred to it by the Assembly or Council of the League of Nations. Accordingly, on 13 February 1920 the Council of the League established the Advisory Committee of Jurists to prepare plans as provided in Article 14 of the Covenant (further in § 2.1). That was the beginning of the political process that led to the adoption in 1920 of the Statute of the Permanent Court of International Justice, established as a functioning judicial organ in 1922.

46 P. Guggenheim, 'Les mesures conservatoires dans la procédure arbitrale et judiciaire', 40 *Recueil* 648, 670 (1932–II).

47 *See* the *Letelier and Mofitt* case with Chile (1992), 88 ILR 727.

48 For a summary of international thinking at that time, *see* M.O. Hudson, op. cit. in n. 14, 93.

2

The Statutes

I. THE INTERNATIONAL COURT OF JUSTICE

2.1. THE ADVISORY COMMITTEE OF JURISTS (1920)

As required by Article 14 of the Covenant of the League of Nations, which formed Part I of each of the Peace Treaties of 1919, the Council quickly got down to work. At its second session in February 1920 it decided to convene an Advisory Committee of Jurists to prepare plans for the establishment of the Court.[1] The Committee was in session at The Hague from 10 June to 24 July 1920.

For the most part the Committee was concerned with the major issues of the organization and constitution of the Court, its composition, and its contentious jurisdiction, the major issues left open in the 1907 Conference with regard to the proposed Court of Arbitration. The issue of jurisdiction related to the question whether Article 14 of the Covenant required that the Court's jurisdiction over legal disputes should be compulsory. The Committee settled the question of the composition of the Court—the system of the election of the judges and the institution of judges ad hoc and the composition of the Court for any case in the system that has been preserved to this day. The constitution of the Court was left for the Assembly to decide—and that led to the Protocol of Signature as an instrument independent of the Covenant, and hence of the Peace Treaties of 1919. The Committee also proposed that the jurisdiction of the Court to decide legal disputes between parties to the Statute would be compulsory. That, however, was rejected in

[1] PCIJ, Advisory Committee of Jurists, *Procès-Verbaux of the Proceedings of the Committee, June 16th–July 24th 1920 with Annexes* (The Hague, 1920) (hereafter PV); League of Nations, PCIJ, *Documents concerning the action taken by the Council of the League of Nations under Art. 14 of the Covenant and the Adoption of the Statute of the Permanent Court* (Geneva, 1921) (hereafter *Action taken*). That Committee was composed of the following eminent jurists, several of whom had taken part in the 1907 Peace Conference: Baron Descamps (Belgium) (President), Loder (Netherlands) (Vice-President), Adatci (Japan), Altamira (Spain), Bevilaqua, replaced by Raul Fernandes (Brazil), Hagerup (Norway), Albert de Lapradelle (France), Lord Phillimore (Great Britain), Ricci-Busatti (Italy) and Elihu Root, with J.B. Scott as legal adviser (U.S.A.). The Secretary-General of the League appointed D. Anzilotti as Secretary-General of the Committee and, to replace him in case of impediment, Åke Hammarskjöld. Anzilotti was elected a member of the Court in 1921, a position which he held until the Court's dissolution in 1946. He was President from 1928 to 1930. Hammarskjöld was Registrar from 1922 to 1936 when he was elected a member of the Court. He died in 1937. For a recent reassessment of the work of that Committee, *see* O. Spiermann, '"Who attempts too much does nothing well": The 1920 Advisory Committee of Jurists and the Statute of the Permanent Court of International Justice', 73 BYIL 187 (2002).

the Council of the League, which insisted on maintaining the traditional rule of arbitration, that the Court's jurisdiction to determine any case required the consent of the parties to that dispute, and that, following Article 14 of the Covenant, the Court could only hear cases that the parties submitted to it. Although the draft prepared by the Advisory Committee assumed throughout that the jurisdiction would be compulsory, the Council did not require a second look at the text when it decided to maintain the traditional approach of *ad litem* consent to the jurisdiction. One of the consequences is that in the new context not all of the proposals of the Advisory Committee are applicable as they stand.

The League Secretariat presented the Committee with a detailed memorandum setting out the different plans for the Court.[2] Given the Committee's preoccupation with those essential matters, it did not have much time for procedural issues, especially as these had to a large extent been settled in the 1907 Conference. At its fifteenth meeting, on 3 July 1920, the Committee established a Drafting Committee to draw up rules for procedure. Those rules were to be considered at unofficial meetings with no procès-verbaux. In that memorandum, minor attention was paid to the question of provisional measures, which was presented under the heading: *Is the Court competent to decree, as regards the subject-matter of the dispute, the fixation of the* status quo *pending its decision?* In that context the memorandum described the experience of the Central American Court of Justice quoting Article 18 of the Convention (*see* § 1.5) and the Bryan Treaties (*see* § 1.6), Article 12 of the Phillimore Plan of March 1918,[3] and one new proposal by the German Government to empower the tribunal to settle by a provisional arrangement the relations arising from the dispute for the duration of the proceedings (Article 34).[4] That is how the matter came before the Advisory Committee of Jurists.

This Drafting Committee presented its text at the twenty-fifth meeting, on 19 July.[5] In the section on procedure it included what was then Article 2 *bis* as follows:

> If the dispute arises out of an act which has already taken place or which is imminent, the Court shall have the power to suggest, if it considers that circumstances so require, the provisional measures that should be taken to preserve the respective rights of either party.
>
> Pending the final decision, notice of the measures suggested shall forthwith be given to the parties and the Council.

[2] PCIJ, Advisory Committee of Jurists, *Documents presented to the Committee relating to existing plans for the establishment of a Permanent Court of International Justice* (1920) (hereafter *Documents*).

[3] For the Phillimore Plan, *see* David Hunter Miller, *The Drafting of the Covenant* 2 doc.1, 3–6 (New York: Putnam, 1928).

[4] *Documents* 127.

[5] PV 551, 561.

As seen, the 1899 and 1907 Conventions contained nothing like this. That proposal, although apparently inspired by the Statute of the Central American Court of Justice which contained a similar provision, nevertheless differed from it and possibly could have given the Court a right of initiative if it considered that the circumstances required its intervention. A brief discussion of this proposal took place at the Committee's twenty-eighth meeting, on 20 July, but it does not throw much light on its interpretation.[6] Fernandes proposed a revised text to read:

> In case the cause of the dispute should consist of certain acts already committed or about to be committed, the Court may, provisionally and with the least possible delay, order adequate provisional measures to be taken, pending the final judgment of the Court.[7]

That was a reproduction of the text included in the three Bryan Treaties with China, France, and Sweden. It was adopted in principle and referred to the Drafting Committee whose text was adopted 'with some modifications in the wording', which are not set out in the record. This text is available in French only. It reads:

> Dans le cas où la cause du différend consiste en un acte effectué ou sur le point de l'être, la Cour a le pouvoir d'indiquer, si elle estime que les circonstances l'exigent, quelles mesures conservatoires du droit de chacun doivent être prises à titre provisoire.
>
> En attendant l'arrêt, cette indication de ces mesures est immédiatement transmise aux parties et au Conseil.[8]

As finally adopted on first reading, what became Article 39 read (the English being a translation):[9]

If the dispute arises out of acts which have already taken place or which are imminent, the Court shall have the power to suggest, if it considers that circumstances require it, the measures that must be taken provisionally to ensure that the respective rights be not prejudiced.	Dans le cas où la cause du différend consisterait en un acte effectué, ou sur le point de l'être, la Cour a le pouvoir d'indiquer, si elle estime que les circonstances l'exigent, quelles mesures conservatoires du droit de chacun doivent être prises à titre provisoire.
Pending the decision, notice of the measures suggested shall forthwith be given to the parties and the Council.	En attendant l'arrêt, l'indication de ces mesures est immédiatement transmise aux parties et au Conseil.

[6] Ibid. 587, 588.

[7] Ibid. 609. He accompanied this proposal, clearly based on the Bryan Treaty with Sweden, with a long explanatory memorandum.

[8] Ibid. 637.

[9] Ibid. 659, 666.

In a brief discussion at the thirty-first meeting, on 22 July, Ricci-Busatti proposed that the first portion of the first paragraph be deleted, so that the provision could also be applied in other circumstances. The proposal was rejected and the article was adopted with a slight modification in wording.[10] The Committee gave a long explanation for this article in its report:[11]

At the very outset of the case, circumstances may exist requiring that provisional measures be taken to ensure that the rights of each party are not prejudiced. This is the case in the event of a dispute arising out of an act just performed, for instance, the seizure of an object or the invasion of a territory. If such an act has just been, or is on the point of being, put into execution, it may be highly desirable to undo the consequences for the time being, or to prevent it from taking place if there is still time.

The Committee, drawing its inspiration from a provision contained in the treaties between the United States and certain other States (France, China and Sweden) which were signed in 1914 on behalf of the former by Mr Bryan, the then Secretary of State, gives the Court the power of suggesting the measures to be taken provisionally, to ensure that the respective rights are not prejudiced.

There is no question here of a definite order, even of a temporary nature, which must be carried out at once. Great care must be exercised in any matter entailing the limitation of sovereign powers. It is sufficiently difficult to ensure compliance with a definite decision; it would be much more difficult to ensure the putting into effect of a purely temporary decision. The decisions of this kind taken in transit cases, in accordance with the view of the Communications and Transit Committee, are a valuable guide in this connection owing to the prudence shown in them; the Bryan treaties, from which the idea of giving such a power to the Court is borrowed, were also very prudent in their expressions, and only gave the Court the right of suggesting the measures to be taken provisionally, pending the report of the international commission of enquiry, entrusted with the task of reporting on the dispute.

Whereas, however, in the Bryan treaties, the suggested measures to be taken to preserve existing rights, were simply communicated by the Court to the parties, in the present case these measures are, once they have been suggested by a Court of the League of Nations, indicated to the Council of the League as the body most competent to take such action, in order that it may suggest that the measures calculated to ensure the effect of sentences of Arbitration be carried out.

As mentioned, all this discussion took place in a general context of a complete proposal for a court that would have compulsory jurisdiction over legal disputes.

A contemporary assessment of that proposal by one who participated in the work of the Advisory Committee, after observing that the Committee 'transferred bodily' the provision from the Bryan Treaties, concluded:

[10] Ibid. 619. In the final text the opening sentence in English was slightly modified to read: 'If the dispute arises out of an act'.

[11] Ibid. 693, 735; *see further* Ch. 7 text to n. 86.

This is a modest beginning to what may prove to be a very useful remedy. It is at present an indication, a suggestion, and the duty of the Court stops with notice to the parties and to the Council.[12]

The report of the Advisory Committee does not mention the discretionary nature of the power conferred on the Court although that is implicit in the report. Furthermore, it is the only document to suggest what the functions of the Council would be, namely to take such action in order that it may suggest that the measures calculated to ensure the effect of the Court's final decision (in the report called 'sentences of Arbitration') be carried out. Implicit in that statement is that the Council of the League would act in accordance with its general powers under the Covenant of the League of Nations, and would not have special powers when taking action to give effect to an order indicating provisional measures. This is consonant with the discretionary nature of the Court's power. However, no case of this nature came before the League Council.

2.2. THE ADOPTION OF THE STATUTE AND PROTOCOL OF SIGNATURE (1920)

The League Council took no further action in regard to this proposal, which came before the first Assembly of the League in 1920. There the topic of the establishment of the Permanent Court was allocated to the Third Committee which, in turn, referred the detailed examination of the draft statute to a Sub-Committee. The International Court of Justice has given the following description of what then occurred:

106. When the draft article 39 was examined by the Sub-Committee of the Third Committee of the first Assembly of the League of Nations, a number of amendments were considered. Raul Fernandes suggested again to use the word 'ordonner' in the French version. The Sub-Committee decided to stay with the word 'indiquer', the Chairman of the Sub-Committee [Hagerup] observing that the Court lacked the means to execute its decisions. The language of the first paragraph of the English version was then made to conform to the French text: thus the word 'suggest' was replaced by 'indicate', and 'should' by 'ought to'. However, in the second paragraph of the English version the phrase 'measures suggested' remained unchanged.[13]

[12] J.B. Scott, *The Project of a Permanent Court of International Justice and Resolutions of the Advisory Committee of Jurists: Report and Commentary* 118 (Washington DC: Carnegie Endowment for International Peace, 1920). For a word of caution in accepting Scott's interpretations of the work of the Advisory Committee of Jurists, *see* the dissenting opinion of Judge Schwebel in the *Military and Paramilitary Activities in and against Nicaragua* (Merits) case, ICJ Rep. 1986, 14, 259, 319.

[13] *LaGrand* case, ICJ Rep. 2001, 466, 501 (para. 106). I should here disclose an interest, having been Counsel to the United States delegation in that case. For the original discussion in the Sub-Committee, *see Action taken* 134.

Another amendment was made in the Third Committee. The representative of Panama wished to see a stipulation that would ensure that all Members of the League should be notified of the provisional measures to be taken, but this was not accepted. In reply to questions it was explained that this article covered cases where an omission to act, and not an act which had already been committed or was imminent, threatened the rights of one of the parties, but the representative of the British Empire protested against this extended interpretation of the word *act*. That led Ricci-Busatti to suggest the deletion of the initial words 'if the dispute arises out of an act which has already taken place or is imminent', a suggestion which he had made previously in the Advisory Committee of Jurists. That amendment was adopted after a vote, details of which are not given in the published record, and the article, now numbered 41, was then adopted in what is virtually its current form.[14]

The Statute and related documents were finally adopted at the twenty-first plenary meeting of the first Assembly of the League of Nations on 13 December 1920. There is nothing in the official records to indicate whether the Statute was given any final scrutiny by any kind of drafting committee, or whether, as is normal practice today, the Secretariat was asked to ensure the concordance of the French and English texts of the Statute as a whole: multilingual drafting of multilateral treaties was in its infancy in those days, and the international community had little experience of its complex problems. In 2001 the International Court of Justice found that the two texts were not in 'total harmony'.[15]

The context of this discussion was different from that in which the Advisory Committee had worked, since the Council of the League had rejected the idea of compulsory jurisdiction over legal disputes and replaced it with the requirement of consent *ad litem* of the parties to the dispute. However, that change in context was not directly reflected in the discussion in the League Assembly, nor was it noted by the International Court in the passage quoted above.

The issue of the constitution of the Court was resolved by annexing its Statute to an instrument entitled Protocol of Signature.[16] That was a treaty, and a State became a party to the Statute by signature of the Protocol followed by ratification. The Protocol of Signature as a legal instrument was separate from the Covenant of the League of Nations, so the Permanent

[14] Ibid. 103, 107, 169 (final text as approved by the Sub-Committee).

[15] *LaGrand* case, above n. 13 (para. 101). The first judicial reference to the possibility that the two texts of Art. 41 were not in harmony seems to have been made by Judge ad hoc Thierry in the *Arbitral Award of 31 July 1989* (Provisional Measures) case, ICJ Rep. 1990, 64, 79. He found that the English version 'differs substantially' from the French. The lack of harmony between the two texts was not confined to Art. 41, but has troubled the application of other provisions of the Statute. In 1945 the Washington Committee of Jurists and the San Francisco Conference made some attempt to bring the two texts into closer harmony, but did not touch Art. 41.

[16] 6 LNTS 379.

Court was not an organ of the League, notwithstanding that it was established by the actions of the Council and Assembly of the League, that the members of the Court were elected by the Council and Assembly of the League, that the Court's budget was covered by the League acting through the Assembly, and that only the Assembly and Council of the League were authorized to request an advisory opinion of the Court on any dispute or question. The Protocol of Signature contained an undertaking by its parties to accept the jurisdiction of the Court in accordance with the terms and subject to the conditions of the Statute. That covered the Court's incidental jurisdiction and, after the Statute was amended in 1931, its advisory competence as well.

As a direct consequence, the international judicial community consisted of those States that were parties to the Protocol of Signature, and was distinct from the international community formed by membership in the League of Nations. The act of ratifying the Protocol of Signature symbolized a general commitment to the idea of the judicial settlement of legal disputes and in many cases was accompanied by a declaration accepting the so-called 'optional clause' of what is now Article 36, paragraph 2, of the Statute. There is no explanation on the record for this second acceptance of the jurisdiction in accordance with the Statute. However, it is generally understood as referring to all those different provisions of the Statute which give the Court power to decide matters arising out of or otherwise relating to the trial of a case, now going under the general name of the incidental jurisdiction (*see* § 1.2), together with its power to give advisory opinions. That included the Court's jurisdiction to indicate provisional measures under Article 41 of the Statute.

The constitutional provisions regarding the Court were completed by Article 13, paragraph 4, of the Covenant (as revised with effect from 26 September 1924), by which the Members of the League agreed that they would carry out in full good faith any [arbitral] award or [judicial] decision that may be rendered. In the event of any failure to carry out such an award or decision, the Council was to propose what steps should be taken to give effect to it. Technically that obligation was imposed only on members of the League, and there was no similar provision as regards those parties to the Protocol of Signature of the Statute that were not members of the League, a theoretical matter which did not arise in practice.[17] The expression 'judicial decision' was broad enough to encompass relevant interlocutory decisions,

[17] On 17 May 1922, the Council of the League adopted a resolution on the conditions on which the Permanent Court would be open to a State which was not a member of the League or one mentioned in the Annex of the Covenant. Such a State was to deposit with the Registrar of the Court a declaration by which it accepted the jurisdiction of the Court in accordance with the Covenant and with the terms and subject to the conditions of the Statute and Rules of Court, and undertook to carry out in full good faith the decision or decisions of the Court and not to resort to war against any State complying therewith. *See* also Art. 36 of the Rules of the Permanent Court of 11 March 1936, PCIJ, Ser. D 1, 4th edn, 1940.

including decisions indicating provisional measures. However, the question of non-compliance with those decisions did not arise in the period of the League and the Council did not have to deal with it. The absence of practice notwithstanding, controversy over whether an order of the Permanent Court indicating provisional measures was in any way binding, or was simply a recommendation, was in full swing. Indeed, the leading position in this controversy was occupied by no less an authority than Åke Hammarskjöld, the Registrar of the Permanent Court, who published a major article in which he contended that the orders did not impose binding obligations on the parties.[18] This controversy was based on three main elements, the report of the Advisory Committee of Jurists which was ambivalent, the unusual terminology employed in Article 41 following the amendments adopted in the First Assembly in 1920, and the divergence between the French and English texts of the provision, the English-speaking world being inclined to follow the English version in which the element of obligation is less emphatically expressed.

In the two diplomatic Conferences about the Permanent Court that were held in 1926[19] and 1929,[20] concerning primarily the accession of the United States to the Statute, little attention was paid to Article 41.

2.3. THE 1929 COMMITTEE OF JURISTS

On 28 September 1928 the League Assembly, noting the ever-increasing number of cases being referred to the Permanent Court, decided that the Statute should be examined with a view to the introduction of any amendments as may be judged advisable, the necessary proposals being submitted to the next ordinary session of the Assembly. On 14 December the Council established a committee of jurists for this purpose.[21] The Committee held a

[18] 'Quelques aspects de la question des mesures conservatoires en droit international positif', 5 *Zeitschrift für ausländisches öffentliches Recht und Völkerrecht* 5 (1935): reproduced in his *Juridiction internationale* 299 (Leiden: Sijthoff, 1938).

[19] Minutes of the Conference of States Signatories of the Protocol of Signature of the Statute of the Permanent Court of International Justice, Geneva, September 2nd to 23rd, 1926, League of Nations Publication 1926 V.26.

[20] Committee of Jurists on the Statute of the Permanent Court of International Justice, Geneva, March 11th to 19th, 1929, League of Nations Publication V Juridical Questions V.5, doc. C.166 M.66.1929 V.4; Minutes of the Conference regarding the Revision of the Statute of the Permanent Court of International Justice and the Accession of the United States of America to the Protocol of Signature of the Statute, Geneva, September 4th to 12th, 1929, doc. C.514 M. 172 1929, Publication V Legal 1929 V.18.

[21] The members of this Committee were Fromageot (France), Gaus (Germany), Sir Cecil Hurst (United Kingdom), Ito (Japan), Pilotti replacing Scialoja (Italy), Politis (Greece), Raestad (Norway), Rundstein (Poland), Urrutia (Uruguay), van Eysinga (the Netherlands), and an American jurist, later nominated, Elihu Root. The President (Adatci) and Vice-President (Huber) of the Permanent Court were also invited to participate in the Committee's work. The

brief discussion on Article 41 at its tenth meeting. Huber explained the practice to date, and reported that no difficulty had arisen, and in the opinion of the Court the article was sufficiently elastic. Experience had not shown that any amendment was necessary, and such amendment might lead to an extensive discussion. Most of the discussion that followed was concerned with the powers of the President under the relevant Rule. The Chairman (Scialoja) summed up the discussion saying that it was undesirable to amend Article 41. It should, however, be recognized that Article 30 of the Statute empowered the Court to decide what action the President might take, and those indications were given in the Rules of Court. The Rules of Court thus acquired a legal basis under Article 30.[22] The Committee made no reference to Article 41 in its report. The Permanent Court considered the remarks about the powers of the President when it started re-examining its Rules of Court after the meetings of 1929 (*see* § 3.4).

As the Appendix shows, the Permanent Court had little experience of the application of Article 41. No difficulties have been reported over compliance with any of the provisional measures indicated by the Permanent Court which, however, was not faced with the problem of the 'unwilling respondent' to the extent that this has been a feature of the activities of States in the present ICJ.[23]

2.4. THE WASHINGTON COMMITTEE OF JURISTS AND THE SAN FRANCISCO CONFERENCE (1945)

As the Second World War approached its end, the four great powers of the time, China, the Union of Soviet Socialist Republics, the United Kingdom, and the United States of America engaged in negotiations regarding the future institutional arrangements to be put in place on the restoration of peace. Those negotiations led to the Dumbarton Oaks Proposals—Proposals for the Establishment of a General International Organization—published on 9 October 1944.[24] Chapter IV, paragraph 1, of those Proposals envisaged

Committee's secretary was Nisot, then a member of the Legal Section of the League's Secretariat. Its report was submitted to the 1929 Conference (*see* previous note).

[22] For this discussion, *see* n. 20 at 53.

[23] During the 1931 revision of the Rules the problem of compliance with orders on provisional measures was discussed in some detail. Judge Schücking was definitely of the opinion that 'measures of protection, being only interim measures, had no binding force'. His colleagues, it seems, thought that the decision of the Court indicating interim measures was binding on the States concerned. PCIJ, Ser. D 2 Add. 2 (1931), particularly pp. 198–200. In the 1929 session of the Committee of Jurists on the Statute of the Permanent Court of International Justice, Mr Root had expressed a point of view similar to that of Judge Schücking (n. 20 at 53).

[24] 3 UNCIO 10. The use of lower-case letters for the international court of justice in those Proposals was deliberate, and was designed not to prejudice the question of whether to continue the Permanent Court or to create a new one. The solution ultimately adopted was to create a new

an international court of justice as a principal organ of the new international organization. Chapter VII was devoted to the court, and went in detail into the institutional aspects of the court as an integral part of the new Organization.

These Proposals presaged a major change in the constitutional position of the Court—now a new Court under the name of the International Court of Justice. In the Charter of the United Nations the Protocol of Signature was replaced by Article 7, paragraph 1, establishing the Court as one of the principal organs of the United Nations and by Article 93, by which all members of the United Nations are *ipso facto* parties to the Statute. The Statute is by Article 92 annexed to the Charter and is no longer a separate instrument. The revised Article 10 of the Covenant of the League of Nations is replaced by Article 94 of the Charter. By paragraph 1, each member of the United Nations undertakes to comply with the decision of the Court in any case to which it is a party, and by paragraph 2 provision is made for recourse to the Security Council if any party fails to perform the obligations incumbent upon it under a judgment, the Security Council being given a discretionary power to make recommendations or decide upon measures to be taken to give effect to the judgment. In consequence, any undertaking to observe all the obligations of the Charter automatically constitutes an undertaking to observe all the obligations arising from the Statute. This difference in wording between the two paragraphs of Article 94 has led many commentators to the conclusion that paragraph 1 also applies to relevant interlocutory decisions, including orders on provisional measures.[25]

court on the basis of a statute that was based on the Statute of the Permanent Court. *See Law and Practice*, vol. I, 52.

[25] I once took the view that 'on the whole, these indications were of an advisory character, imposing upon the States to which they are directed no more than an obligation to examine them in good faith'. *Procedure in the International Court: A Commentary on the 1978 Rules of the International Court of Justice* 149 (The Hague: Martinus Nijhoff, 1983). But on further reflection I could not sustain that position, and later I wrote that it seems that the word *decision* in Art. 94 of the Charter refers to all decisions of the Court, regardless of their form. *Law and Practice*, vol. I, 216. *See* also B. Simma (ed.), *The Charter of the United Nations: A Commentary*, 2nd edn, vol. II, 1175 (Oxford: Oxford University Press, 2002): *contra*, P. Cot and A. Pellet (eds.), *La Charte des Nations Unies: Commentaire article par article*, 2nd edn, 1283 (Paris: Economica, 1991). For judicial discussion of this issue, *see* in the *Application of the Genocide Convention* (Further Provisional Measures) case, separate opinions of Judges Shahabuddeen, Weeramantry, and Ajibola, ICJ Rep. 1993, 325, 365, 374, and 397. In those opinions a distinction is made between the binding character of the order and its enforceability. What is the scope of a binding decision of an unenforceable character? *See* also the powerful plea of Sir Hersch Lauterpacht in favour of the binding quality of these indications in his 'Report on the Revision of the Statute of the International Court of Justice', 1 *The Law and Practice of International Courts and Tribunals* 55, 94 (2002). Lauterpacht reported that writers on the subject were practically unanimous that the pronouncements of the Court under Art. 41 do not bind the parties to the dispute, and he sought to remedy that situation. On a related issue, he thought that the Court ought to be able to make non-binding recommendations to the parties, proposing an addition to Art. 38 of the Statute to that effect (p. 96).

A recent commentary on the Charter explains that the enumeration of the principal organs in Article 7 'does not place them in any hierarchical order, but rather assigns them equal status in their capacity as "principal organs" '.[26] This arrangement preserved one feature of the previous arrangements: the new Court, like its predecessor, was not directly linked to any peace settlement after the Second World War. The relevant Peace Treaties were concluded later, in 1946, 1947, and 1951.

No doubt unintentionally, as a result of this change in the constitutional position of the International Court of Justice that element of direct commitment to the idea of the judicial settlement of international disputes has become depreciated in the broader acceptance of the Charter. Indeed, it is further depressed thanks to the freedom of choice provision of Article 33 of the Charter, duplicated as far as concerns judicial organs by Article 95.[27] What is more, through a complicated political development, admission to the United Nations is frequently regarded as the final act in a process of decolonization. Many new States seek admission to the United Nations as a formality and without considering the implications in terms of obligations deriving from the Statute.

In preparation for the Conference on International Organization, the San Francisco Conference, the Sponsoring Powers decided to have the Statute of the Permanent Court examined by a Committee of Jurists. Convened by the United States on behalf of the Sponsoring Powers the Committee of Jurists—to which all members of the anti-Axis coalition of the United Nations were invited—met at Washington in April 1945.[28]

No suggestions were made or amendments proposed to Article 41 in the preparatory work undertaken during the Second World War in connection with the question of the revival of the Court after the restoration of peace. That is surprising. The lack of harmony between the English and French texts of Article 41 had been noticed. No substantive changes were proposed for Article 41 in the Washington Committee of Jurists. The Committee reported it out with only the last word of the second paragraph being changed to refer to the Security Council. No attention was given to any possible lack of harmony between the English and French texts of the article, although elsewhere changes were proposed especially to the English text to

[26] Simma, op. cit. in previous note, 217. That section of the Commentary was prepared by Professor G. Jaenicke.

[27] *See* Sh. Rosenne, 'Article 95 of the Charter of the United Nations Revisited', *Studi di diritto internazionale in onore di Arangio-Ruiz*, vol. II, 1387 (Naples: Editoriale Scientifica, 2004).

[28] For the proceedings of the Washington Committee of Jurists, *see* UNCIO 14. Of the fighting United Nations, only India and South Africa declined to attend the Committee. On the difference between the United Nations as the name of the wartime fighting coalition and the United Nations as the name of the international organization created at the San Francisco Conference, *see* Sh. Rosenne, *The Perplexities of Modern International Law* 399 (Leiden: Martinus Nijhoff, 2004).

bring it into closer harmony with the French. Likewise, at the San Francisco Conference, where the questions relating to the Court were allocated to Committee IV/1, no further changes were proposed or made.[29]

In its final form, Article 41 reads:

1. The Court shall have the power to indicate, if it considers that circumstances so require, any provisional measures which ought to be taken to preserve the respective rights of either party.	1. La Cour a le pouvoir d'indiquer, si elle estime que les circonstances l'exigent, quelles mesures conservatoires du droit de chacun doivent être prises à titre provisoire.
2. Pending the final decision, notice of the measures suggested shall forthwith be given to the parties and to the Security Council.	2. En attendant l'arrêt définitif, l'indication de ces mesures est immédiatement notifiée aux parties et au Conseil de sécurité.

It was not until 2001 that the Court considered the meaning of Article 41 in the context of the object and purpose of the Statute. In *LaGrand* it wrote:

> 102. The object and purpose of the Statute is to enable the Court to fulfil the functions provided for therein, and, in particular, the basic function of judicial settlement of international disputes by binding decisions in accordance with Article 59 of the Statute. The context in which Article 41 is to be seen within the Statute is to prevent the Court from being hampered in the exercise of its functions because the respective rights of the parties to a dispute before the Court are not preserved. It follows from the object and purpose of the Statute, as well as from the terms of Article 41 when read in their context, that the power to indicate provisional measures entails that such measures should be binding, inasmuch as the power in question is based on the necessity, when the circumstances call for it, to safeguard, and to avoid prejudice to, the rights of the parties as determined by the final judgment of the Court. The contention that provisional measures indicated under Article 41 might not be binding would be contrary to the object and purpose of that Article.[30]

While Article 41 certainly empowers the Court to indicate provisional measures for the purpose of preserving the respective rights of each party, it does little more than that, and leaves it to the Court to develop the law. The Court has done this in two ways, by regulating the matter in successive versions of the Rules of Court (1922, 1931, 1936, 1946, 1978), and by its judicial pronouncements (see the list in the Appendix). In fact, it can be said that the whole of the substantive law of the International Court on provisional measures of protection and its procedure (virtually inseparable) is judge-made law, with the minimum of outside interference.

[29] UNCIO 13.

[30] *LaGrand* case, ICJ Rep. 2001, 466, 502 (para. 102). But *see* the dissenting opinion of Judge Oda at p. 537. The Court continued with a reference to the Judgment of the Permanent Court in the *Electricity Company of Sofia and Bulgaria* case quoted in Ch. 1 n. 2.

The fundamental change in the status of the Court dispensed with the need for a separate Protocol of Signature of the Statute. For the original members under Article 3 of the Charter, signature of the combined Charter and Statute of the Court followed by ratification in accordance with Article 110 was required for those States to become parties to the Charter and bound by all of its provisions and all the provisions of the annexed Statute that give the Court incidental jurisdiction, including Article 41. For a new State admitted to the Organization under Article 4 of the Charter, Part XIV (Rules 134 to 137) of the Rules of Procedure of the General Assembly governs the process of admission.[31] The new member is required to deposit with the Secretary-General a formal instrument in which it declares acceptance of the obligations contained in the Charter. That includes the obligations contained in the annexed Statute. The automatic participation in the Statute of the present Court follows from membership in the United Nations and as such does not imply any direct and separate commitment to the principle of the judicial settlement of international disputes.

2.5. THE BINDING FORCE OF PROVISIONAL MEASURES IN THE INTERNATIONAL COURT OF JUSTICE

As seen in connection with the interpretation of the Statute of the Permanent Court and the Covenant of the League of Nations, the question of the binding force of an order of the Permanent Court was controversial, with major opinion of the writers answering the question in the negative. The controversy was not resolved under the Charter, and remained whether, given the language of Article 41 and its drafting history together with Article 94 of the Charter, an indication of provisional measures by the ICJ imposes binding obligations on the addressees of the order, and what was the effect of a State's non-compliance with such an order. The controversy was theoretical in the period of the Permanent Court. It has become practical in the present Court, following the appearance of the 'unwilling respondent', first in the crisis over the Iranian nationalization of the Anglo-Iranian Oil Company, and the subsequent proceedings in the Court and in the Security Council.[32] It has since become aggravated with the attempts to invoke proceedings for provisional measures in a political context and with what were widely seen as political objectives. To some extent, that ambiguity was once recognized by the present Court. In the merits phase of the *Military and Paramilitary Activities in and against Nicaragua* case the Court said:

[31] A/520/Rev.15 + Amends 1 and 2.

[32] *See Law and Practice*, vol. I, 260. *See also* A. Azar, *L'Exécution des décisions de la Cour internationale de Justice* (Brussels: Bruylant, 2003).

When the Court finds that the situation requires that measures of this kind should be taken, it is incumbent on each party to take the Court's indications seriously into account, and not to direct its conduct solely by reference to what it believes to be its rights. Particularly is this so in a situation of armed conflict where no reparation can efface the results of conduct which the Court may rule to have been contrary to international law.[33]

For a long time the Court avoided directly pronouncing itself on the issue, mainly because it found that it had no need to decide it in the case before it. The Court maintained its position by repeating in the English text of the operative clauses of the orders the language of *ought* and the like, while in French using a verb like *devoir* (as in the French text of Article 41) in the conditional or subjunctive mode. It acted in this way regardless of which version of the order was authoritative. In English legal usage, *ought* is normally the language of a recommendation or exhortation, not of a binding instruction. The position is further complicated by the limited practice of the Security Council which, when it has dealt with these issues, has tended to approach the question before it as a political question, not as one necessarily requiring it to make every effort to ensure compliance with the Court's decision. The unusual language of Article 41, with words such as (in English) *indicate*, *which ought to be taken*, and *suggested* not directly corresponding to the French words, *doivent être prises*, *indication de ces mesures*, coupled with the last-minute changes made in the League Assembly just before the final adoption of the Statute (without careful examination by a drafting committee), and the rapid and somewhat summary proceedings usual on a request for provisional measures, constituted the axis around which this controversy was centred. The confusion is well illustrated in the *Restatement of the Law of the Foreign Relations of the United States* which has written:

The Court has not ruled on whether an order 'indicating' provisional measures is mandatory on the parties. It is not clear what effect the failure of a state to comply with provisional measures has on the decision in the principal case.[34]

And:

As the Statute of the Court uses the ambiguous word 'indicate' rather than 'order' or 'determine', there has been uncertainty as to whether the Court's orders indicating provisional measures are binding.[35]

[33] ICJ Rep. 1986, 114, 144 (para. 289).

[34] The American Law Institute, Restatement of the Law Third, *Restatement of the Law of the Foreign Relations of the United States* vol. II, § 903, Comment *e* on p. 358 (St Paul, Minnesota: 1987).

[35] Ibid., Reporters' Note 6 on p. 368. As late as 1991 the Court expressed similar doubts in a communication to the Preparatory Commission for ITLOS. UN Press Release SEA/1284, 29 August 1991, reproduced in R. Platzöder, *The Law of the Sea Documents 1983–1992*, vol. XIII, 510 (Dobbs Ferry, NY: Oceana, 1992). It is believed that those statements in an authoritative American publication influenced the United States authorities, both federal and state, when they

However, controversy has now been set at rest by the Judgment in *LaGrand*, holding that an order of the ICJ indicating provisional measures is binding and that non-compliance with it could give rise to a claim for reparation as an internationally wrongful act.[36] Let us take a closer look at that case.

In *LaGrand* Germany included a final submission No. 3 to the effect that the United States had violated its international legal obligation to comply with the Court's Order on provisional measures of 4 March 1999,[37] and to refrain from any action which might interfere with the subject-matter of the dispute while judicial proceedings were pending. Against this, the United States submitted that all Germany's submissions should be dismissed, and it raised a number of objections in the form of pleas in bar with which the Court had to deal before it could decide on the merits. In its Counter-Memorial, the United States argued that the German submission was inadmissible in light of the circumstances of that Order and the action taken in response to it, and in particular that the Order by its terms did not create binding legal obligations incumbent on the United States.[38] Against this background, the Court had to deal head-on with an issue that it had been able to avoid over a long period of time. Paragraphs 45, 57, together with paragraphs 92 to 116 and operative paragraphs 128 (1), (2)(*c*), and (5), of the Judgment are the Court's answer, dismissing the American contentions.

On its jurisdiction to deal with that submission the Court said that where it has jurisdiction to decide a case, it also has jurisdiction to deal with submissions requesting it to determine that an order indicating measures which seeks to preserve the rights of the parties to this dispute has not been complied with (paragraph 45). The United States also argued that the third submission was inadmissible because of the manner in which those proceedings had been brought before the Court by Germany. Germany's late filing of the case compelled the Court to respond to the request for provisional measures by acting *ex parte*, without full information, and that procedure was inconsistent with the principles of the equality of the parties and of giving each party sufficient opportunity to be heard (paragraph 55). On this, the Court included the following passage in its Judgment:

> 57. The Court recognizes that Germany may be criticized for the manner in which these proceedings were filed and the manner of their timing. The Court recalls, however, that notwithstanding its awareness of the consequences of Germany's

had to deal with provisional measures addressed to state authorities in the series of capital punishment cases (*see* § 8.5).

[36] ICJ Rep. 2001, 466. For a serious critique of that Judgment, *see* H. Thirlway, 'The Law and Procedure of the International Court of Justice, 1960–1989', 27 BYIL 37, 113 (2001). For further interpretation of that Judgment, *see* the *Avena and other Mexican Nationals* case, ICJ Rep. 2004, 31 March, *passim.*

[37] ICJ Rep. 1999 (I), 9.

[38] Counter-Memorial of 27 March 2000, paras. 103 ff., and in particular from para. 128 onwards.

> filing at such a late date it nevertheless considered it appropriate to enter the Order of 3 March 1999, given that an irreparable prejudice appeared to be imminent. In view of these considerations, the Court considers that Germany is now entitled to challenge the alleged failure of the United States to comply with the Order. Accordingly, the Court finds that Germany's third submission is admissible.

On the merits of that submission, the Court first pointed out that neither the Permanent Court nor the present Court had been called upon to determine the legal effects of orders made under Article 41 of the Statute. Germany's submission referred specifically to the Order of 3 March 1999, and as the United States disputed the existence of any such obligation 'the Court was now called upon to rule expressly on this question' (paragraph 92). The Court explained that the dispute between the parties essentially concerned the interpretation of Article 41 'which is worded in identical terms in the Statute of each Court (apart from the respective references to the Council of the League of Nations and the Security Council)'.

> This interpretation has been the subject of extensive controversy in the literature. The Court will therefore now proceed to the interpretation of Article 41 of the Statute. It will do so in accordance with customary international law, reflected in Article 31 of the 1969 Vienna Convention on the Law of Treaties. According to paragraph 1 of Article 31, a treaty must be interpreted in good faith in accordance with the ordinary meaning to be given to its terms in their context and in the light of the treaty's object and purpose. [paragraph 99][39]

The Court first turned directly to the French text of Article 41. It pointed out that the terms *indiquer* and *indication* may be deemed to be neutral as to the mandatory character of the measures concerned. By contrast the words *doivent être prises* have an imperative character. The Court then examined the English text. It took up the American argument that the use of the words *indicate* instead of *order*, of *ought* instead of *must*, must be understood as implying that a decision under Article 41 lacks mandatory effect, and replied that it might be argued, having regard to the fact that in 1920 the French text was the original version, that such terms have a meaning equivalent to *order* and *must* or *shall* (paragraph 100).[40]

[39] 1155 UNTS 331. The provisions of that Convention on interpretation, while they are usually understood as giving preference to textual and literal interpretation provided that it is performed in good faith, do not exclude teleological interpretation if that is justified by reference to the object and purpose of the treaty.

[40] This argument assumes that because the French text was the original of the Statute of the PCIJ in 1920 it also constituted the original of the Statute of the ICJ in 1945. While this may be a matter for discussion, it is to be regretted that the Court did not explain why it decided to rely on the 1920 French text for a treaty that was adopted in 1945. All the pleadings in *LaGrand* were in English (except for two oral statements in French) and English is the authoritative text of the Judgment. The UNCIO records, being summary records, do not indicate the language in which any delegate spoke. However, it is believed that in 1945 most of the delegates in the Washington Committee of Jurists and later in the San Francisco Conference used English as their working language. The Conference Committee of Jurists assumed responsibility for the English and

The Court then subjected Article 41 to thorough analysis. Accepting that the two versions were not in total harmony, in the absence of any other directives it applied Article 33, paragraph 4, of the Vienna Convention on the Law of Treaties as reflecting customary international law for the interpretation of a treaty authenticated in more than one language, when a comparison of the authentic texts discloses a difference of meaning which cannot be removed by application of the normal rules of interpretation. In such a case the Court may adopt a meaning which best reconciles the texts, having regard to the object and purposes of the treaty. This led it to the passage from paragraph 102 quoted at note 30. The Court interpreted the preparatory work of Article 41 as showing that preference was given in the French text to *indiquer* and *indication* by the consideration that the Court did not have the means to assure the execution of its decisions. The Court continued:

However, the lack of means of execution and the lack of binding force are two different matters. Hence, the fact the Court does not itself have the means to ensure the execution of orders made pursuant to Article 41 is not an argument against the binding nature of such orders.[41]

Having thus found that the Order was binding in character and created a legal obligation for the United States, the Court examined the question whether the United States had complied with that obligation. The Government had simply transmitted the Order to the Governor of the state of Arizona (where the crime had been committed, the trial held, and where the execution was scheduled to take place). On this the Court said:

112. The Court observes . . . that the mere transmission of its Order to the Governor of Arizona without any comment, particularly without even so much as a plea for a temporary stay and an explanation that there is no general agreement on the position of the United States that orders of the International Court of Justice on provisional measures are non-binding, was certainly less than could have been done even in the short time available. The same is true of the United States Solicitor General's categorical statement in his brief letter to the United States Supreme Court that 'an order of the International Court of Justice indicating provisional measures is not binding and does not furnish a basis for judicial relief . . . '. This statement went substantially further than the amicus brief

French texts only, 17 UNCIO 90. The other authentic language versions of the Charter and Statute were settled by the Conference Advisory Committee on Languages, 5 UNCIO 543. Probably French can be regarded as the original text of the provisions of the Statute taken over unchanged from the Statute of the Permanent Court, while English is the original text of all the new provisions introduced into the Statute at San Francisco. Cf. *Sovereignty over Pulau Litigan and Pulau Sipadan* (Application of the Philippines for Permission to Intervene) case, ICJ Rep. 2001, 575, 596 (para. 47).

[41] Para. 107. This overlooks that it is not the Court's function to assure the execution of its decisions. The fact that by Art. 41, para. 2, notice of provisional measures has to be given to the Security Council indicates that the Court is not expected to assure the execution of its decisions on provisional measures. The same can be said of the Permanent Court, where notice of provisional measures had to be given to the Council of the League of Nations. *See further* in § 7.9 below.

referred to in a mere footnote in his letter, which was filed on behalf of the United States in earlier proceedings before the United States Supreme Court in the case of Angel Francisco Breard (see *Breard* v. *Greene*, United States Supreme Court, 14 April 1998, 118 S. Ct. 1352). In that amicus brief, the same Solicitor General had declared less than a year earlier that 'there is substantial disagreement among jurists as to whether an ICJ order indicating provisional measures is binding... The better reasoned position is that such an order is not binding'.

After further review of different steps taken by United States authorities before the execution of LaGrand, the Court concluded this part of the Judgment with the following:

116. The Court observes finally that in the third submission Germany requests the Court to adjudge and declare only that the United States violated its international legal obligation to comply with the Order of 3 March 1999; it contains no other request regarding that violation. Moreover, the Court points out that the United States was under great time pressure in this case, due to the circumstances in which Germany had instituted the proceedings. The Court notes moreover that at the time when the United States authorities took their decision the question of the binding character of orders indicating provisional measures had been extensively discussed in the literature, but had not been settled by its jurisprudence. The Court would have taken these factors into consideration had Germany's submission included a claim for indemnification.

With that, and whatever controversies that part of the Judgment might engender, the Court finally put an end to a controversy which had occupied a prominent place in the literature, but which had not loomed so large in diplomatic practice which frequently, to remove doubts, had made it plain in treaties providing for the peaceful settlement of disputes (including judicial settlement), that provisional measures, where the court or tribunal (or other body such as a conciliation commission) was empowered to issue them, would be binding.[42] The latest indication of this was in the United Nations

[42] A prominent instance of this was the General Act for the Pacific Settlement of International Disputes of 26 September 1928, 93 LNTS 343. That was revised by the General Act of 28 April 1949, 72 UNTS 101. There is however widespread doubt whether either version is still in force, since the original instrument was closely related to the Covenant of the League of Nations and the 1949 text is little more than a technical revision. The General Act was invoked as an alternative title of jurisdiction in the *Nuclear Tests* (Provisional Measures) cases in 1973, but in reply to a question from the Court Australia stated that in the provisional measures proceedings it was relying 'first and foremost' on another title of jurisdiction, not on the General Act. ICJ Rep. 1973, 99, 103 (para. 18). New Zealand worded its position differently and pleaded the General Act in the alternative. ICJ Rep. 1973, 135, 139 (para. 19). The General Act was also invoked in the *Aegean Sea Continental Shelf* (Provisional Measures) case, but the Court did not find it necessary there to reach a final decision on whether it was in force as between the two parties although it largely based its decision on a Greek reservation to the original instrument. That reservation would have excluded the jurisdiction had the General Act been applicable. ICJ Rep. 1976, 3, 9 (para. 21). The Judgment in the *Aerial Incident of 10 August 1999* case was also largely concerned with a similar question. ICJ Rep. 2000, 12. The Court has shown a marked disinclination to pronounce itself on whether the General Act, in any form, is still in force.

Convention on the Law of the Sea of 1982 which includes elaborate provisions to deal with this.[43] It is this strong affirmation by the Court on the one hand and by a major diplomatic conference on the other, that provisional measures indicated under Article 41 of the Statute, together with the formal provision in Article 290, paragraph 6, of the Convention on the Law of the Sea, with the consequence that non-compliance with such an order is an internationally wrongful act within the context of the law on the responsibility of States, that has made it necessary to re-examine the law and practice of the Court in dealing with provisional measures.

Lest one might think that this Judgment was inarticulately coloured by the fact that human life was at stake, in the *Land and Maritime Boundary between Cameroon and Nigeria* case, a dispute about territory and maritime boundaries, the Court took the opportunity to confirm and clarify the *LaGrand* Judgment on this question. Here Cameroon contended that Nigeria had failed to comply with the Order indicating provisional measures handed down by the Court on 15 March 1996 and had thereby breached its international obligations. The Court recalled that in its Judgment in the *LaGrand* case it had reached 'the conclusion that orders on provisional measures under Article 41 [of the Statute] have binding effect'. The burden of proof was on Cameroon, to show that Nigeria had acted in violation of the provisional measures indicated in the Order. As Cameroon had not established the facts which it bears the burden of proving, its submission on this point must be rejected.[44]

2.6. THE NEW FORM OF THE OPERATIVE CLAUSE OF AN ORDER INDICATING PROVISIONAL MEASURES

With the settlement of the controversy over the obligation to comply with an order made under Article 41 indicating provisional measures, the question has arisen of the appropriate verb to use in the operative clause of the order. We have already mentioned that the usual practice was to use ambiguous auxiliary verbs in the English text of the operative clause of these orders, and a more definite verbal expression in the French text, regardless of which version of the order was authoritative.

Signs of a change in the Court's position began to appear in 1993. In its second Order in the *Application of the Genocide Convention* (Further Provisional Measures) case the Court ordered that each one of the provisional measures indicated in the previous order 'should be [*doit être*] immediately

[43] 1183 UNTS 3. The relevant provisions are found in Part XI, section 5 (Arts. 186 to 191) and Part XV (Arts. 279 to 299 together with Annexes V, VI, VII, and VIII).

[44] *Land and Maritime Boundary between Cameroon and Nigeria* case, ICJ Rep. 2002, 303, 453 (para. 321). For the provisional measures in this case, *see* ICJ Rep. 1996 (I), 13.

and effectively implemented'.[45] In 2000 it used the word *must* to render the verb *devoir* in the authoritative French text of the Order in the *Armed Activities on the Territory of the Congo* (Uganda) (Provisional Measures) case.[46] In the *Avena and Other Mexican Nationals* (Provisional Measures) case, the first indication of provisional measures after *LaGrand*, the Court carried *LaGrand* to its logical conclusion. It retained the initial word *indicates* to introduce the operative clause, that being the language of Article 41 of the Statute.[47] For the provisional measures themselves, in the authoritative English text it used the auxiliary verb *shall*, and in the French text the future simple of the appropriate verb.[48]

The confirmation that an order indicating provisional measures is binding with appropriate consequences in the event of non-compliance places such an order on a footing similar to that of a judgment. In 1927 the Permanent Court declined to give effect to a request for the indication of provisional measures which was designed to obtain an interim judgment in favour of part of the claim for damages set out in the application. As such, it was not covered by Article 41 of the Statute and the relevant provision of the Rules of Procedure then in force.[49] Given those facts, that case is not a general statement that an indication of provisional measures cannot be made if its effect would be to meet in whole or in part the main claim in the case, and in some recent cases

[45] *Application of the Convention on the Prevention and Punishment of the Crime of Genocide* (Further Provisional Measures) case, ICJ Rep. 1993, 325, 349 (para. 61). This Order contained three identical operative paragraphs corresponding to each one of the three measures indicated in the earlier Order. For that Order, *see* ibid. 3.

[46] ICJ Rep. 2000, 111, 129 (para. 47). This rendition of *devoir* does not correspond to the English version of Article 41, which uses the verb *ought*.

[47] ICJ Rep. 2003, 77.

[48] In English legal drafting *shall* is used to indicate obligation. Sir Humphrey Waldock, special rapporteur on the law of treaties, once explained to the International Law Commission that '[i]n English the "shall" form was used in statute law to denote imperative rules'. International Law Commission, 872nd meeting 17 June 1966, YBILC, 1966, vol. I, Part II, 199. The United Nations Secretariat and, for instance, the Drafting Committee of the Third United Nations Conference on the Law of the Sea, carefully studied all the authentic texts whenever an auxiliary verb of this kind appeared in the English text. ITLOS has always used *shall* when prescribing provisional measures. This has not prevented that Tribunal from including a recommendation in such an order. The *Saiga No. 2* (Provisional Measures) case, and *see* the declarations of Judge Vukas. ITLOS Rep. 1998, 24 at 40 (operative para. 2), and 41.'The *minus* is always included in what is greater (*plus*)', and 'He who is allowed to do what is greater (*plus*) should not be prohibited from doing what is less.' A. Berger, *Encyclopedic Dictionary of Roman Law*, Transactions of the American Philosophical Society, NS 43, Part 2, s.v. *minus* 583, citing Digest D.50.17.110 pr and D. 50.17.21 (Philadelphia, 1953). The *MOX Plant* arbitration also distinguished between the binding provisions of its Order No. 3 relating to the provisional measures requested by Ireland and its recommendations to the parties, for which it used the expressions 'Calls on the Parties . . .' and 'Requests . . .' On that Order, *see* Ch. 3, n. 46. MOX—Mixed Oxide Plant.

[49] *Chorzów Factory (Indemnities)* case, PCIJ Ser. A 12 (1927). *See further* Ch. 8 text to nn. 5, 6. In principle that approach was followed in the *Military and Paramilitary Activities in and against Nicaragua* (Merits) case in respect to a claim for a definite sum of money on account of reparations due after further proceedings. The Court refused to do this. ICJ Rep. 1986, 14, 143 (para. 287). Here the money claimed was included in the submissions on the merits.

that has been the real effect of the provisional measures requested and indicated. Thus in the *United States Diplomatic and Consular Staff in Tehran* (Provisional Measures) case, the indicated provisional measure was that Iran should ensure the immediate release, without any exception, of all persons of United States nationality who were or had been held as hostages in the Embassy or elsewhere. This corresponded closely to the main claim in the application instituting the proceedings, that Iran was under a particular obligation immediately to secure the release of all United States nationals currently being detained within the premises of the Embassy, quoted verbatim in the Order.[50] The Court did not refer to this aspect in *LaGrand*.

However, there is no reason to suppose that the Court would in an appropriate case not continue to follow the decision of its predecessor and refuse to grant as a provisional measure a defined sum of money on account of damages to be assessed fully in future proceedings, while following the *Hostages* case in other circumstances if that would be appropriate. In fact a binding provisional measure requiring the respondent to take action similar to the *petitum* of the original claim may have the effect of rendering the continuation of the proceedings redundant. That, however, may require a closer examination of the measures requested in light of the claim as it stands at the time when the provisional measures have to be decided. Provisional measures binding on the parties would seem to be more justified if the Court should be provisionally satisfied that the claimant State has a reasonable probability of success (as is required in some domestic legal systems), even though there may be an element of hazardous guesswork in making such an assessment.

A question arises as to what is 'binding' in an order indicating provisional measures. The same question arises as regards a judgment, in connection with the application of Article 94 of the Charter and Articles 60 and 61 of the Statute (on interpretation of a judgment and revision respectively). Here it is normally assumed that it is the operative clause (*dispositif*) that is binding in the sense that if it is executory the operative clause formulates the conduct that is to be observed by either or both of the parties. The reasons, although essential in a modern judgment under provisions such as Article 56, paragraph 1, of the Statute and Annex VI, Article 30, paragraph 1 of the Convention on the Law of the Sea, are not part of the binding element of a judgment, unless the operative clause should directly incorporate any specific passage from the reasons. It may be assumed that the same practice will be followed as regards the binding force of the operative clause of an order indicating provisional measures of protection.[51]

[50] ICJ Rep. 1979, 7.

[51] For a discussion of the relation between the reasons and the operative clause of a judgment, *see* the Judgment in the *Sovereignty over Pulau Litigan and Pulau Sipadan (Application of the Philippines for Permission to Intervene)* case. That Judgment described the findings and reasons as constituting 'the necessary steps to the *dispositif*'. ICJ Rep. 2001, 575, 596 (para. 47).

It should also be noted that even if endowing orders on provisional measures with binding force may place them on a similar footing to that of a judgment, they differ from judgments in major respects. The binding order does not create a *res judicata*. Under Article 60 of the Statute of the International Court of Justice a judgment is final and without appeal. Under Article 296 of the Convention on the Law of the Sea, any decision rendered by a court or tribunal under Part XV, section 2 (Articles 286 to 296) shall be final. Special, and exceptional, provisions exist in both instruments for the interpretation and the revision of judgments. Under Annex VI, Article 32, of the Convention, a judgment of ITLOS is final, and under Article 39, the decisions of the Seabed Disputes Chamber 'shall be enforceable in the territories of the States Parties in the same manner as judgments or orders of the highest court of the State Party in whose territory the enforcement is sought'.[52] This could produce a complex situation for a binding order on provisional measures made under the Convention. But one thing is certain: these orders are not final and without appeal. The provisions regarding the interpretation and the revision of a judgment are not applicable to them. To the contrary, the law governing provisional measures, whether in the Rules of Court of the ICJ, the Rules of the Tribunal for ITLOS, or in the Convention for all courts and tribunals acting under the Convention, the Convention itself provides for modification and revocation of such an order should circumstances change. The analogy of a binding order on provisional measures and a binding judgment should not be pushed too far.

Questions have arisen regarding the position when the title of jurisdiction invoked, whether a compromissory clause under Article 36, paragraph 1, of the Statute or the so-called compulsory jurisdiction under Article 36, paragraph 2, of the Statute, contains a reservation which on its face is relevant to the case being instituted. When the jurisdiction under Article 36, paragraph 2, is invoked, the case is regularly entered in the General List and the normal procedure is followed, leaving to the respondent to raise the question of jurisdiction (or admissibility) in whatever form it finds appropriate, frequently as a preliminary objection. The present Court has also applied the same principle when there is a reservation by the respondent to the compromissory clause of the treaty invoked in the title of jurisdiction. If in

[52] In Annex VI, Art. 39, the word *decisions* (*décisions*) may be ambiguous, since Art. 153 and Annex III (basic conditions of prospecting, exploration, and exploitation of the Area), Art. 21, refer to 'final decisions' (*décisions définitives*). Cf. University of Virginia, Center for Oceans Law and Policy, *United Nations Convention on the Law of the Sea 1982: A Commentary* (hereafter Virginia *Commentary*) vol. V, M.H. Nordquist, Sh. Rosenne, and L. Sohn (eds.) 414 (Dordrecht: Martinus Nijhoff, 1989); vol. VI, S.N. Nandan, M.W. Lodge, and Sh. Rosenne (eds.) 751 (The Hague: Martinus Nijhoff, 2002). However, whatever it might mean in Annex III, it would seem that in Annex VI it does encompass decisions on requests for the prescription of provisional measures, given the special role of the Seabed Disputes Chamber in relation to activities in the international seabed Area.

provisional measures proceedings at an early stage of the case the respondent invokes the reservation and the Court is satisfied that through the reservation the absence of jurisdiction under that title is manifest, it will find that it has no jurisdiction to indicate provisional measures under that title, and may order the case to be removed from the General List.[53] A case has also risen in which the applicant requested the indication of provisional measures, but the named respondent challenged whether the case was legitimately brought before the Court. Here the Court, after consulting the parties, ordered the case to be entered in the General List solely for the purpose of enabling it to hold a hearing on the matter. The Court found that the case must be dismissed, and with it the request for the indication of provisional measures.[54]

II. THE UNITED NATIONS CONVENTION ON THE LAW OF THE SEA AND THE INTERNATIONAL TRIBUNAL FOR THE LAW OF THE SEA

2.7. ARTICLE 290 OF THE UNITED NATIONS CONVENTION ON THE LAW OF THE SEA

The compulsory settlement of disputes on the interpretation or application of the Convention, as set out in Part XI, section 5 (Articles 186 to 191)[55] and Part XV (Articles 279 to 299 together with Annexes V, VI, VII, and VIII), was an essential part of the 'package deal' embodied in the Convention. Accordingly, the main provisions for the settlement of disputes are found in the Convention, with Annexes V (conciliation), VI (ITLOS), VII (arbitration), and VIII (special arbitration) containing specifics applicable to different machineries created by the Conference for this purpose. Under Part XI, section 5, non-State entities are also given a procedural standing in connection with activities in the international seabed Area, a major innovation in the general law of the sea. As only States can be parties to cases in the International Court of Justice, an alternative mechanism had to be found to which those non-State entities, including regional organizations of economic co-operation, could have access for the settlement of a dispute over the

[53] *See* § 4.7.

[54] *Request for an Examination of the Situation in accordance with Paragraph 63 of the Court's Judgment of 20 December 1974 in the* Nuclear Tests *Case*, ICJ Rep. 1995, 288. This is a truly unusual case.

[55] Part XI, section 5, is also applicable to the settlement of disputes under the Regulations on Prospecting and Exploration for Polymetallic Nodules in the Area (Regulation 39) International Seabed Authority doc. LSBA/6/A/18, 4 October 2000, ISBA, *The Law of the Sea: Basic Documents* 226 (Kingston, Jamaica: 2001), and under draft Regulations on Prospecting and Exploration for Polymetallic Sulphides and Cobalt-rich Ferromanganese Crusts in the Area (Regulation 42, doc. ISBA/10/LTC/WP.1 [2004]).

interpretation or application of the convention. Above all to meet that requirement the Conference decided to create a new tribunal, the International Tribunal for the Law of the Sea (ITLOS), as the ultimate safeguard always available for all purposes to ensure that recourse to compulsory dispute settlement procedures under the Convention would not be frustrated on technical grounds. That explains why the main rules, substantive and procedural, are in the Convention.

To understand the provisional measures of the Convention, a brief account of its dispute settlement mechanism is required. The main approach is based on the principle of the freedom of choice of dispute settlement procedure embodied in Articles 33 and 95 of the Charter. This is reflected in Article 287 of the Convention. Briefly, if the parties to a dispute on the interpretation or application of the Convention have not reached agreement on any other means for the pacific settlement of that dispute, they are obliged to have recourse to one of the following: the International Court of Justice, the International Tribunal for the Law of the Sea, an arbitral tribunal constituted under Annex VII, or a special arbitral tribunal constituted under Annex VIII, two standing bodies and two ad hoc bodies, with special provisions for an appointing authority to prevent frustration through the non-appointment of arbitrators. On becoming a party to the Convention, a State should indicate its choice. If both parties to the dispute have made the same choice, recourse to that procedure is compulsory. If the parties to a dispute have not accepted the same procedure, recourse to arbitration under Annex VII is compulsory. If a party has made no choice, it is deemed to have accepted Annex VII arbitration. In addition, the Seabed Disputes Chamber of ITLOS has exclusive jurisdiction under Part XI (Articles 133 to 191 and Annexes III and IV) for disputes with respect to activities in the international seabed Area falling within the categories set out in Article 187. As a consequence, there is a large number of existing or ad hoc arrangements with compulsory jurisdiction over disputes arising out of the Convention. Some of these are standing bodies with their own provisions regarding provisional measures.

In this context, it was necessary for special arrangements for provisional measures of protection, both to cover the multiplicity of courts and tribunals with compulsory jurisdiction under the Convention and to avoid possible earlier ambiguity over the question of the binding force of an order of the ICJ indicating provisional measures. That is the basis for Article 290 of the Convention. The structure of that provision, together with Annex VI, Article 25, has an orientation that is altogether different from that of Article 41 of the Statute of the ICJ. Those two provisions contain marked departures from the patterns established by that Statute, and it is in some important respects an open question how far ITLOS, and other dispute settlement courts and tribunals, when applying the Convention will follow the precedents established by the ICJ. At the same time it is also to be kept in mind that in negotiating these provisions, the Conference was closely influenced by its understanding of the law and practice of the International Court, which, as seen, is largely judge-made law. When introducing into the Convention the concept of prima facie jurisdiction over the merits, the Conference certainly had in mind the development of that notion by the ICJ. Article 290, paragraphs 1 to 4, of the Convention are widely regarded as a codification or as a consolidation or restatement of the law and practice of the ICJ. Paragraph 6 is a major innovation (followed by the International Court only in the *LaGrand* Judgment of 2001 (*see* § 2.5)). It is unambiguous in providing that the parties to the dispute shall comply promptly with any provisional measures prescribed under Article 290.

Although Annex VI of the Convention is entitled *Statute of the International Tribunal for the Law of the Sea*, the substantive law regarding provisional measures is set out in Article 290, which is applicable to all the courts and tribunals given competence under the Convention.[56] That jurisdiction is unlimited *ratione materiae* to a dispute concerning the interpretation or application of the Convention (Articles 279, 286, and 288, paragraph 1) or a dispute concerning the interpretation or application of an international agreement related to the purposes of the Convention which is submitted to the competent court or tribunal in accordance with the agreement (Article 288, paragraph 2), and provisional measures are requested for that dispute. Article 290 accordingly envisages two distinct types of proceedings for provisional measures. Proceedings under paragraph 1 may be regarded as normal provisional measures proceedings. That paragraph was modelled on what was accepted as the general practice of the International Court of Justice, and is intended to afford protection to the rights of all parties so long as the proceedings are in progress. However, there is a major addition to the purposes for which provisional measures may be requested. Paragraph 1 allows for provisional measures not only to preserve the respective rights of the parties. but also 'to prevent serious harm to the marine environment'. That reference to the protection of the marine environment

[56] On Art. 290, *see* Virginia *Commentary* (n. 52), vol. V, 52. For a more detailed account of the difference between the two provisions, *see* Sh. Rosenne, 'The International Tribunal for the Law of the Sea and the International Court of Justice: Some Points of Difference'; R. Platzöder and Ph. Verlaan (eds.), *The Baltic Sea: New Developments in National Policies and International Cooperation* 200, 206 (Dordrecht: Kluwer Law International, 1996). *And see* the Separate Opinion of Judge Laing in the *Saiga No. 2* (Provisional Measures) case, ITLOS Rep. 1998, 40; G. Eiriksson, *The International Tribunal for the Law of the Sea* 215 (The Hague: Martinus Nijhoff, 2000); R. Wolfrum, 'Provisional Measures of the International Tribunal for the Law of the Sea'; P. Chandrasekhara Rao and E. Khan (eds.), *The International Tribunal for the Law of the Sea: Law and Practice* 173 (The Hague: Kluwer Law International, 2001); P. Gautier, 'Interim Measures of Protection before the International Tribunal for the Law of the Sea'; M.H. Nordquist and J.N. Moore (eds.), *Current Marine Environmental Issues and the International Tribunal for the Law of the Sea* 243 (The Hague: Martinus Nijhoff, 2001).

presumably has in mind the protection of the marine environment in the context of the dispute of which the court or tribunal is seised, and is distinct from the protection of the rights of the parties. That was appropriate in an instrument dealing with the whole of the law of the sea and which devotes one Part—Part XII (Articles 192–237)—to the protection of the marine environment as an integral part of the new law of the sea. Following that, some of the additional agreements with compulsory dispute settlement provisions contain other objectives for which provisional measures may be requested (*see* § 2.10). Here too the specific objective must stand in some relationship to the principal claim.

Paragraph 1 is applicable to all the judicial bodies empowered to render binding decisions on the interpretation or application of the Convention mentioned in Article 287 to which a dispute has been submitted; that includes the International Court of Justice, the International Tribunal for the Law of the Sea, an ad hoc arbitration, and arbitration under Annex VII or Annex VIII of the Convention. However, in respect of the International Court of Justice, ITLOS, and any other court or tribunal operating under a constituent instrument of its own, it is to be assumed that that court or tribunal would first apply its constituent rules with regard to the conditions under which it may order provisional measures of protection. Annex VI accordingly addresses various procedural aspects connected with the constitution and operation of ITLOS and the Seabed Disputes Chamber, much in the same way that Annexes VII and VIII deal with procedural aspects of the two forms of compulsory arbitration that they envisage. It is therefore necessary here to address separately the Convention and Annex VI.

Article 290 provides:

Provisional measures

1. If a dispute has been duly submitted to court or tribunal which considers that *prima facie* it has jurisdiction under this Part [Part XV, Settlement of Disputes] or Part XI, section 5 [The Area, Settlement of Disputes and Advisory Opinions], the court or tribunal may prescribe any provisional measures which it considers appropriate under the circumstances to preserve the respective rights of the parties to the dispute or to prevent serious harm to the marine environment.

Mesures conservatoires

1. Si une cour ou tribunal dûment saisi d'un différend considère, *prima facie*, avoir compétence en vertu de la présente partie [la Partie XV, Règlement des différends] ou de la section 5 de la partie XI [La Zone, Règlement des différends et avis consultatifs], cette cour ou ce tribunal peut prescrire toutes mesures conservatoires qu'il juge appropriées en la circonstance pour préserver les droits respectifs des parties en litige ou pour empêcher que le milieu marin ne subisse de dommages graves en attendant la décision définitive.

2. Provisional measures may be modified or revoked as soon as the circumstances justifying them have ceased to exist.
3. Provisional measures may be prescribed, modified or revoked under this Article only at the request of a party to the dispute and after the parties have been given an opportunity to be heard.
4. The court or tribunal shall forthwith give notice to the parties to the dispute, and to such other States Parties as it considers appropriate, of the prescription, modification or revocation of provisional measures.
5. Pending the constitution of an arbitral tribunal to which a dispute is being submitted under this section [Section 2, Compulsory procedures entailing binding decisions, Articles 286–296], any court or tribunal agreed upon by the parties or, failing such agreement within two weeks from the date of the request for provisional measures, the International Tribunal for the Law of the Sea or, with respect to activities in the Area, the Seabed Disputes Chamber, may prescribe, modify or revoke provisional measures in accordance with this Article if it considers that *prima facie* the tribunal which is to be constituted would have jurisdiction and that the urgency of the situation so requires. Once constituted, the tribunal to which the dispute has been submitted may modify, revoke or affirm those provisional measures, acting in conformity with paragraphs 1 to 4.
6. The parties to the dispute shall comply promptly with any provisional measures prescribed under this article.

2. Les mesures conservatoires peuvent être modifiées ou rapportées dès que les circonstances les justifiant ont changé ou cessé d'exister.
3. Des mesures conservatoires ne peuvent être prescrites, modifiées ou rapportées en vertu du présent article qu'à la demande d'une partie au différend at après que la possibilité de se faire entendre a été donnée aux parties.
4. La cour ou le tribunal notifie immédiatement toute mesure conservatoire ou toute décision la modifiant ou la rapportant aux parties au différend et, s'il le juge approprié, à d'autres Etats Parties.
5. En attendant la constitution d'un tribunal arbitral saisi d'un différend en vertu de la présente section [Section 2, Procédures obligatoires aboutissant à des décisions obligatoires, Articles 286–296], toute cour ou tout tribunal désigné d'un commun accord par les parties ou, à défaut d'accord dans un délai de deux semaines à compter de la date de la demande de mesures conservatoires, le Tribunal international du droit de la mer ou, dans le cas d'activités menées dans la Zone, la Chambre pour le règlement des différends relatifs aux fonds marins, peut prescrire, modifier ou rapporter des mesures conservatoires conformément au présent article s'il considère, *prima facie*, que le tribunal devant être constitué aurait compétence et s'il estime que l'urgence de la situation l'exige. Une fois constitué, le tribunal saisi du différend, agissant conformément aux paragraphes 1 à 4, peut modifier, rapporter ou confirmer ces mesures conservatoires.
6. Les parties au différend se conforment sans retard à toutes mesures conservatoires prescrites en vertu du présente article.

Paragraphs 1 to 4, as stated, are a consolidation of the law and practice of the International Court of Justice. Paragraph 1 embodies the temporal element which in the ICJ Rules is comprehended in the phrase in Article 73, paragraph 1, of the Rules of Court: 'During the course of the proceedings'. But it should be noted that as in the case of the ICJ, that refers to the period of time within which provisional measures can be prescribed, not to the period of time within which duly prescribed provisional measures are in force or are operative (*see* § 6.1). Paragraphs 2 and 3 embody Article 74, paragraph 3, and Article 76 of those Rules, and paragraph 4 corresponds to their Article 77 with appropriate changes and to the normal practice of the Court. Paragraph 6 was an innovation when it was introduced in 1982, but following *LaGrand* is now the accepted rule for the ICJ. The Secretariat has expressed the view that Article 290, paragraphs 2 to 6, had no comparable provisions in the Statute of the International Court of Justice and that in some respects the provisions of Article 290 are stronger than those of Article 41 of the Statute of the ICJ.[57]

Paragraph 5 of Article 290 is a major innovation. It is believed to be the first occasion on which a standing international tribunal is given a compulsory residual jurisdiction to prescribe binding provisional measures of protection when the principal dispute is submitted to another tribunal which, when the provisional measures are requested, has not yet been constituted although the procedure leading to the constitution of the arbitral tribunal, which includes the definition of the dispute that it is being asked to settle, has been set in motion. The idea is not new. Dumbauld, for instance, was of the opinion that jurisdiction to grant protection *pendente lite* was not dependent upon jurisdiction in the principal action. From that it followed that interim measures may be granted before a plea to the jurisdiction is disposed of, and that one court may prescribe a remedy *pendente lite* in aid of an action of which another court has cognizance.[58] Hudson too in his authoritative work on the Permanent Court thought that jurisdiction to indicate provisional measures was not dependent upon a previous determination of the Court's jurisdiction to deal

[57] Report of the Preparatory Commission ... of the Convention regarding practical arrangements for the establishment of the International Tribunal for the Law of the Sea (LOS/PCN/152, 4 vols., 1995) (hereafter PrepCom Report), vol. III (LOS/PCN/SCN.4/L.3/Add.1, 1985) 51. It is true that Art. 290 is more complex than Art. 41 of the Statute of the ICJ. One of the reasons for this is that to some extent, except for paragraphs 5 and 6, it attempts to consolidate or codify the substance of the main features of the case law developed by the ICJ.

[58] E. Dumbauld, *Interim Measures of Protection in International Controversies* 186 (The Hague: Martinus Nijhoff, 1932). However, he relied on *doctrine* and on some internal legislation, and cited no international precedents. He probably had in mind the complex relations that existed between the Permanent Court and the different judicial bodies established by the Treaty of Versailles and the other Peace Treaties, including the different Mixed Arbitral Tribunals. What is believed to be the first use of the word *prescribe* in a treaty was in Art. 10 of the Treaty of Friendship, Conciliation and Judicial Settlement between Austria and Italy, Rome, 6 February 1930, 105 LNTS 97. *See* United Nations, *Systematic Survey of Treaties for the Pacific Settlement of International Disputes 1928–1948* 282 (Lake Success, NY: 1948) Sales No. 1949.V.5. It had been used earlier in writings. *See also* Ch. 1 n. 22 and related text.

with the merits of the case.[59] Nevertheless, it was not certain that the International Court of Justice could exercise jurisdiction under that provision, and those doubts could have undermined the general compromise of the Convention, for which guaranteed freedom of navigation and overflight according to the terms of the Convention backed by a system of compulsory jurisdiction was a counterbalance to acceptance of the exclusive economic zone (where the compulsory settlement of disputes is less emphatic). Paragraph 6 completes the compromise. Accordingly, the four provisional measures cases to date in ITLOS, all initiated on the basis of Article 290, paragraph 5, and Annex VI, Article 25, of the Convention, are of an entirely different order from those hitherto encountered in the International Court of Justice.

It is also necessary to keep in mind the provision of Article 288, paragraph 6, of the Convention: 'In the event of a dispute as to whether a court or tribunal has jurisdiction, the matter shall be settled by decision of *that* [emphasis supplied] court or tribunal.' This has a special function in the relations between proceedings in ITLOS and an arbitration under Annexes VII and VIII (recourse to which can be compulsory), and it highlights the fundamental difference between an ITLOS finding that the arbitral tribunal could prima facie have jurisdiction over the dispute and a definitive finding on jurisdiction by the competent arbitral tribunal. Given that provision, it would appear very difficult for ITLOS, after the usual summary and rapid proceedings on a request for provisional measures, not to find that the low threshold of prima facie jurisdiction of the tribunal to be constituted has been reached. Indeed, in the first instance of this kind, after ITLOS had found that the Annex VII arbitral tribunal might have jurisdiction, the parties agreed that the arbitral tribunal would first deal with the respondent's preliminary objections on jurisdiction.[60] The Arbitral Tribunal held that it was without jurisdiction to rule on the merits of the case. In the course of its reasoning it remarked that the parties' agents and counsel had plumbed the depths of those holdings [of ITLOS on the prima facie jurisdiction of the arbitral tribunal] with a profundity that the time pressures of the ITLOS processes did not permit. 'In any

[59] M.O. Hudson, *The Permanent Court of International Justice 1920–1942* 425 (New York: Macmillan, 1943). Hudson had expressed this view in the first edition of his book, adding that 'perhaps the Court should hesitate to make an indication in any case in which its jurisdiction has been or is likely to be challenged'. *The Permanent Court of International Justice: A Treatise* 415 (New York: Macmillan, 1934). Those words were dropped in the second edition.

[60] *Southern Bluefin Tuna* award, 4 August 2000, 119 ILR 508, 511 (para. 7); B. Kwiatkowska, 'The Australia and New Zealand v Japan Southern Bluefin Tuna (Jurisdiction and Admissibility) Award of the First Law of The Sea Convention Annex VII Arbitral Tribunal', 16 *Int'l J. Marine and Coastal L.* 239 (2001); D. Colson and P. Hoyle, 'Satisfying the Procedural Prerequisites to the Compulsory Dispute Settlement Mechanisms of the 1982 Law of the Sea Convention: Did the *Southern Bluefin Tuna* Tribunal Get it Right?', 34 *Ocean Development and Int'l L.* 59 (2003); Kwiatkowska, 'The *Southern Bluefin Tuna* Arbitral Tribunal Did Get It Right: A Commentary and Reply to the Article by David A. Colson and Dr. Peggy Hoyle', ibid. 369. I must disclose an interest, as counsel for Japan in that arbitration.

event, the ITLOS holdings upheld no more than the jurisdiction *prima facie* of this Tribunal. It remains for it to decide whether it has jurisdiction to pass upon the merits of the dispute.'[61] Both those decisions were correct. There is no contradiction between the holding of ITLOS that the Arbitral Tribunal prima facie could have jurisdiction and the final decision of the Arbitral Tribunal that it was without jurisdiction to rule on the merits of the dispute. There is no question of the Arbitral Tribunal 'overruling' ITLOS. A finding by one court or tribunal that another court or tribunal might have jurisdiction over the merits, so as to enable the first court or tribunal to exercise its power (and its duty) to prescribe provisional measures pending the determination of the case and the unreserved jurisdiction of the second court or tribunal over all aspects of the merits of the case (including any question of provisional measures) are two entirely different legal concepts unrelated to each other. Article 288, paragraph 6, of the Convention emphasizes this.

2.8. THE LEGISLATIVE HISTORY OF ARTICLE 290

At this point it is appropriate to recall the legislative history of Article 290. For this purpose, the Virginia *Commentary* on the Convention has been taken, almost in its entirety.[62]

290.1. Article 290 was discussed thoroughly at several sessions of the Conference . . . and it was revised considerably as a result of these discussions. While the need for provisional measures was accepted quickly, without any strong dissent, it proved difficult to agree on some of the issues associated with such measures.

[. . .]

290.3. The informal working group which prepared the 1975 working paper in Geneva[63] decided to depart from the wording of the Statute of the International Court of Justice because it considered:

(a) that the word 'indicate' was insufficient, did not clearly convey the binding character of the provisional measures, and as a result had not only led to some disputes about the obligation to comply with those measures, but also resulted in non-compliance by States with the indicated measures;

[61] *Southern Bluefin Tuna* award, para. 37.

[62] Virginia *Commentary* (n. 52), vol. V. For the Commentary on Art. 290, *see* p. 32; and on Annex VI, Art. 25, *see* p. 385. Art. 290 was for the most part finally negotiated in the Informal Plenary meetings of the Conference, which operated as a fourth Main Committee for the settlement of disputes and the final clauses, but without official records. Annex VI was for the most part negotiated through the Drafting Committee and a working party of the French Language Group of the Drafting Committee, also without official records.

[63] Informal document SD.Gp/2nd Session/No. 1/Rev.5 (1975, mimeo) reissued as A/CONF.62/Background Paper 1 (1976, mimeo) Art. 12. Reproduced in R. Platzöder (ed.), *Third United Nations Conference on the Law of the Sea: Documents*, vol. XII, 108, 194 (Dobbs Ferry, NY: Oceana, 1984).

(b) that, consequently, the word 'prescribe' should be used instead, and there should be an explicit provision that the prescribed measures 'shall be binding upon the parties to the dispute';[64]
(c) that in any case in which the International Court of Justice has jurisdiction under the Convention, 'any provisional measures indicated by that Court shall be binding on the parties to the dispute';
(d) that provisional measures should not be prescribed by a tribunal *proprio motu*, but should be considered by the tribunal only upon the request of a party to the dispute and only after giving the parties to the dispute the opportunity to be heard;
(e) that the provisional measures should not only preserve the respective rights of the parties, but also minimize damage to any party pending final adjudication; and
(f) that special arrangements need to be made if the dispute is to be submitted not to a permanent tribunal but to an *ad hoc* one.

290.4. In his initial draft,[65] President Amerasinghe took into account certain criticisms of the informal group's approach, but in general he accepted most of its suggestions. He made it clearer than it was in the earlier draft:

(a) that the provisional measures can be granted either by the International Court of Justice or the International Tribunal for the Law of the Sea, or by some other permanent tribunal;
(b) that the tribunal or the International Court of Justice 'as the case may be' shall have the power 'to indicate or prescribe' provisional measures;
(c) that any provisional measures indicated by the International Court of Justice or prescribed by a tribunal 'shall be binding upon the parties to the dispute';
(d) that the prescribed measures are intended 'to preserve the respective rights of the parties to the dispute' while at the same time preventing 'serious harm to the marine environment'; and
(e) that if the dispute has been submitted to a procedure for the settlement of disputes under the Convention and the tribunal has not yet been constituted or does not have the power to prescribe provisional measures, and if the parties to the dispute disagree as to the need for provisional measures or as to the content of such measures, a party may request the Law of the Sea Tribunal to step in and to prescribe temporary measures until the other organ can take over and itself review the need for such measures (and if necessary revise or terminate them).[66]

Paragraph 290.5 of the *Commentary* goes on to describe the complicated negotiations that took place in 1976 and 1977 that led to Article 290 assuming its current form, and the various issues that arose in that connection. One

[64] The idea of 'binding interim measures' had already appeared in a 1973 proposal by the United States doc. A/AC.138/97, reproduced in the Report of the Committee on the Peaceful Uses of the Sea Bed and Ocean Floor beyond the Limits of National Jurisdiction for 1973, 28 GAOR Sup. 21 (A/9021), 2, 23.

[65] A/CONF.62/WP.9 (Informal Single Negotiating Text [ISNT], Part IV, 1975), Third UN Conference on the Law of the Sea, V *Official Records* 111.

[66] Such a reference to ITLOS was first suggested in slightly different circumstances in the United States proposal of 1973 (n. 64) and was elaborated in a form similar to that of President Amerasinghe in the 1985 report of the informal working group (n. 63).

of those issues calls for special mention. In the words of paragraph 290.5 of the *Commentary*:

fear was expressed that the Law of the Sea Tribunal might interfere unnecessarily in some cases, asserting its allegedly superior authority over other tribunals. To restrict the Tribunal's intervention, it was provided that the Tribunal should prescribe provisional measures only 'if it considers that the urgency of the situation so requires.' This change did not prove sufficient, however, as some delegations contended that the Tribunal might act even if the tribunal to which the dispute was submitted obviously had no jurisdiction. To prevent this occurrence, another provision was added that the Law of the Sea Tribunal should prescribe provisional measures only 'if it considers *prima facie* that the tribunal to which the dispute has been submitted would have jurisdiction.'

The *Commentary* continues:

290.6. As a result of all these changes, article 290 became a rather complex provision, trying to ensure, on the one hand, that provisional measures will be available promptly when needed and, on the other hand, that this special power will be exercised with caution and will not interfere too much with the rights of the States concerned. Thus, when the dispute is submitted to a tribunal which cannot act immediately because time is required to constitute it, the parties are given only two weeks (from the date of the request for provisional measures) to reach agreement as to which pre-existing court or tribunal should prescribe such measures. If they do not agree within two weeks on any other court or tribunal, the International Tribunal for the Law of the Sea (or in seabed mining cases the Sea-Bed Disputes Chamber) would be authorized to prescribe provisional measures, if so requested by a party to the dispute and after giving the parties an opportunity to be heard. However, that Tribunal can only act if it considers (a) that the tribunal to which the dispute has been submitted would seem to have *prima facie* jurisdiction over the parties and the subject matter of the dispute; (b) that the urgency of the situation requires provisional measures; or (c) that such measures are needed to preserve the respective rights of the parties to the dispute, or that they are required to prevent serious harm to the marine environment.

290.7. The situation is more straightforward when the dispute is submitted to an existing court or tribunal which can immediately exercise the special jurisdiction to prescribe provisional measures. Apart from the International Court of Justice and the International Tribunal for the Law of the Sea or any of their preconstituted chambers, the parties might have agreed in advance that some permanent court or tribunal—such as the Court of Justice of the European Economic Community—should decide law of the sea disputes between them (in accordance with article 282 of the Convention). Any such court or tribunal, when exercising jurisdiction under Part XV of the Convention (as distinguished from any other jurisdiction it may exercise under some other international agreement), would have power to prescribe 'any provisional measures which it considers appropriate under the circumstances.' However, under article 290, any such court or tribunal would also have to comply with the following general conditions for prescribing provisional measures: (a) it can act only upon the request of a party to the dispute and after giving the parties an opportunity to be heard (paragraph 3); and (b) the measures must be needed 'to preserve the respective rights of the parties to the dispute or to prevent serious harm to the marine environment' (paragraph 1).

290.8. The decisions relating to provisional measures are by their nature provisional. They are prescribed 'pending final adjudication,' and the final judgment or award determines their fate. Such judgment or award may terminate them, or continue them for a specified period or permanently, or modify them to fit the terms of the final adjudication. Even before the final decision, circumstances which originally justified the prescription of provisional measures may change or completely disappear. In such a case, the court or tribunal in charge of the settlement of the dispute may modify or revoke the provisional measures. Again this can be done only upon the request of a party, and after giving the parties an opportunity to be heard. If the circumstances should change before the competent tribunal has been established, the International Tribunal for the Law of the Sea, or any other court or tribunal having special jurisdiction to prescribe provisional measures in accordance with article 290, paragraph 5, would have to decide whether these measures should be changed or revoked. As soon as the tribunal to which the dispute has been originally submitted is constituted, it takes over the question of provisional measures; it can modify, revoke, or affirm such measures, subject to the general conditions specified in article 290, paragraphs 1 to 4. If the provisional measures originally prescribed by the court or tribunal functioning under article 290, paragraph 5, have been revoked by that court or tribunal before the tribunal to which the dispute has been submitted has been constituted, the latter tribunal may, as soon as it is established, reconsider the matter and prescribe the provisional measures which it considers appropriate. It may then either restore the revoked measures or prescribe different ones (subject again to the conditions specified in article 290, paragraphs 1 to 4).

This part of the *Commentary* concludes (paragraph 290.9) by pointing out that paragraph 6 makes it clear that the parties to the dispute are obliged to comply promptly with any provisional measures prescribed (or modified) under Article 290. It goes on to explain that in order to strengthen the pressure of public opinion on the parties with respect to the provisional measures, all the notices are sent not only to the parties to the dispute, but also to such other States Parties to the Convention as the court or tribunal considers appropriate (Article 290, paragraph 4).[67]

The *MOX* (Provisional Measures) case was the occasion for important interpretations by the judges of Article 290, and especially the relations between paragraphs 1 and 5. Thus, Judge Mensah said that in considering a request for the prescription of provisional measures under Article 290 ITLOS is governed by both paragraphs 1 and 5 of Article 290. 'Paragraph 1 sets out the parameters and conditions for the prescription of provisional measures in general.' He went on:

[67] In the *Southern Bluefin Tuna* (Provisional Measures) case, one of the entities participating in that fishery was Taiwan. One of the provisional measures prescribed required the three States parties to the litigation to make further efforts with other States 'and fishing entities' engaged in fishing for that stock with a view to ensuring conservation and promoting the objective of optimum utilization of the stock. ITLOS Rep. 1999, 280, 299 (operative para. (*f*)).

But whatever may be the considerations for determining that the prescription of provisional measures is appropriate under paragraph 1 of article 290 of the Convention, it is important to recognize that they are not the only factors that need to be taken into account when dealing with a request for provisional measures under paragraph 5 of article 290. In other words, although the conditions for provisional measures under paragraph 1 are necessary for prescription of measures under paragraph 5, they are not sufficient. This is because the situations dealt with under the two paragraphs are different from each other in two important respects. The first difference arises from the facts that, whereas a request for the prescription of provisional measures under paragraph 1 of article 290 is dealt with by the court or tribunal to which 'the dispute has been duly submitted' (and which, therefore, is expected to deal with the substance of the dispute, including as appropriate, questions of jurisdiction, admissibility and merits), a request for provisional measures under paragraph 5 is considered by a court or tribunal that will not deal with any of the substantive aspects of the dispute, except the relatively simple issue of whether or not there is reason to believe that *prima facie* the court or tribunal to which the dispute is to be submitted would have jurisdiction to adjudicate upon the dispute. The second difference is that a court or tribunal dealing with a request for provisional measures under paragraph 1 is required to consider measures that are appropriate to preserve rights or prevent harm 'pending the final decision' in the case. On the other hand, a court or tribunal considering a request for provisional measures under paragraph 5 of article 290 has power only to prescribe measures pending the constitution of the arbitral tribunal to which the dispute is being submitted, i.e. the Annex VII arbitral tribunal. These are not mere technical differences: they have significant implications not only with regard to the considerations and factors that need to be taken into account by the respective courts or tribunals but also with regard to the approach to be adopted in considering the evidence adduced before them. ... That court or tribunal is only required and empowered to determine whether, on the evidence adduced before it, it is satisfied that there is a reasonable possibility that a prejudice of rights of the parties (or serious damage to the marine environment) might *occur prior to the constitution of the arbitral tribunal to which the substance of the dispute is being submitted* [italics in original]. This difference in the temporal dimension of the competence of the tribunal imposes a measure of constraint on a court or tribunal dealing with a request for provisional measures under article 290, paragraph 5, of the Convention. That constraint applies fully to this Tribunal in the present case.[68]

Judge Wolfrum also devoted an important part of his separate opinion to the issue of urgency in the context of the Tribunal's jurisdiction. He said that paragraph 5 has to be read in conjunction with paragraph 1, and that when interpreting the notion 'to preserve the respective rights of the parties' account has to be taken of the fact that two different types of provisional measures have to be distinguished, one dealing with a future event and its consequences, and one where the event in question has already occurred. In the former case it is necessary to assess future

[68] ITLOS Rep. 2001, 95, 118, 119. MOX—Mixed Oxide Plant.

developments. 'Such future developments do not have to be certain: probability is sufficient.'[69]

Article 290, paragraph 5, has to be read together with Annex VII, Article 3 (e), and Annex VIII, Article 3 (e). Those provisions are designed to prevent the frustration of the obligation to resort to arbitration. Annex VII requires the President of ITLOS to appoint arbitrators within a specified time-limit from receipt of the request for the appointment where an Annex VII arbitration is the competent dispute settlement organ in the circumstances.[70] Annex VIII contains a similar provision for the appointment to be made by the Secretary-General of the United Nations in the case of what is termed a special arbitration. The existence of these time-limits in those circumstances may be one of the circumstances to be considered by the Tribunal in exercising its discretion whether to prescribe provisional measures.

2.9. ANNEX VI, ARTICLE 25

The procedure to enable ITLOS to exercise the special jurisdiction to prescribe provisional measures is set out in Annex VI, Article 25, as follows:

Provisional measures

1. In accordance with article 290, the Tribunal and its Seabed Disputes Chamber shall have the power to prescribe provisional measures.
2. If the Tribunal is not in session or a sufficient number of members is not available to constitute a quorum, the provisional measures shall be prescribed by the chamber of summary procedure formed under article 15, paragraph 3, of this Annex. Notwithstanding article 15, paragraph 4, of this Annex, such provisional measures may be adopted at the request of any party to the dispute. They shall be subject to review and revision by the Tribunal.

Mesures conservatoires

1. Conformément à l'article 290, le Tribunal et la Chambre pour le règlement des différends relatifs aux fonds marins ont le pouvoir de prescrire des mesures conservatoires.
2. Si le Tribunal ne siège pas ou si le nombre des membres disponibles est inférieure au quorum, les mesures conservatoires sont prescrites par la chambre de procédure sommaire constituée conformément à l'article 15, paragraphe 3, de la présente annexe. Nonobstant l'article 15, paragraph 4, de cette même annexe, ces mesures conservatoires peuvent être prescrites à la demande de toute partie au différend. Elles sont sujettes à appréciation et à revision par le Tribunal.

[69] ITLOS Rep. 2001, 95, 133.

[70] The first instance of this was the appointment by the President of ITLOS (Judge Nelson) of the arbitrators and the President of the arbitral tribunal for the dispute between Malaysia and Singapore concerning land reclamation by Singapore in and around the Straits of Johor. *See* the statement of Judge Nelson at the fifty-eighth session of the General Assembly, 24 November 2003, A/58/PV.64, 33.

Annex VI, Article 25, is the link between the norm-setting provision of Article 290 of the Convention and the procedural pattern of ITLOS.[71] It confirms that ITLOS has power to prescribe provisional measures, but only in accordance with Article 290. In one sense, therefore, this is a restriction on the Tribunal's power, which is limited by the provisions of Article 290. Article 25 also confirms that the Seabed Disputes Chamber, established by Article 186 of the Convention and Annex VI, Article 14, is for the purposes of provisional measures an independent judicial organ whose general jurisdiction is governed by Article 187 of the Convention.[72]

The introduction in paragraph 2 of the Chamber of Summary Procedure as a reserve organ for provisional measures proceedings is another major innovation. It is the continuation of the compromise regarding the place of the compulsory settlement of disputes in the general 'package deal' represented by the Convention as a whole. To some extent this may be regarded as an unusual provision, and it is offset by the last sentence of Article 25, paragraph 2, that provisional measures prescribed by that Chamber are subject to review and revision by the Tribunal itself, presumably as soon as a quorum of its elected members can be attained. This special power of the Chamber for Summary Procedure does not affect the power of any ad hoc or special chamber of either the Tribunal itself under Annex VI, Article 15 (the Tribunal) or Article 36 (the Seabed Disputes Chamber) to prescribe provisional measures in a case of which the chamber is duly seised. Any of those chambers would be a 'court or tribunal' within the meaning of Article 287 and Article 290, paragraph 1. Until such a chamber has been created by the Tribunal or the Seabed Disputes Chamber as the parent body, the parent body would have jurisdiction to make an initial prescription of provisional measures under Article 290, paragraph 1. Subsequent action in regard to those provisional measures would, however, be within the competence of the relevant chamber. In fact one might think that this provision has been introduced through an excess of caution. Given modern communications and travel facilities, it is unlikely that there would be difficulty in convening at least a quorum of members of the Tribunal, whether for a provisional measures case or for any other purpose.

When the Convention was being negotiated, it was not known how ITLOS would organize itself. The Rules of the Tribunal do not provide for 'sessions': by Article 41, paragraph 2, of the Rules, members shall hold themselves permanently available to exercise their functions and shall attend all such meetings, unless they are absent on leave as provided elsewhere in the Rules, or prevented from attending by illness or for other serious reason duly

[71] *See* Virginia *Commentary* (n. 52), vol. V, 389.

[72] On those two provisions of Part XI, *see* Virginia *Commentary* (n. 52), vol. VI, 605 (Art. 186) and 608 (Art. 187). This jurisdiction extends *ratione personae* both to the International Seabed Authority and to individuals in contractual relations with it. ITLOS cannot exercise that extended jurisdiction.

explained to the President who shall inform the Tribunal. Article 41, paragraph 4, of the Rules empowers the Tribunal to fix judicial vacations, but if the practice of the ICJ is followed, a request for provisional measures filed during a judicial vacation would require the attendance of as many members of the Tribunal as possible. In light of this, there is little likelihood of the Tribunal's Chamber of Summary Procedure being called upon to hear a request for provisional members. Furthermore, that Chamber is not empowered to act for the Seabed Disputes Chamber in the eventuality contemplated by Article 25, paragraph 2, if the case is one that comes within the exclusive jurisdiction of the Seabed Disputes Chamber.

Eleven elected members constitute the quorum required for the Tribunal (Annex VI, Article 13, paragraph 1). The quorum required for the Seabed Disputes Chamber, which consists of eleven members selected by a majority of the elected members of the Tribunal, is seven of the selected members (Annex VI, Article 35, paragraphs 1 and 7). Judges ad hoc are not included in the calculation of the quorum.

The details of the proceedings for provisional measures are regulated in the Rules of the Tribunal. The original draft rules for the Tribunal were prepared by the Secretariat.[73] In the discussion of that initial draft there was general agreement that the rules regarding provisional measures and the rules regarding the prompt release of vessels and crews should as far as possible be brought into line with each other, and as the Chamber for Summary Procedure was regarded as essential for the prompt release of vessels, so should it be brought into the rules for provisional measures.[74] The Secretariat therefore introduced this idea in Article 84, paragraph 2, of its revised draft of the Rules of the Tribunal prepared for the Preparatory Commission.[75] The main difference is that provisional measures are prescribed in an order, and questions of prompt release are decided in a judgment.

2.10. THE EXTENSION OF THE CONVENTION'S PART XV

Since the conclusion of the Law of the Sea Convention on 10 December 1982, the dispute settlement provisions of Part XV have been incorporated in other

[73] PrepCom Report, LOS/PCN/SCN.4/WP2, 27 July 1987, reproduced in R. Platzöder, op. cit. in n. 63, vol. VII, 209.

[74] Supplement to the draft rules of the Tribunal (LOS/PCN/SCN.4/WP2/Add.1, 23 March 1985), reproduced in Platzöder, op. cit. in n. 63, vol. VII, 324. Explanatory statement by the Secretariat (LOS/PCN/SCN.4/1985/CRP.11, 2 April 1095, ibid. 444. Chairman's summary of discussion on the draft rules of the International Tribunal for the Law of the Sea (LOS/PCN/SCN.4/L.4/Add.1, 28 February 1986, art. 88B), PrepCom Report vol. III, 66. Art 291 of the Convention, on the prompt release of vessels and crews, does not mention the Chamber as the residual judicial organ in that type of case.

[75] Final draft rules of the Tribunal (LOS/PCN/SCN.4/WP16/Add.1), ibid., vol. I, 28.

multilateral treaties related to the purposes of the Convention within the meaning of Article 288, paragraph 2, of the Convention, relating to the jurisdiction of the dispute settlement organs recognized by the Convention. Article 288, paragraph 2, provides that any court or tribunal referred to in Article 287 shall also have jurisdiction over any dispute concerning the interpretation or application of an international agreement related to the purposes of this Convention, which is submitted to it in accordance with the agreement. That provision is completed by Article 291 on access, by which the dispute settlement processes of Part XV shall be open to entities other than States Parties only as specifically provided for in the Convention. More particularly as regards ITLOS, Annex VI, Article 21, on its jurisdiction, provides that the jurisdiction of the Tribunal comprises all disputes and all applications submitted to it in accordance with this Convention and all matters specially provided for in any other agreement which confers jurisdiction on the Tribunal. In addition, Article 22 goes further and provides that if all the parties to a treaty or convention already in force (*déjà en vigueur)* and concerning the subject-matter covered by this Convention so agree, any disputes concerning the interpretation or application of such treaty or convention may, in accordance with such agreement, be submitted to the Tribunal. That provision is similar to Article 37 of the Statute of the Permanent Court in that it enables ITLOS to exercise jurisdiction over disputes concerning the interpretation or application of treaties *already* in force. As the Virginia *Commentary* has put it, Article 22 introduces the possibility of adding to a treaty already in force a jurisdictional provision, where none existed before.[76] In this connection, Annex VI, Article 19, paragraph 2, provides that when an entity other than a State Party or the International Seabed Authority is a party to a case submitted to it, ITLOS shall fix the amount which that party is to contribute towards the expenses of the Tribunal. This includes both conventions concluded under the auspices of the United Nations and others concluded elsewhere.[77] These agreements usually contain special provisions for the case where a party to the agreement is not a party to the Law of the Sea Convention.

The basic pattern was set in the Agreement for the Implementation of the Provisions of the United Nations Convention on the Law of the Sea of 10 December 1982 relating to the Conservation and Management of Straddling Fish Stocks and Highly Migratory Fish Stocks of 4 August 1995.[78] That Agreement fully incorporates Part XV of the Law of the Sea

[76] Virginia *Commentary* (n. 52), vol. V, 363. The expression 'already in force' is ambiguous. Prima facie it should mean 'in force when the Convention entered into force', but it can also mean 'in force when the proceedings are instituted', or even later. Ibid.

[77] Particulars are given in ITLOS Yearbook 2002 at 125, and on the Tribunal's website. At the time of writing seven agreements containing such provisions have been concluded, but not all of them are in force.

[78] UNTS 37924; *Law of the Sea Bulletin* No. 29 (1995) 25.

Convention *mutatis mutandis* to any dispute between States parties to the Agreement, whether or not they are parties to the Law of the Sea Convention (Article 30). It also contains a special provision in Article 31 regarding provisional measures:

1. Pending the settlement of a dispute in accordance with this Part, the parties to the dispute shall make every effort to enter into provisional arrangements of a practical nature.
2. Without prejudice to article 290 of the Convention, the court or tribunal to which the dispute has been submitted under this Part may prescribe any provisional measures which it considers appropriate under the circumstances to preserve the respective rights of the parties to the dispute or to prevent damage to the stocks in question, as well as in the circumstances referred to in article 7, paragraph 5, and article 16, paragraph 2.[79]
3. A State Party to this Agreement which is not a Party to the Convention may declare that notwithstanding article 290, paragraph 5, of the Convention, the International Tribunal for the Law of the Sea shall not be entitled to prescribe, modify or revoke provisional measures without the agreement of such State.

The expression of Article 290, paragraph 1, 'to prevent serious harm to the marine environment' has been replaced here by 'to prevent damage to the stocks in question'. It is not clear why this change was made. That was followed by the Honolulu Convention of 5 September 2000 on the Conservation and Management of Highly Migratory Fish Stocks in the Western and Central Pacific Ocean.[80] Article 31 on the settlement of disputes applies Part VIII of the 1995 Agreement *mutatis mutandis* between members of the Commission established by that Convention, whether or not they are parties to the 1995 Agreement, and, once removed, whether or not they are parties to the 1982 Convention.

The Convention on the Protection of the Underwater Cultural Heritage, concluded under the auspices of UNESCO on 2 November 2001 is similar.[81] Article 25 on the settlement of disputes provides that if after a process of mediation through UNESCO machinery or otherwise the dispute is not settled, the provisions of Part XV of the Law of the Sea Convention shall apply *mutatis mutandis* whether or not the parties to the dispute are parties to that Convention. It goes further. Paragraph 4 provides that any procedure chosen by a State Party to the 1982 Convention by a State Party to the UNESCO Convention under Article 387 of the 1982 instrument shall apply *mutatis mutandis* to the settlement of disputes under the UNESCO

[79] Those articles deal with the compatibility of conservation and management measures, and with the special problem of areas of high seas surrounded entirely by an area under the national jurisdiction of a single State.

[80] *Law of the Sea Bulletin* No. 45 (2000), 79.

[81] Not yet in force. For text, *see* UNESCO, General Conference, 31st session, Resolutions 50; *Law of the Sea Bulletin* No. 48 (2002), 29.

Convention unless that State, when ratifying, accepting, approving, or acceding to the UNESCO Convention or at any time thereafter may choose another procedure pursuant to Article 297 for the settlement of disputes arising out of the UNESCO Convention.

The Windhoek Convention for the Conservation and Management of Fishery Activities in the South-East Atlantic Ocean of 20 April 2001 provides in Article 24 for dispute settlement and by paragraphs 4 and 5:[82]

4. Where a dispute is not referred for settlement within a reasonable time of the consultations referred to in paragraph 2, or where a dispute is not resolved by recourse to other means referred to in this article within a reasonable time, such dispute shall, at the request of any party to the dispute, be submitted for binding decision in accordance with procedures for the settlement of disputes provided in Part XV of the 1982 Convention or, when the dispute concerns one or more straddling stocks, by provisions set out in Part VIII of the 1995 Agreement. The relevant part of the 1982 Convention and the 1995 Agreement shall apply whether or not the parties to the dispute are also Parties to these instruments.
5. A court or panel to which any dispute has been submitted under this article shall apply relevant provisions of the Convention, of the 1982 Convention, of the 1995 Agreement, as well as generally accepted standards for the conservation and management of living marine resources and other rules of international law, compatible with the 1982 Convention and the 1995 Agreement, with a view to ensuring the conservation of the fish stocks concerned.

Those are the most comprehensive to date in incorporating and adapting the provisions of Part XV for the settlement of disputes arising out of them. Clearly, no single or simple formula is used, but the reference in all these texts to Part XV of the 1982 Convention is sufficient to bring these agreements within the scope of Article 288, paragraph 2, and Annex VI, Article 21.

It may be assumed that with these multiple choice provisions and the various options that are given to the parties to a dispute, the court or tribunal first seised will have jurisdiction, and that this would exclude the right of any other party to make a different choice. *Una via selecta, altera non datur*.

[82] ITLOS Yearbook 2002 131.

3

The Rules

I. THE INTERNATIONAL COURT OF JUSTICE

3.1. STATUTE AND RULES

As seen, the sparse axiomatic statement of Article 41 of the Statute of the International Court of Justice left the development of the law and practice relating to provisional measures of protection in the hands of the Court. Article 30 of the Statute requires the Court to frame rules for carrying out its functions, and by paragraph 2 the rules may provide for assessors to sit with the Court or with any of its chambers, without the right to vote. The avulsive judicial experience has to a great extent been generalized in successive versions of the Rules of Court, in which the substantive and the adjectival law are sometimes intermixed. The 1929 Committee of Jurists (§ 2.3 above) drew attention to the function of the Rules in dealing with provisional measures of protection. Since 2001 the Court has also been issuing formal Practice Directions for use by the States appearing before it, additional to the Rule of Court.[1] None of the Practice Directions directly concerns provisional measures, but they are all of general application to the conduct of all litigation in the International Court of Justice.

On the basis of Article 30 of the Statute, the Permanent Court of International Justice first adopted Rules of Court in 1922. They were amended in 1926, 1927, and 1931, and thoroughly revised in 1936. The PCIJ published the records of its deliberations on these sets of Rules, now mainly of historical interest. That Court's limited experience of provisional measures meant that those Rules were to a large extent an abstraction. The present International Court of Justice adopted its initial Rules of Court in 1946, for the most part an adaptation of the Rules of 1936 with a few changes.[2] They were amended in 1972[3] and were thoroughly revised in 1978 (with a further

[1] The Practice Directions are available on the Court's website. *See also* the Court's Report to the 57th session of the General Assembly, 57 GAOR Sup. 4 (A/57/4) at 98, and T. Gill, *Rosennes's The World Court: What It Is and How It Works* 303 (Leiden: Martinus Nijhoff, 2003).

[2] *See* on this M.O. Hudson, 'The Twenty-Fifth Year of the World Court', 41 AJIL 1 (1947).

[3] An authoritative account of the amendments of the Rules of 1972 is E. Jiménez de Aréchaga, 'Amendments to the Rules of Procedure of the International Court of Justice', 67 AJIL 1 (1973). *See also* G. Guyomar, *Commentaire du Règlement de la Cour internationale de Justice: Interprétation et pratique* (Paris: Pedone, 1973); Sh. Rosenne, 'The 1972 Revision of the Rules of the International Court of Justice', 8 *Israel L. Rev.* 197 (1973).

amendment not relevant here in 2000), and those are the Rules in force today.[4] No records of the Court's deliberations on those Rules have been published. By the time the 1978 Rules were adopted there was already an accumulation of judicial experience, and those Rules were accordingly less 'abstract' than the previous versions.

3.2. THE RULES OF THE INTERNATIONAL COURT

In considering the early Rules and practice of the Permanent Court and of the present Court, one should keep in mind that the members of the Courts were not required to live at or near The Hague and that initially the Permanent Court carried out its business in judicial sessions. This has changed radically. Today, with the increase in its workload, the present Court is virtually in continuous session except during normal judicial vacations, and many of its members have taken up residence in The Hague. Before the advent of air travel, time would be required to convene the Court if it were not in session when a request for provisional measures was made. In addition, communications in general were not as speedy or as reliable as they are today, when facsimile and e-mail together with efficient courier services provide almost instantaneous and accurate transmission of texts and documents worldwide, and modern telephonic equipment enables interested persons to conduct video conference calls also the world over. The prevailing physical conditions led to the problems which the Permanent Court faced, and which continued in the present Court until the last decade or so (except for the ease of modern travel by air greatly facilitating the urgent convening of a court or tribunal).

Neither the present International Court of Justice nor ITLOS seems to have experienced any difficulties in convening at short notice. On the other hand, these technical developments and the geographical spread of international litigation, much of which is intercontinental, are bringing new problems inseparable from the globalization of contemporary international relations. One of these is found in the large time differences which must be taken into account in assessing intercontinental litigation. This is not limited to provisional measures cases, and its impact is being felt in other branches of

[4] For an account of the revision of 1978, *see* M. Lachs, 'The Revised Procedure of the International Court of Justice', *Essays on the Development of the International Legal Order in Memory of Haro F. Panhuys* 21 (Alphen aan den Rijn: Sijthoff & Noordhoff, 1980). *And see* G. Guyomar, *Commentaire du Règlement de la Cour internationale de Justice adopté le 14 avril 1978: Interprétation et pratique* (Paris: Pedone, 1983); Sh. Rosenne, *Procedure in the International Court of Justice: A Commentary on the 1978 Rules of the International Court of Justice* (The Hague: Martinus Nijhoff, 1983). On the revision of 2000 *see* Sh. Rosenne, 'The International Court of Justice: Revision of Articles 79 and 80 of the Rules of Court', 14 *Leiden J. Int'l L.* 77 (2001).

the law of international litigation, notably the time of the entry into force of treaty action with the depositary in New York (or elsewhere) which confers jurisdiction on the Court or removes it and the capital of a State affected by that treaty action. There are two decisions of the present Court concerning the acceptance of jurisdiction under Article 36, paragraph 2, of the Statute, which do not make any allowance for this time difference.[5] One case is pending in which the time difference between the capitals concerned and The Hague may be relevant for the institution of proceedings, the applicant State not having known of the withdrawal by the respondent of its declaration accepting the compulsory jurisdiction.[6] The application in that case was not accompanied by a request for the indication of provisional measures.

3.3. THE RULES OF 1922

On 24 March 1922 the Permanent Court adopted its first Rules, before it had acquired any judicial experience. For what it designated 'Interim Protection' (a term retained in the Rules until 1978), Article 57 simply laid down that when the Court was not sitting, any measures for the preservation in the meantime of the respective rights of the parties should be indicated by the President, and that any refusal by the parties to conform to the suggestions of the Court or of the President with regard to such measures should be placed on record.[7] As a matter of substantive law it appears to grant the President of the Court power to indicate provisional measures when the Court is not sitting. In the first case heard under those Rules, the *Denunciation of the Treaty of 2 November 1865 between China and Belgium* case, the President (Huber) indicated a series of substantive measures to be undertaken by China pending the final decision of the Court. Following agreement between the parties he revoked that Order a month later.[8] The question did not arise in the second case under those Rules, the *Chorzów Factory (Indemnities)* case.[9]

[5] *Right of Passage over Indian Territory* (Preliminary Objections) case, ICJ Rep. 1957, 125; *Land and Maritime Boundary between Cameroon and Nigeria* (Preliminary Objections) case, ICJ Rep. 1998, 275.

[6] The *Territorial and Maritime Dispute between Nicaragua and Colombia* case, in which a preliminary objection based on this factor has been raised, is an illustration of this problem. The preliminary objection is pending at the time of writing.

[7] For the Rules of 1922, *see* International Intermediary Institute The Hague, *The Permanent Court of International Justice: Statute and Rules*, 1922 (published on behalf of the Court). For the deliberations preceding those Rules, *see* PCIJ Ser. D, Acts and Documents concerning the Organization of the Court, No. 2, *Preparation of the Rules of Court: Minutes of Meetings held during the Preliminary Session of the Court with Annexes (January 30th to March 24th 1922)*.

[8] Orders of 8 January and 15 February 1927, PCIJ Ser. A 8, 6, 8. The case was later discontinued. Order of 25 May 1929, Ser. A 18. For the Treaty of 1865 *see* 131 CTS 373.

[9] PCIJ Ser. A 12 (1927).

3.4. THE RULES OF 1931

That provision remained in force until 1931, when a new version of the Article was adopted. (There were amendments in 1926 and 1927 but they are not relevant here.) Following the 1929 meeting of the Committee of Jurists, the League Assembly on 25 September 1930 requested the Permanent Court to examine various suggestions made by the Jurists regarding sessions of the Court. The Court took this up and found that Article 57 was among the articles that called for re-examination. The underlying change required here was to introduce the idea that the judges are, in principle, always at the disposal of the Court, and that the Court is always at the disposal of the parties.[10] Following a discussion running over several meetings of the Court, Article 57 was completely revised, to read:

> IV—*Interim Protection*
>
> An application made to the Court by one or both of the parties, for an indication of interim measures of protection, shall have priority over all other cases. The decision thereon shall be treated as a matter of urgency, and if the Court is not sitting, it shall be convened without delay by the President for the purpose.
>
> If no application is made, and if the Court is not sitting, the President may convene the Court to submit to it the question whether such measures are expedient.
>
> In all cases, the Court shall only indicate measures of protection after giving the parties an opportunity of presenting their observations on the subject.

There are several interesting aspects of that text, which on close inspection is seen to combine elements both of substance and of procedure. The powers of the President were reduced and limited to convening the Court without delay if it was not sitting when the request was made. Urgency is introduced ostensibly as a question of procedure, although it is also a matter of substance in that the Court requires to be satisfied as to the urgency of the matter as one of the ingredients for the determination that the circumstances could justify the indication of provisional measures. As a matter of procedure, the decision is to be treated as a matter of urgency, meaning that even if the Court is working on another case at the time, the hearing, deliberation of the Court, and its decision on the provisional measures are to have priority. Striking in this version of the Rule is its dropping of any possible sanction for non-compliance with the suggestions for measures of protection, although the sanction of the 1922 Rules was mild enough. The second element of substance is in the middle paragraph, which recalls the power of the Central American Court of Justice to take the initiative in indicating provisional measures, as well as President Huber's initiative in the *Belgium–China*

[10] From the letter of the Registrar of 21 February 1931 to the Secretary-General of the League, forwarding the revised Rules of that date. Reproduced in PCIJ Ser. D 2 Add. 2, 5. For the discussion on provisional measures, *see* pp. 188 to 200. For the Rules of 1931, *see* PCIJ Ser. D 1, 2nd edn (1931).

case in 1927.[11] This is perhaps surprising, not only on account of the political difficulties to which that initiative led during the short time in which the Central American Court was functioning, but also because there is nothing in the Statute in general, and in Article 41 in particular (in the context of consensual jurisdiction *ad litem* for contentious cases), allowing the Court to undertake any such initiative.

The main element of procedure is in the third paragraph, requiring both parties to be given an opportunity of presenting their observations on the subject. The Rule contained no provision regarding the form those observations should take. In the three cases that were heard under those Rules, the *Legal Status of the South-Eastern Territory of Greenland*,[12] the *Administration of the Prince von Pless*,[13] and the *Polish Agrarian Reform and the German Minority*[14] cases, different procedures were followed. In *South-Eastern Greenland* the Court held a hearing and received written summaries of the parties' statements. In *Prince von Pless*, when the President (Adatci) convened the Court he also envisaged a hearing. At the same time he took the initiative and telegraphed to the President of Poland with some suggestions regarding possible action by Poland pending the hearing.[15] But in the course of a written exchange that followed the filing of the request the parties reached an agreement that made the provisional measures unnecessary. In *Polish Agrarian Reform* the Court held a hearing and found that the request was not in conformity with Article 41.

3.5. THE RULES OF 1936, 1946, AND 1972

The Rules of 1931 only dealt with part of the recommendations of the 1929 Committee of Jurists, and the Court continued with the work, later taking into account the amendments to the Statute adopted by the League Assembly in 1929. One of the purposes was to codify the Court's practice.[16] The Rules then adopted served the Permanent Court and the present Court (with a minor change in 1946) until the entry into force of the Rules of 1978,[17] and it is therefore under their regime that most of the major early developments in

[11] Above n. 8. [12] PCIJ Ser. A/B 48 (1932). [13] PCIJ Ser. A/B 52 (1933).
[14] PCIJ Ser. A/B 58 (1933).
[15] PCIJ Ser. E 9, 165, note. This is not mentioned in the Order of 11 May 1933 (above n. 13).
[16] PCIJ Ser. D 2 Add. 3, 5. This addendum is entitled *Elaboration of the Rules of Court of March 11th, 1936*. In 1940 the Court published a Fourth Addendum to No. 2, consisting of extracts from the Minutes of 1934, 1935 and 1936 systematically arranged according to the articles of the Rules. On what was discussed as Art. 57, *see* that Fourth Addendum at 234. The Article was renumbered 61. For the Rules as adopted on 11 March 1936, *see* PCIJ Ser. D 1, 4th edn (1940), 31.
[17] International Court of Justice, Acts and Documents concerning the Organization of the Court, No. 1, *Charter of the United Nations, Statute and Rules of Court*, 2nd edn, 54 (May 1947). The numbering of the paragraphs was introduced in 1946.

the substantive and procedural law of provisional measures took place. In those Rules Article 61, on interim protection, was placed first in Heading I—Contentious procedure, Section I—Procedure before the full court, II—Occasional rules. Article 61 (in its 1946 version) read:

1. A request [*demande*] for the indication of interim measures of protection may be filed at any time during the proceedings in the case in connection with which it is made. The request shall specify the case to which it relates, the rights to be protected and the interim measures of which the indication is proposed.
2. A request for the indication of provisional measures shall have priority over all other cases. The decision thereon shall be treated as a matter of urgency.
3. If the Court is not sitting, the members shall be convened by the President forthwith. Pending the meeting of the Court and a decision by it, the President shall, if need be, take such measures as may appear to him necessary in order to enable the Court to give an effective decision.
4. The Court may indicate interim measures of protection other than those proposed in the request.
5. The rejection of a request for the indication of interim measures of protection shall not prevent the party which has made it from making a fresh request in the same case based on new facts.
6. The Court may indicate interim measures of protection *proprio motu*. If the Court is not sitting, the President may convene the members in order to submit to the Court the question whether it is expedient to indicate such measures.
7. The Court may at any time by reason of a change in the situation revoke or modify its decision indicating interim measures of protection.
8. The Court shall only indicate interim measures of protection after giving the parties an opportunity of presenting their observations on the subject. The same rule applies when the Court revokes or modifies a decision indicating such measures.

[9. When the President has occasion to convene the members of the Court, judges who have been appointed under Article 31 of the Statute [judges ad hoc] shall be convened if their presence can be assured at the date fixed by the President for hearing the parties.]

(Paragraph 9 was dropped in 1946.)

Only one case, the *Electricity Company of Sofia and Bulgaria* case, was heard under this provision.[18] A request was first filed on 4 July 1938 shortly after the filing of the memorial, and a hearing was held on that request, which

[18] *Electricity Company of Sofia and Bulgaria* (Interim Measures) case, PCIJ Ser. A/B 79 (1939). At that time the so-called 'phoney war' was in full progress, and while the President was laudably anxious to protect the international judicial organ and required it to continue functioning regardless of what was happening all around it, the fact remains that Eastern Europe (Poland) had been overrun and the remainder of the continent was gearing up for the armed hostilities to begin after winter had passed. The Bulgarian Government of the day was justified in raising the issue of *force majeure* to explain the non-participation of its nationals in the proceedings of December 1939. Indeed, in a later order of February 1940—the last it made—the Permanent Court fixed 16 May 1940 for the opening of the hearing on the merits of that case. PCIJ Ser. A/B 80 (1940). By that date the invasion of the Netherlands was in full swing and the Court, or what was left of it, had evacuated itself to Geneva.

the Bulgarian agent did not attend. The Court adjourned that hearing to a date to be fixed. Shortly afterwards, Bulgaria sent a telegram to the Court and that led to the withdrawal of the request for provisional measures. On 27 August 1938 the President made an Order recording that withdrawal and stating that in the circumstances there was no occasion to fix a date for the public hearing.[19] That withdrawal was subject to a condition, and later, when that condition was not met, Belgium, on 14 October 1939 (after the Second World War had broken out in Europe but while both Belgium and Bulgaria were still neutral, as was the Netherlands, the seat of the Court), filed a second incidental request for the indication of provisional measures of protection. The President fixed 4 December as the date for the hearing to which the Bulgarian Judge ad hoc was summoned. Neither the Bulgarian agent nor that judge attended the hearing, contending the existence of *force majeure* which prevented their travelling to The Hague and, in the case of the agent, the difficulties of consulting with foreign (French) counsel. Nevertheless the Court relying on Article 61, paragraph 4, of the Rules, indicated some provisional measures which were different from those requested by Belgium. The war prevented the continuation of that litigation on the international level, and with the dissolution of the Permanent Court in 1946 the international dispute was terminated.

The present Court adopted the Rules of 1936 with only a minor change in Article 61 in the Rules of 6 May 1946. That change consisted in the dropping of paragraph 9, thereby allowing the attendance of the judges ad hoc in all cases of provisional measures.[20] The Rule was retained unchanged in the revision of 1972, being renumbered as Article 66.[21]

3.6. THE RULES OF 1978

In 1978 the Court completely revised all its Rules, largely based on experience gained since the previous Rules.[22] Experience shows that the accumulated judicial action continues to regulate the Court's activities in this matter. Instead of being concentrated in a single Rule, the material is now spread over Articles 73 to 78, giving the impression of a codification or consolidation of the law as it had evolved up to 1978. The Rules currently in force are as follows:

[19] *Electricity Company of Sofia and Bulgaria* (Preliminary Objections) case, PCIJ Ser. A/B 77 (1939), 66–67; Ser. E 14 (1938), 180.

[20] ICJ, *Acts and Documents concerning the Organization of the Court, No. 1,* 2nd edn, 54, 74 (1947).

[21] ICJ, *Acts and Documents concerning the Organization of the Court, No. 3*, 93, 133 (1977).

[22] ICJ, *Acts and Documents concerning the Organization of the Court*, No. 5, 93, 133 (1989), reissued as *Rules of Court (1978): as amended on 5 December 2000* (2000).

Section D. Incidental Proceedings

Subsection 1. Interim Protection

Article 73

1. A written request for the indication of provisional measures may be made by a party at any time during the course of the proceedings in the case in connection with which the request is made.
2. The request shall specify the reasons therefor, the possible consequences if it is not granted, and the measures requested. A certified copy shall forthwith be transmitted by the Registrar to the other party.

1. Une partie peut présenter une demande en indication de mesures conservatoires par écrit à tout moment de la procédure engagée en l'affaire au sujet de laquelle la demande est introduite.
2. La demande indique les motifs sur lesquels elle se fonde, les conséquences éventuelles de son rejet et les mesures sollicitées. Copie certifiée conforme de la demande est immédiatement transmise par le Greffier à la partie adverse.

Article 74

1. A request for the indication of provisional measures shall have priority over all other cases.
2. The Court, if it is not sitting when the request is made, shall be convened forthwith for the purpose of proceeding to a decision on the request as a matter of urgency.
3. The Court, or the President if the Court is not sitting, shall fix a date for a hearing which will afford the parties an opportunity of being represented at it. The Court shall receive and take into account any observations that may be presented to it before the closure of the oral proceedings.
4. Pending the meeting of the Court, the President may call upon the parties to act in such a way as will enable any order the Court may make on the request for provisional measures to have its appropriate effects.

1. La demande en indication de mesures conservatoires a priorité sur toutes autres affaires.
2. Si la Cour ne siège pas au moment de la présentation de la demande, elle est immédiatement convoquée pour statuer d'urgence sur cette demande.
3. La Cour ou, si elle ne siège pas, le président fixe la date de la procédure orale de manière à donner aux parties la possibilité de s'y faire représenter. La Cour reçoit et prend en considération toutes observations qui peuvent lui être présentées avant la clôture de cette procédure.
4. En attendant que la Cour se réunisse, le président peut inviter les parties à agir de manière que toute ordonnance de la Cour sur la demande en indication de mesures conservatoires puisse avoir les effets voulus.

Article 75

1. The Court may at any time decide to examine *proprio motu* whether the circumstances of the case require the indication of provisional measures which ought to be taken or complied with by any or all of the parties.

1. La Cour peut à tout moment décider d'examiner d'office si les circonstances de l'affaire exigent l'indication de mesures conservatoires que les parties ou l'une d'elles devraient prendre ou exécuter.

2. When a request for provisional measures has been made, the Court may indicate measures that are in whole or in part other than those requested, or that ought to be taken or complied with by the party which has itself made the request.

2. Lorsqu'une demande en indication de mesures conservatoires lui est présentée, la Cour peut indiquer des mesures totalement ou partiellement différentes de celles qui sont sollicitées, ou des mesures à prendre ou à exécuter par la partie même dont émane la demande.

3. The rejection of a request for the indication of provisional measures shall not prevent the party which made it from making a fresh request in the same case based on new facts.

3. Le rejet d'une demande en indication de mesures conservatoires n'empêche pas la partie qui l'avait introduite de présenter en la même affaire une nouvelle demande fondée sur des faits nouveaux.

Article 76

1. At the request of a party the Court may, at any time before the final judgment in the case, revoke or modify any decision concerning provisional measures if, in its opinion, some change in the situation justifies such revocation or modification.

1. A la demande d'une partie, la Cour peut, à tout moment avant l'arrêt définitif en l'affaire, rapporter ou modifier toute décision concernant des mesures conservatoires si un changement dans la situation lui paraît justifier que cette décision soit rapportée ou modifiée.

2. Any application by a party proposing such a revocation or modification shall specify the change in the situation considered to be relevant.

2. Toute demande présentée par une partie et tendant à ce qu'une décision concernant des mesures conservatoires soit rapportée ou modifiée indique le changement dans la situation considéré comme pertinent.

3. Before taking any decision under paragraph 1 of this Article the Court shall afford the parties an opportunity of presenting their observations on the subject.

3. Avant de prendre une décision en vertu du paragraphe 1 du présent article, la Cour donne aux parties la possibilité de présenter des observations à ce sujet.

Article 77

Any measures indicated by the Court under Articles 73 and 75 of these Rules, and any decision taken by the Court under Article 76, paragraph 1, of these Rules, shall forthwith be communicated to the Secretary-General of the United Nations for transmission to the Security Council in pursuance of Article 41, paragraph 2, of the Statute.

Toutes mesures indiquées par la Cour en vertu des articles 73 et 75 du présent Règlement et toute décision prise par la Cour en vertu de l'article 76, paragraphe 1, sont immédiatement communiquées au Secrétaire général de l'Organisation des Nations Unies pour transmission au Conseil de sécurité conformément à l'article 41, paragraphe 2, du Statut.

Article 78

The Court may request information from the parties on any matter connected with the implementation of any provisional measures it has indicated.

La Cour peut demander aux parties des renseignements sur toutes questions relatives à la mise en œuvre de mesures conservatoires indiquées par elle.

Those Rules constitute what is now denominated Part III (*Proceedings in Contentious Cases*), Section D (*Incidental Proceedings*), Subsection 1, *Interim Protection*. Articles 73 to 78 are the first group of articles in Part III of the revised Rules of Court of 1978. In the heading of this section, the term *Incidental Proceedings* replaces *Occasional rules*. That more accurately reflects the place of proceedings for provisional measures in the context of judicial proceedings. It corresponds to the widely used expression *Incidental jurisdiction* to describe that jurisdiction which the Statute authorizes the Court to exercise in relation to the parties to the Statute, without the degree of specific consent of the parties required for the principal jurisdiction to determine the merits (*see* § 1.2). The hearing, which is now obligatory,[23] ensures that the respondent has an opportunity to give the Court some idea of how it sees the case as a whole. Nevertheless, the Court, acting *proprio motu*, can decide, as it did in the provisional measures phase of the *LaGrand* case, to forego all proceedings and proceed to indicate a provisional measure *ex parte* and only on the basis of the applicant's statements in the application instituting the proceedings and in the request. That procedure can only be justified, if at all in the light of modern communication facilities, by the extreme urgency that the Court saw in the case, one of the capital punishment cases (§ 8.5 below).

As is now clarified in the Rules, in these incidental proceedings the Court requires the party making the request to establish the existence of a case in which the Court has at least prima facie jurisdiction over the merits of the claim that the party is advancing.[24] That prima facie jurisdiction, discussed in Chapter 4, is frequently established after rapid proceedings and without full examination of all the facts concerning the merits or all the possible arguments regarding jurisdiction and admissibility. It is, therefore, provisional and rebuttable, although instances of this are rare. It really means little more

[23] Despite the categorical language of the Rule, there may be doubt whether oral proceedings will always be held. A similar provision appeared in the 1978 version of Art. 80 on counter-claims, but the Court has refused to hold a hearing when there was opposition to the admissibility of the counter-claims, on the ground that it was sufficiently well informed of the position of the parties. *Application of the Genocide Convention* (Counter-claims) case, ICJ Rep. 1997, 247, 256 (para. 25): and *see* the separate opinion of Judge Sir E. Lauterpacht at 278. Art. 80 was accordingly revised in 2000, and the requirement for a hearing was dropped.

[24] The only instance in which a request for provisional measures was not acted upon because of uncertainty over the existence of a case was in the *Request for Examination of the Situation in Accordance with Paragraph 63 of the Court's Judgment of 20 December 1995 in the Nuclear Tests (New Zealand* v *France)* case, ICJ Rep. 1995, 291, 306 (paras. 6, 67).

than that the lack of jurisdiction is not manifest on the face of things. In the history of the present Court, there is only one case in which the Court indicated provisional measures on the basis of a prima facie finding of this nature and later found that it had no jurisdiction to entertain the merits of the case—the *Anglo-Iranian Oil Co.* case. There are two cases in which in the later substantive phase the Court found that since the claims were first made and provisional measures had been indicated the claims no longer had any object and that the Court was therefore not called upon to give any decision on them—the *Nuclear Tests* cases, although the decisions were not based on purely jurisdictional grounds.[25]

Article 73 corresponds to Article 61, paragraph 1, of the 1946 Rules (Article 66 of the 1972 Rules). In this paragraph, although the words 'during the course of the proceedings in the case' are unchanged, their meaning may have become modified as the consequence of the new language of Article 38, paragraphs 2 and 5, of the Rules.[26] In the first sentence of paragraph 2, the expression 'the possible consequences if it is not granted' replaces 'the rights to be protected'. At first glance this may involve some departure from the language of the Statute. Closer examination discloses that it brings the procedure nearer the phrase in the Statute 'if it [the Court] considers that circumstances so require'. The Court has always attached importance to that factor, which in practice links urgency to the anticipated harm likely to result if the requested measures are not granted. (This is discussed in § 8.7.) It is arguable that this also can imply some assessment by the Court of the nature of the decision on the merits and the chances of each party on the merits. But speculation of that nature is hardly compatible with the international judicial function. As an arbitration of the International Centre for the Settlement of Investment Disputes recently put it: 'While hypothetical issues are stimulating and academically challenging, they are beyond the ken of an arbitral tribunal determining real issues of fact and law.' And: 'Expectations of success or failure in an arbitration or judicial case are conjectures.'[27]

Article 74, paragraphs 1, 2, and 4, correspond to Article 61, paragraphs 2 and 3, of the 1946 Rules with drafting changes. Paragraph 1 echoes Article 54, paragraph 2, regarding the opening of oral proceedings in any case.[28] Paragraph 2 repeats Article 20, paragraph 6, by which in case of urgency the President may convene the Court at any time. Paragraph 3 is new, replacing former Article 61. Here the Court faces the challenge which has been presented to it in many cases of a request for the indication of provisional measures since

[25] *Anglo-Iranian Oil. Co* case, ICJ Rep. 1952, 91. *Nuclear Tests* cases, *Australia* v *France*, ICJ Rep. 1974, 253; *New Zealand* v *France*, ibid. 457. *See* § 6.3 below.

[26] *See* Ch. 4 n. 5 and in general, Ch. 6.

[27] *Marffezini* v *Kingdom of Spain* (Case No. ARB/97/7), Procedural Order No. 2 (28 October 2000) 124 ILR 6 at 8.

[28] On the application of Art. 74 in proceedings for the indication of provisional measures, *see* Ch. 7 n. 30. On para. 3, *see* § 7.4. Practice Direction VI is applicable to the oral proceedings on a request for provisional measures.

1946, in which the named respondent at that stage of the proceedings has declined to acknowledge the jurisdiction of the Court and did not appear at the hearings on the provisional measures. The first instance of this was the *Anglo-Iranian Oil Co.* case in 1951. Since then, in the two *Fisheries Jurisdiction* cases, the two *Nuclear Tests* cases, the *Trial of Pakistani Prisoners of War*, and the *Aegean Sea Continental Shelf* cases (in the last two cases the Court declined to indicate provisional measures) the Court also decided that the first written pleadings should address issues of jurisdiction and, if necessary, admissibility, a new procedure similar to but not identical with preliminary objection procedure. The Court has never applied Article 53 of the Statute in proceedings for provisional measures in which the respondent has not appeared or has failed to defend its case.[29] In the present Court, there have been fifteen cases in which the respondent, while disputing the jurisdiction of the Court, has nevertheless taken part in the proceedings on provisional measures.[30]

Article 75, paragraph 1, corresponds to Article 61, paragraph 6, of the 1946 Rules. It has been revised and its language brought closer to that of Article 41 of the Statute. The phrase 'which ought to be taken or complied with' appears as an attempt to strengthen the authority of the indication of provisional measures, the word *ought* following the English version of Article 41 of the Statute as a rendition of the French *doivent*. Neither the Permanent Court nor the present Court, however, has taken the initiative which paragraph 1 envisages. Each, however, acted *proprio motu* when requests for the indication of provisional measures are already before it.[31] Paragraph 2 corresponds partly to Article 61, paragraph 4, of the 1946 Rules, the last phrase being new. It reflects the continuous practice of the Permanent Court and the present Court. It also opens the way for the adverse party to suggest to the Court measures which ought to be taken by the party requesting the provisional measures without its being seen to have accepted the jurisdiction over the principal claim (*forum prorogatum*), as occurred in both provisional measures phases of the *Application of the Genocide Convention* (Bosnia and Herzegovina *v* Yugoslavia) case.[32] This is because Article 41 of the Statute refers to the respective rights of either party (stronger in the French—*[le] droit de chacun*). Paragraph 3 reproduces Article 61, paragraph 5, and its application is examined in § 7.5.

[29] H.W.A. Thirlway, *Non-appearance before the International Court of Justice* 83 (Cambridge: Cambridge University Press, 1985); A.Z. Pagnetta, *La non-comparizione davanti alla Corte internazionale di Giustizia* 157 (Milan: Giuffré, 1996).

[30] *Interhandel*, *Military and Paramilitary Activities in and against Nicaragua*, the two *Questions of Interpretation and Application of the 1971 Montreal Convention arising from the Aerial Incident at Lockerbie*, the *Application of the Convention on the Prevention and Punishment of the Crime of Genocide* case, and the ten *Legality of Use of Force* cases of 1999.

[31] *See* § 7.6.

[32] On the possibility of a counter-claim in provisional measures proceedings, see *Land and Maritime Boundary between Cameroon and Nigeria* (Provisional Measures) case, ICJ Rep. 1996, 13, 20 (para. 26); and cf. *U.S. Diplomatic and Consular Staff in Tehran* (Provisional Measures) case, ICJ Rep. 1979, 3, 17 (para. 29).

Article 76 consolidates and generalizes the actions of the Court in the *Fisheries Jurisdiction* cases.[33] Paragraph 1 corresponds to Article 61, paragraph 7, of the 1946 Rules, with the difference that the addition of the opening words 'At the request of a party' may restrict the Court's power to act *proprio motu* unless that remains covered by Article 75. Paragraph 2 is new and corresponds to the new wording of Article 73, paragraph 2. Paragraph 3 corresponds to Article 61, paragraph 8, of the 1946 Rules. Another change was made in paragraph 1, which limits to the parties the power to request revocation or modification of any decision concerning provisional measures. I have interpreted that change as possibly depriving the Court of its power to act *proprio motu*, unless that remains covered by Article 75. However, an authoritative writer on provisional measures has interpreted that paragraph as apparently indicating that the Court had in mind some *possibility* of action on its own initiative.[34] The Court has used this phrase when it has not accepted the original claims regarding provisional measures, but has indicated different provisional measures on its own initiative, especially measures to be observed by both parties.[35]

Article 78 of the 1978 Rules, a major innovation, appears as a renewed attempt by the Court to strengthen the authority of an indication of provisional measures. It reflects the decision in the provisional measures phase of the *Fisheries Jurisdiction* cases, and has opened the way to a requirement that the State or States concerned should report to the Court on its compliance with an order indicating provisional measures, a matter discussed more fully in § 7.7.

II. THE UNITED NATIONS CONVENTION ON THE LAW OF THE SEA AND THE INTERNATIONAL TRIBUNAL FOR THE LAW OF THE SEA

3.7. CONVENTION AND RULES

In the Convention on the Law of the Sea, Article 290, paragraphs 1 and 5, and (for ITLOS) Annex VI, Article 25, are similar to Article 41 of the Statute of the International Court of Justice in that they too, although fuller, are axiomatic statements of the power of any authorized court or tribunal to prescribe provisional measures within the framework of the applicable paragraph. Although they initiate two major innovations, they also leave developments in the hands of the competent court or tribunal. Annex VI, Article 16, of the Convention follows Article 30 of the Statute of the International Court of Justice. It provides that ITLOS shall frame rules for carrying out its functions. In particular it shall lay down rules of procedure. There is no provision

[33] ICJ Rep. 1972, 12, 30; 1973, 302, 313.

[34] J. Stuzki, *Interim Measures in the Hague Court* 196 (Deventer: Kluwer Law and Taxation, 1983); L. Daniele, *Le misure cautelare davanti alla Corte internazionale di Giustizia* 133 (Milan: Giuffré, 1993).

[35] This is particularly evident in the practice of ITLOS. *See* § 4.6.

regarding assessors either in the Convention or in Annex VI. However, Article 289 of the Convention more generally envisages the appointment of scientific or technical experts to sit with the court or tribunal having jurisdiction under the Convention in any dispute involving scientific or technical matters, without the right to vote. There is no reason why such experts should not sit with the Tribunal in a case of provisional measures. Three of the requests for provisional measures submitted to the Tribunal to date, although based on Article 290, paragraph 5, of the Convention, raised serious technical questions, one about the health of an important stock of highly migratory fish, one about radioactive pollution of an important area of the sea and the adjoining coastal areas, and the third relating to environmental pollution as a result of certain construction works being undertaken by the respondent State.

ITLOS on its inauguration, with the experience of the ICJ to guide it, initially adopted Rules of the Tribunal prepared by Special Commission 4 of the Preparatory Commission.[36] The Report of the Preparatory Commission gives a full account, though not a verbatim record, of their development. No case was heard under those Rules.

The Preparatory Commission explained that it was always intended and understood that the general procedures for the functioning of the Tribunal and its powers are on the lines of the Statute of the International Court of Justice and other judicial tribunals. To remain consistent with this guideline, which was adopted by Special Commission 4, the Rules of the Tribunal should as far as possible follow the practice of the International Court of Justice and the usage of the Rules of Court.[37]

3.8. THE RULES OF 1997

Although the Preparatory Commission interpreted its mandate as requiring it to produce draft rules for the Tribunal, to enable it to function as soon as it was constituted, it was never intended that the Commission would usurp the powers of the Tribunal, under Annex VI, Article 16, of the Convention, itself to frame rules for carrying out its functions.[38] Accordingly, as soon as it was constituted in October 1996, the Tribunal turned to its Rules of the Tribunal. On 28 October 1977 the Tribunal adopted its own Rules of the Tribunal.[39] These were slightly amended on 21 September 2001 (not relevant here) and are currently in force. Here too, as in the case of the ICJ, there are

[36] Report of the Preparatory Commission ... of the Convention regarding practical arrangements for the establishment of the International Tribunal for the Law of the Sea (LOS/PCN/152, 4 vols. 1995), *passim*.

[37] Ibid., vol. I, 27 doc. LOS/PCN/SCN.4/WP16/Add. 2, 27 (para 2).

[38] For the final draft rules of the Tribunal (LOS/PCN/SCN.4/WP16/Add.2, 19 January 1994) *see* ibid., vol. I, 26. Arts. 83 to 88 dealt with provisional measures.

[39] For text of the Rules as adopted, *see* ITLOS, *Basic Texts* 16 (The Hague: Kluwer Law International, 1999).

no published records of the Tribunal's deliberations preceding the adoption of the Rules. They may be regarded as the most advanced rules for proceedings on provisional measures available to international tribunals (including arbitral tribunals) today. ITLOS has not published any Practice Directions as such, but it has issued Guidelines concerning the preparation and presentation of cases before the Tribunal.[40]

The Rules relating to provisional measures appear in Part III (*Procedure*), section C (*Incidental Proceedings*), subsection I (*Provisional Measures*), and like the rules of the ICJ are spread over several Articles, Articles 89 to 95, as follows:

Article 89

1. A party may submit a request for the prescription of provisional measures under Article 290, paragraph 1, of the Convention at any time in the course of the proceedings in a dispute submitted to the Tribunal.	1. Une partie peut présenter une demande en prescription de mesures conservatoires conformément à l'article 290, paragraphe 1, de la Convention, à tout moment de la procédure engagée relative au différend soumis au Tribunal.
2. Pending the constitution of an arbitral tribunal to which a dispute is being submitted, a party may submit a request for the prescription of provisional measures under article 290, paragraph 5, of the Convention:	2. En attendant la constitution d'un tribunal arbitral saisi d'un différend, une partie peut présenter une demande en prescription de mesures conservatoires conformément à l'article 290, paragraphe 5, de la Convention:
(a) at any time if the parties have so agreed;	(a) à tout moment si les parties en conviennent ainsi;
(b) at any time after two weeks from the notification to the other party of a request for provisional measures if the parties have not agreed that such measures be prescribed by another court or tribunal.	(b) à tout moment après un délai de deux semaines à compter de la notification à la partie adverse d'une demande en prescription de mesures conservatoires, si les parties ne conviennent pas de soumettre la question à toute autre cour ou tout autre tribunal.
3. The request shall be in writing and specify the measures requested, the reasons therefor and the possible consequences, if it is not granted, for the preservation of the respective rights of the parties or for the prevention of serious harm to the marine environment.	3. La demande est présentée par écrit et indique les mesures sollicitées, les motifs sur lesquels elle se fonde et les conséquences éventuelles de son rejet en ce qui concerne la préservation des droits respectifs des parties ou la prévention de dommages graves au milieu marin.

[40] ITLOS *Basic Texts* (n. 39), 78.

4. A request for the prescription of provisional measures under article 290, paragraph 5, of the Convention shall also indicate the legal grounds upon which the arbitral tribunal which is to be constituted would have jurisdiction and the urgency of the situation. A certified copy of the notification or of any other document instituting the proceedings before the arbitral tribunal shall be annexed to the request.

4. La demande en prescription de mesures conservatoires présentée conformément à l'article 290, paragraphe 5, de la Convention, indique également les moyens de droit sur la base desquels le tribunal arbitral devant être constitué aurait compétence, ainsi que l'urgence de la situation. Une copie certifiée conforme de la notification ou de tout autre document introduisant l'instance devant le tribunal arbitral est annexée à la demande.

5. When a request for provisional measures has been made, the Tribunal may prescribe measures different in whole or in part from those requested and indicate the parties which are to take or to comply with each measure.

5. Lorsqu'une demande en prescription de mesures conservatoires lui est présentée, le Tribunal peut prescrire des mesures totalement ou partiellement différentes de celles qui sont sollicitées, et indiquer les parties qui doivent prendre ou exécuter chaque mesure.

Article 90

1. Subject to article 112, paragraph 1 [on the prompt release of vessels and crews], a request for the prescription of provisional measures has priority over all other proceedings before the Tribunal.

1. Sans préjudice de l'article 112, paragraphe 1 [prompte mainlevée de l'immobilisation du navire ou prompte libération de son équipage], la demande en prescription de mesures conservatoires a priorité sur toutes autres procédures devant le Tribunal.

2. The Tribunal, or the President if the Tribunal is not sitting, shall fix the earliest possible date for a hearing.

2. Le Tribunal ou, s'il ne siège pas, le Président fixe la date de la procédure orale au plus tôt.

3. The Tribunal shall take into account any observations that may be presented to it by a party before the closure of the hearing.

3. Le Tribunal prend en considération toutes observations qui peuvent lui être présentées par une partie avant la clôture de cette procédure.

4. Pending the meeting of the Tribunal, the President of the Tribunal may call upon the parties to act in such a way as will enable any order the Tribunal may make on the request for provisional measures to have its appropriate effects.

4. En attendant que le Tribunal se réunisse, le Président du Tribunal peut inviter les parties à agir de manière que toute ordonnance du Tribunal sur la demande en prescription de mesures conservatoires puisse avoir les effets voulus.

Article 91

1. If the President of the Tribunal ascertains that at the date fixed for the hearing referred to in article 90, paragraph 2, a sufficient number of Members will not be available to constitute a quorum, the Chamber of Summary Procedure shall be convened to carry out the functions of the Tribunal with respect to the prescription of provisional measures.
2. The Tribunal shall review or revise provisional measures prescribed by the Chamber of Summary Procedure at the written request of a party within 15 days of the prescription of the measures. The Tribunal may also at any time decide *proprio motu* to review or revise the measures.

1. Si le Président du Tribunal constate qu'à la date fixée pour a procédure orale visée à l'article 90, paragraphe 2, un nombre suffisant de ses Membres ne sera pas disponible pour constituer un quorum, la Chambre de procédure sommaire est convoquée afin de remplir les fonctions du Tribunal pour la prescription de mesures conservatoires.
2. Le Tribunal réexamine ou révise les mesures conservatoires prescrites par la Chambre de procédure sommaire à la demande d'une partie, faite par écrite dans un délai de 15 jours après la prescription de ces mesures. Le Tribunal peut également à tout moment décide d'office de réexaminer ou de réviser ces mesures.

Article 92

The rejection of a request for the prescription of provisional measures shall not prevent the party which made it from making a fresh request in the same case based on new facts.

Le rejet d'une demande en prescription de mesures conservatoires n'empêche pas la partie qui l'avait introduite de présenter en la même affaire une nouvelle demande fondée sur des faits nouveaux.

Article 93

A party may request the modification or revocation of provisional measures. The request shall be submitted in writing and shall specify the change in, or disappearance of, the circumstances considered to be relevant. Before taking any decision on the request, the Tribunal shall afford the parties an opportunity of presenting their observations on the subject.

Une partie peut faire une requête tendant à ce qu'une décision concernant des mesures conservatoires soit rapportée ou modifiée. La requête doit être présentée par écrit et doit indiquer que les circonstances les justifiant ont changé ou cessé d'exister. Avant de prendre une décision concernant cette requête, le Tribunal donne aux parties la possibilité de présenter des observations à ce sujet.

Article 94

Any provisional measures prescribed by the Tribunal or any modification or revocation thereof shall forthwith be notified to the parties and to such other States Parties as the Tribunal considers appropriate in each case.

Toute mesure conservatoire prescrite par le Tribunal ou toute décision du Tribunal la modifiant ou la rapportant est immédiatement notifiée aux parties et, selon le cas d'espèce et si le Tribunal le juge approprié, à d'autres Etats Parties.

Article 95

1. Each party shall inform the Tribunal as soon as possible as to its compliance with any provisional measures the Tribunal has prescribed. In particular, each party shall submit an initial report upon the steps it has taken or proposes to take in order to ensure prompt compliance with the measures prescribed.

2. The Tribunal may request further information from the parties on any matter connected with the implementation of any provisional measures it has prescribed.

1. Chaque partie informe le Tribunal au plus tôt des dispositions qu'elle a prises pour mettre en œuvre les mesures conservatoires prescrites par le Tribunal. En particulier, chaque partie présente un rapport initial sur les dispositions qu'elle a prises ou quelle se propose de prendre pour se conformer sans retard aux mesures prescrites.

2. Le Tribunal peut demander aux parties un complément d'information concernant toutes questions relatives à la mise en œuvre des mesures conservatoires prescrites par lui.

Article 112, paragraph 1, to which Article 90 refers, deals with a matter which in some respects may be seen as closely linked to provisional measures, namely the prompt release of vessels or crews. It provides that the Tribunal shall give priority to applications for the release of vessels or crews over all other proceedings before the Tribunal. However, if the Tribunal is seised of an application for release of a vessel or crew and of a request for the prescription of provisional measures, it shall take the necessary measures to ensure that both the application and the request are dealt with without delay. It would be for the Court, in consultation with the parties, to ensure this.

The main difference between the Rules adopted by the Tribunal and the draft of the Preparatory Commission and the Rules of the International Court of Justice is in the separation of the two types of provisional measures proceedings. In the Preparatory Commission's final draft rules of the Tribunal, Article 83, paragraph 1, treated the two together. In the Tribunal's Rules they are in two separate paragraphs, 1 and 5, of Article 89. A second change was the introduction of the obligation to report in Article 95, in place of the Preparatory Commission's Article 85 which, following Article 78 of the Rules of Court of the ICJ, was limited to a requirement to supply the Tribunal with information if requested by the Tribunal. Article 95 requires each party to inform the Tribunal as soon as possible as to its compliance with any provisional measures that the Tribunal has prescribed. In particular, each party is to submit an initial report upon the steps it has taken or proposes to take in order to ensure prompt compliance with the measures prescribed.[41]

[41] This provision was of the Tribunal's initiative. For its Rules, *see* § 3.8. In the *Land Reclamation by Singapore in and around the Straits of Johor* (Provisional Measures) case, ITLOS extended the duty to report to include reporting to the Annex VII arbitral tribunal unless

In the four provisional measures cases so far heard by the Tribunal, this obligation to report does not appear to have caused any difficulties, although some of the Judges have uttered warnings about the delicacy of this operation.

There has in the nature of things been little practice and not much comment by the Tribunal on these Rules. In the *Saiga No. 2* (Provisional Measures) case it recalled Article 95, paragraph 2, and considered that it would be appropriate to authorize the President to request further information on the implementation of the provisional measures prescribed in that Order. It included a sentence to that effect in the operative provision of the Order.[42] A similar provision was included in the Orders on provisional measures in the *Southern Bluefin Tuna* (Provisional Measures) cases,[43] the *MOX Plant* (Provisional Measures) case,[44] and the *Reclamation of Land by Singapore in and around the Straits of Johor* (Provisional Measures) case.[45] This creates an impression that the inclusion of this provision is becoming a matter of routine when the Tribunal prescribes provisional measures. It is open to question whether Article 290 of the Convention intends to give the Tribunal (or any other court or tribunal authorized by the Convention to prescribe provisional measures) carte blanche to request reports from parties in cases before it as to their implementation of orders prescribing provisional measures. It is even less clear what the Tribunal intends to do with the reports it receives, since by Article 290, paragraph 3, of the Convention provisional measures may be prescribed, modified, or revoked only at the request of a party to the dispute and after the parties have been given an opportunity to be heard.

3.9. PROVISIONAL MEASURES IN ANNEX VII ARBITRATIONS

It follows from Article 290, paragraph 1, of the Convention that an Annex VII arbitration tribunal (also an Annex VIII arbitration and any ad hoc arbitration tribunal) possesses an original jurisdiction to prescribe

that tribunal should decide otherwise. ITLOS Rep. 2003, Order of 8 October (para. 104). To the extent that the reporting is in implementation of Art. 290, para. 5 of the Convention, it is not a matter for comment here. To the extent that issues of compliance with an indication of provisional measures by the ICJ remain open despite the ruling in *LaGrand*, the question arises whether the International Court could not introduce something similar in its Rules.

[42] ITLOS Rep. 1998, 24, 39 (para. 50). And note the declarations of Judges Vukas at p. 42 and Warioba at p. 44, and the latter's hope that the Tribunal would use its discretion to request information under Art. 95, para. 2, of the Rules 'with circumspection lest it unwittingly contribute to aggravation or extension of the dispute'. He also warned the Tribunal to use its discretion under Art. 89, para. 5, only when there are compelling reasons borne out by facts.

[43] ITLOS Rep. 1999, 280, 297.

[44] ITLOS Rep. 2001, 95.

[45] ITLOS Rep. 2003, 8 October.

provisional measures, independently of its jurisdiction under paragraph 5, to modify, revoke, or affirm provisional measures already prescribed by ITLOS. How the arbitral tribunal does this will depend on its Rules of Procedure (if any).

The question arose in the second Annex VII arbitration under the Convention—the *MOX Plant* arbitration—where ITLOS had declined to prescribe a measure requested by Ireland, but had nevertheless prescribed other measures.[46] The proceedings here were complicated. Ireland instituted the arbitration proceedings on 25 October 2001. On 9 November it submitted a request to ITLOS for the prescription of provisional measures. In its Order, ITLOS declined to prescribe the provisional measures requested by Ireland, but proceeded to prescribe other provisional measures of its own. The Annex VII Tribunal was constituted in February 2002 and the proceedings before it took their normal course in accordance with the Rules of Procedure adopted by the Tribunal. The Tribunal held hearings between 10 and 21 June 2003. Those hearings brought out serious differences over the question of the Tribunal's jurisdiction, and on 13 June the President announced that, after having considered submissions on jurisdiction, the Tribunal had decided to suspend further proceedings in the case until a date in December. The President added that in the circumstances the Tribunal would be willing to consider a request from Ireland for further provisional measures. That request was filed on 16 June, and hearings on it took place between 17 and 23 June.[47]

In its Order No. 3, the Arbitral Tribunal first described the circumstances in which it decided to suspend the proceedings on the merits and to consider the possibility of prescribing provisional measures if it considered that such measures were necessary to preserve the respective rights of the parties or to prevent serious harm to the marine environment (paragraphs 31, 32). The

[46] *MOX Plant* (Provisional Measures) case, ITLOS Rep. 2001, 95. On the Annex VII arbitration in this case, *see Dispute concerning the MOX Plant, International Movements of Radioactive Materials and the Protection of the Marine Environment of the Irish Sea* (Ireland *v* United Kingdom), Order No. 3, 24 June 2003, which together with the other relevant documents cited here can be accessed on the website of the Permanent Court of Arbitration, www.pca-cpa.org. The dispute between the two countries was also subject to another arbitration under the name of *Dispute concerning Access to Information under Article 9 of the OSPAR Convention*, decided by a Final Award of 2 July 2003, also available on the PCA website. The President of that Tribunal was Professor Reisman. In the OSPAR case the ITLOS and Annex VII proceedings were of some relevance. The parties agreed to request the Annex VII Tribunal to permit the disclosure in the OSPAR proceedings of material from Ireland's memorial in the Annex VII proceedings. The request was granted (paras. 62, 63). On one point the majority of this Tribunal found some of the ITLOS reasons helpful in the interpretation of the OSPAR Convention (para. 141). The Tribunal also followed ITLOS in not referring to the parallel procedure approach of the *Southern Bluefin Tuna* arbitration. For the OSPAR (Oslo–Paris) Convention, *see* the Convention for the Protection of the Marine Environment in the North-East Atlantic, 2 September 1992, 23 *Law of the Sea Bulletin* 32 (1993). On 30 October 2003 the Commission commenced proceedings against Ireland in the European Court of Justice, Case No. C-459/03, *see* Official Journal of the European Community C 7 p. 24 (2004).

[47] PCA Press Release of 17 June 2003, referring to President Mensah's statement of 16 June.

Tribunal then turned to the issues of its competence with regard to provisional measures and the applicable rules. It had no difficulty over its jurisdiction prima facie over the dispute submitted to it, and that allowed it to prescribe provisional measures under Article 290, paragraph 1, of the Convention (paragraphs 36 to 41). The Order continues:

42. In considering the Request, the Tribunal is governed by the terms of article 290 of the Convention, the relevant provisions of Annex VII and its Rules of Procedure. Article 1, paragraph 2, of the Rules of Procedure provides that 'to the extent that any question of procedure is not expressly governed by these Rules or by Annex VII to the Convention or other provisions of the Convention, and the Parties have not otherwise agreed, the question shall be decided by the Tribunal after consulting the Parties'. In fact there are no provisions in Annex VII, or in the Rules of Procedure, expressly governing applications for the prescription of provisional measures.
43. In that connection, the Tribunal notes that according to article 89, paragraph 5, of the ITLOS Rules of Procedure, it is open to ITLOS to prescribe provisional measures different in whole or in part from those requested. A similar provision is contained in article 75, paragraph 2, of the Rules of Court of the International Court of Justice. The Tribunal, having drawn these provisions to the attention of the Parties without comment from either, considers that it is also competent to prescribe provisional measures other than those sought by any Party.

That is useful guidance for any future Annex VII (and Annex VIII) arbitral tribunal that might be faced with a similar situation.

PART II

Jurisdiction and Procedure

4
Jurisdiction

4.1. JURISDICTION TO ORDER PROVISIONAL MEASURES

Neither the Statute nor the Rules of the Permanent Court of International Justice had much to say about that Court's jurisdiction to indicate provisional measures of protection. No doubt this was because the original draft of the Advisory Committee of Jurists proposed compulsory jurisdiction generally, and after the League Council had rejected that approach no general re-examination of the draft statute was undertaken.[1] The only case in that Court which might have presented a problem was the provisional measures phase of the *Electricity Company of Sofia and Bulgaria* case in 1939.[2] Underlying that case is a determination to save the cause of the judicial settlement of disputes from the war then in its early stages, and the Permanent Court avoided any major pronouncement on its jurisdiction to deal with the request for provisional measures.

There is no change in the Statute of the present International Court. Following immediately after Article 40 of the Statute on the institution of proceedings, the assumption must be that its jurisdiction to indicate provisional measures under Article 41 will rest on and is incidental and related to its jurisdiction to determine the case brought before it. If the case is instituted by the notification of a special agreement, there should be no problems, whether as regards its jurisdiction *ratione personae* or as regards its jurisdiction *ratione materiae* (assuming that both parties either are parties to the Statute or are otherwise entitled to have recourse to the Court under Article 35, paragraph 2, of the Statute).[3] But when proceedings are instituted unilaterally by the filing of an application instituting the proceedings, the situation may be more difficult, especially if the application is directed against an

[1] *See* § 2.1. For a full comparative discussion of jurisdiction over requests for provisional measures, *see* C. F. Amerasinghe, *Jurisdiction of International Tribunals* 344 (The Hague: Kluwer Law International, 2003).

[2] PCIJ Ser. A/B 77 (1939). *See* Ch. 3 nn. 18, 19.

[3] The term 'special agreement' in this context also applies to a framework agreement which, without defining the dispute or question on which the Court is to rule, permits either party to institute proceedings unilaterally. There has been only one case instituted by the filing of a special agreement in which provisional measures were requested, and that request arose out of an incident that occurred while the proceedings were in progress—the *Frontier Dispute* (Burkina Faso/Mali) (Provisional Measures) case, ICJ Rep. 1986, 3. The *Legal Status of the South-Eastern Territory of Greenland* case was instituted by the simultaneous filing by each party of an application instituting proceedings based on the Optional Clause of the Protocol of Signature of the Statute of the Permanent Court, and was treated as analogous to a case instituted by the filing of a special agreement. PCIJ Ser. A/B 48, 277 (1932).

'unwilling respondent'. Article 38 of the Rules of Court governs the institution of proceedings by means of an application. The application must indicate the party making it, the State against which the claim is brought, and the subject of the dispute (paragraph 1). But on the question of jurisdiction, the application shall also specify as far as possible the legal grounds upon which the jurisdiction of the Court is said to be based. It shall also specify the precise nature of the claim together with a succinct statement of the facts and grounds on which the claim is based (paragraph 2). This may give a tentative character to the application, to be consolidated through the reaction of the respondent to the claim and clarified by both parties in the course of the subsequent proceedings.

Occasionally the respondent has indicated in the provisional measures proceedings that it had reservations over the Court's jurisdiction, but did not wish to broach the jurisdiction over the main case. Likewise, if a party indicates to the Court that in principle it does not accept the jurisdiction but is prepared not to contest it in provisional measures proceedings, there will be no difficulty for the Court.[4] In those cases the Court has found that prima facie it appeared that it had jurisdiction and could entertain the request for provisional measures.[5] The effect of this is that before the Court can exercise its jurisdiction to deal with the request for provisional measures, the case must be one which has been entered in the General List. This also follows from the classification as an incidental proceeding given to these proceedings in the 1978 Rules. There can be no 'case' without that having been done.[6]

An important addition was made in Article 38, paragraph 5, of the Rules of 1978. That introduced formally into the Court's procedure the so-called *forum prorogatum* jurisdiction, by which the respondent State may accept the jurisdiction after the application is filed.[7] The first attempt to invoke this type

[4] For examples, the *Arbitral Award of 31 July 1999* (Provisional Measures) case, ICJ Rep. 1990, 64, 69 (para. 71); *Arrest Warrant of 11 April 2000* (Provisional Measures) case, ICJ Rep. 2000, 182, 191 (para. 32); *Avena and other Mexican Nationals* (Provisional Measures) case, ICJ Rep. 2003, 77 (para. 41). A series of objections to the jurisdiction and to the admissibility was raised in the merits phase of the *Avena and other Mexican Nationals* case, but not as preliminary objections and without suspending the proceedings on the merits. ICJ Rep. 2004, 31 March (paras. 22 to 43).

[5] This allows the jurisdiction of the Court to indicate provisional measures to be perfected by consent given in the course of proceedings (*forum prorogatum*). *Arbitral Award of 31 July 1989* (Provisional Measures) case, ICJ Rep. 1990, 64, 69 (para. 21); *Avena and other Mexican Nationals* (Provisional Measures) case, ICJ Rep. 2003, Order of 77 (para. 41).

[6] Statement of the President (Bedjaoui) in the *Request for Examination* proceedings, CR 95/19 (11 September 1995), 16.

[7] The concept of *forum prorogatum* jurisdiction in this sense has its origin in the Judgment in the *Corfu Channel* (Preliminary Objection) case, ICJ Rep. 1947–48, 15. Art. 38, para. 5, of the Rules reads: 'When the applicant State proposes to found the jurisdiction of the Court upon a consent thereto yet to be given or manifested by the State against which the application is made, the application shall be transmitted to that State. It shall not however be entered in the General List, nor any action be taken in the proceedings, unless and until the State against which such application is made consents to the Court's jurisdiction for the purposes of the case.' Up to the

of jurisdiction together with a request for provisional measures was made by Eritrea in a dispute with Ethiopia for alleged violation of the premises and of the staff of Eritrea's diplomatic mission in Addis Ababa.[8] This was transmitted to the Government of Ethiopia but in the absence of that Government's consent the Court could take no further action. A second attempt of this nature was made by Liberia which, on 5 August 2003, applied to the Court in a dispute with Sierra Leone concerning an international arrest warrant issued by the Special Court for Sierra Leone against the President of Liberia, at the same time requesting provisional measures.[9] As in the previous case, the Court took no further action beyond forwarding the application to the Government of Sierra Leone, unless and until Sierra Leone consented to the jurisdiction in this case. In stating that no action would be taken on the application, the press release stressed that this applied 'in particular on the request for provisional measures'.

Under the Rules of Court the State against which an application is made has other procedural rights. By Article 79 of the Rules (amended in 2000) that State may raise a preliminary objection to the jurisdiction of the Court or to the admissibility of the application, or other objection the decision on which is requested before any further proceedings on the merits. The effect of filing such an objection is to suspend the proceedings on the merits until the Court has ruled on the objection.[10] But that does not prevent either party from filing a request for provisional measures while the proceedings on the merits are suspended. By Article 80 of the Rules (also amended in 2000) the respondent State may present a counter-claim under the conditions laid down. Since by Article 41 the Court's power is to indicate provisional measures 'to preserve the respective rights of either party', there can be an element of uncertainty over the Court's jurisdiction to determine the case brought by application, and that will only become clarified as the proceedings advance.

Given this, proceedings on a request for the indication or prescription of provisional measures of protection possess characteristics that set them apart from all other incidental proceedings in an international court or tribunal. This differentiation finds its fullest expression in the special rules governing

time of writing, the only case in which the Court exercised jurisdiction under this provision is the *Certain Criminal Proceedings in France* (Congo *v* France) case, ICJ Rep. 2003, 102. *And see* S. Yee, '*Forum prorogatum* Returns to the International Court of Justice', 16 *Leiden J. Int'l L.* 701 (2003).

[8] Press Release 99/04, 16 February 1999, *and see* the Court's Report to the General Assembly 1 August 1998–31 July 1999, 54 GAOR Sup. No. 4 (A/54/4) para. 21.

[9] Press Release 2003/26, 5 August 2003.

[10] For an instance of a request for provisional measures by the respondent State, filed while proceedings on preliminary objections were pending, *see* the *Land and Maritime Boundary between Cameroon and Nigeria* (Provisional Measures) case, ICJ Rep. 1996 (I), 13.

jurisdiction of the court or tribunal to act on the request. Several different circumstances can occur, and it is not always possible to differentiate between them as questions of justiciability or questions of admissibility. They are all closely related to the fundamental rule of international litigation, that the jurisdiction of a court or tribunal to determine the merits of a case requires the consent *ad litem* of all the parties to the dispute, together with the general principle that provisional measures are designed to preserve the respective rights of each one of the parties to the case *pendente lite*. This means that the starting point of the jurisdiction of the International Court of Justice to indicate provisional measures of protection rests on the combined effect of Article 36 and Article 41 of its Statute. The specific agreement to have recourse to the ICJ within the terms of Article 36 constitutes the title of jurisdiction, which may permit the institution of proceedings by unilateral application.

The same problem exists for the International Tribunal for the Law of the Sea with, however, the difference that the complicated provisions of Part XV of the Convention on the Law of the Sea relating to the jurisdiction of any competent court or tribunal and the conditions to be met before compulsory proceedings are brought under Article 286 of that Convention are additional to the basic conditions for the prescription of provisional measures under Article 290.

The position under the Convention on the Law of the Sea is accordingly more complex. The general power of any court or tribunal acting under Part XV of the Convention rests in the first instance on Article 290, read together with Articles 281 and 286, and in the case of ITLOS, Annex VI, Articles 21 and 25, while the specific power of the Seabed Disputes Chamber depends on a combination of Article 187 read with Annex VI, Articles 21 and 40, paragraph 1. In both cases any specific title of jurisdiction can be added, but for ITLOS, if there is no such instrument the Convention itself serves as the title of jurisdiction, and that permits unilateral application.

In addition to those statutory requirements, the Rules of Court and the Rules of the Tribunal impose other requirements relating more to the proceedings themselves. If under the Law of the Sea Convention some other compulsory dispute settlement system is competent and that system has its own procedural requirements, account has to be taken of them too. Alleged non-observance of those requirements can add a complication to the jurisdiction to deal with the request for provisional measures.

The ICJ has established two general propositions concerning its competence to indicate provisional measures. The first relates to the situation where there is a question whether a preliminary objection can be made in provisional measures proceedings. That question arose directly in the *Interhandel* (Interim Protection) case, where the respondent, the United States, in the provisional measures phase filed what it called a preliminary objection based on the self-judging clause in its declaration accepting the compulsory jurisdiction, the so-called Connally amendment, and Switzerland for its part challenged that action. The Court said:

> Whereas the procedure applicable to requests for the indication of interim measures of protection is dealt within the Rules of Court by provisions which are laid down in Article 61 [of the Rules of 1946, on interim protection] and which appear along with other procedures, in the section entitled: 'Occasional Rules';
>
> Whereas the examination of the contention of the Government of the United States requires the application of a different procedure, the procedure laid down in Article 62 of the Rules of Court [on preliminary objections], and whereas, if this contention is maintained, it will fall to be dealt with by the Court in due course in accordance with that procedure;
>
> Whereas the request for the indication of interim measures of protection must accordingly be examined in conformity with the procedure laid down in Article 61[.][11]

In line with this, the Court does not automatically give effect to a reservation in the title of jurisdiction but requires the author of the reservation to invoke it. In *Interhandel* the United States invoked the self-judging reservation of domestic jurisdiction in its declaration accepting the compulsory jurisdiction. In the above cited extracts the Court accepted the Swiss argument that the Court would not wish to adjudicate on so complex and delicate a question as the validity of that reservation. It did so over the powerful dissenting opinion of Judge Sir Hersch Lauterpacht, arguing that because of that reservation the United States declaration was not a valid acceptance of the compulsory jurisdiction.[12]

The second general proposition is that the Court will not grant provisional measures if it considers that, in the circumstances of the case, the damage in respect of which the claim is made is not irreparable. In the *Aegean Sea Continental Shelf* (Interim Protection) case, the dispute submitted to the Court concerned the delimitation of the continental shelf between Greece and Turkey in the Aegean Sea. The request for Interim Protection asked the Court to direct both Governments unless with the consent of the other to refrain from all exploration activity or any scientific research, with respect

[11] *Interhandel* (Interim Measures of Protection) case, ICJ Rep. 1957, 105, 111. For further insistence that provisional measures of protection can only be granted if Art. 41 of the Statute is invoked, *see* the concluding paragraph of the Judgment in the *Right of Passage over Indian Territory* (Preliminary Objections) case, ICJ Rep. 1957, 125, 152.

[12] *Interhandel* (Interim Measures of Protection) case, previous note, at 117. Other cases in which the Court deferred its decision on the effect of controversial reservations to the title of jurisdiction on its competence to indicate provisional measures include the *Aegean Sea Continental Shelf* case, ICJ Rep. 1976, 3, the *Questions of Interpretation and Application of the 1971 Montreal Convention* cases, ICJ Rep. 1992, 3, 114, and the eight retained *Legality of the Use of Force* cases, Yugoslavia [Serbia & Montenegro] *v* Belgium, Canada, France, Germany, Italy, Netherlands, Portugal, the United Kingdom, ICJ Rep. 1999, 124, 259, 363, 422, 481, 542, 656, and 826. In all of those cases the court established prima facie jurisdiction to examine the request, but declined to indicate provisional measures.

to the continental shelf areas within which Turkey had granted such licences or permits or adjacent to the Islands, or otherwise in dispute in the case, and to refrain from further military measures or actions which might endanger the peaceful relations between the two countries. The immediate cause of this issue before the Court was the granting by Turkey of permits to the Turkish State Petroleum Company for exploration for petroleum in areas in the Aegean claimed by Greece, in particular seismic research activities. These were claimed to be an infringement of Greece's sovereign rights in the areas concerned. There was no claim that this form of seismic research involved any risk of physical damage to the seabed or subsoil or to their natural resources. Jurisdiction was said to be based on the General Act for the Pacific Settlement of International Disputes of 1928.[13] From the evidence then before it the Court found that the continued seismic activities undertaken by Turkey were all of a transitory character not involving the establishment of installations on or above the seabed of the continental shelf, and that no suggestion had been made that Turkey had embarked upon any operations involving the actual appropriation or other use of the natural resources of the areas of continental shelf which were in dispute. Those activities on Greece's continental shelf might raise a question of infringement of Greece's exclusive right of exploration so that in the event that the Court should uphold Greece's claims on the merits, Turkey's activity in seismic exploration might be considered as such an infringement and invoked as a possible cause of prejudice to the exclusive rights of Greece in those areas found to appertain to Greece. However, the Court continued:

32. Whereas, on the other hand, the possibility of such a prejudice to rights in issue before the Court does not, by itself, suffice to justify recourse to its exceptional power under Article 41 of the Statute to indicate interim measures of protection; whereas, under the express terms of that Article, this power is conferred on the Court only if it considers that circumstances so require in order to preserve the respective rights of either party; and whereas this condition, as already noted, presupposes that the circumstances of the case disclose the risk of an irreparable prejudice to rights in issue in the proceedings;
33. Whereas in the present instance, the alleged breach by Turkey of the exclusivity of the right claimed by Greece to acquire information concerning the natural resources of the areas of continental shelf, if it were established, is one that might be capable of reparation by appropriate means; and whereas it follows that the Court is unable to find in that alleged breach of Greece's rights such a risk of irreparable prejudice to rights in issue before the Court as might require the exercise of its power under Article 41 of the Statute to indicate interim measures for their protection[.][14]

[13] On the General Act, *see* Ch. 2 n. 42.

[14] ICJ Rep. 1976, 3, 11. As the Court put it in the *Passage through the Great Belt* (Provisional Measures) case, 'the power of the Court to indicate provisional measures under Article 41 of the Statute ... presupposes that irreparable prejudice should not be caused to rights which are the subject of dispute in judicial proceedings'. ICJ Rep. 1991, 12, 16 (para. 16).

If the jurisdiction of the court or tribunal to determine the dispute is not challenged, or if there is no obstacle to the admissibility of the claim and the request for the provisional measures meets the requirements of the rules of the court or tribunal, or if the court or tribunal finds that its jurisdiction over the merits is manifest, there is no problem over the jurisdiction of that court or tribunal to deal with that request. Likewise, if it is manifest to the court or tribunal that the respondent to the claim has not accepted the jurisdiction of that court or tribunal for that dispute, or if the court or tribunal adopts a decision to that effect, there is no jurisdiction at all and no provisional measures can be indicated or prescribed.[15] Problems arise when the jurisdiction of the court or tribunal or the admissibility of the case or of the request for provisional measures is challenged by the respondent, or when the respondent declines to take part in the proceedings on that request.[16] It is only in the present International Court of Justice that the Court has had to face the issue whether it can indicate provisional measures in that type of situation. The Court has answered this challenge by developing the concept of prima facie jurisdiction, meaning that on first impression the Court might have jurisdiction over the merits.[17] That has been incorporated and specified in Article 290 of the Law of the Sea Convention.

4.2. THE ORIGIN OF PRIMA FACIE JURISDICTION

In the first provisional measures case before the International Court of Justice, the *Anglo-Iranian Oil Co.* case,[18] a heavily charged case politically,

[15] *Request for an Examination of the Situation in accordance with Paragraph 63 of the Court's Judgment of 20 December 1974 in the* Nuclear Tests case, ICJ Rep. 1995, 288; *Legality of Use of Force* (Provisional Measures) (Yugoslavia [Serbia & Montenegro] *v* Spain, Yugoslavia [Serbia & Montenegro] *v* U.S.A.) cases, ICJ Rep. 1999, 761, 916. Where more than one title of jurisdiction is invoked, the absence of jurisdiction may be manifest under only one of them. *Legality of Use of Force* (Provisional Measures) cases (Yugoslavia *v* Spain, Yugoslavia *v* United Kingdom), ibid. 761, 771 (para. 25), 826, 836 (para. 25).

[16] The Court has never applied Art. 53 of the Statute in provisional measures proceedings. *See* Ch. 3 n. 29.

[17] As Judge Schwebel has pointed out, whether 'might' in this context means 'possibly might', or 'might well', or 'might probably' is a question of some controversy. Dissenting opinion in *Military and Paramilitary Activities in and against Nicaragua* (Provisional Measures) case, ICJ Rep. 1984, 169, 190 at 207. Another former President of the Court has written that provisional measures 'will not be granted unless a majority of judges believes at the time that there will be jurisdiction over the merits'. E. Jiménez de Aréchaga, 'International Law in the Past Third of a Century', 159 *Recueil* 9, 161 (1978-I). As will be seen, in several cases the Court has asserted its prima facie jurisdiction but has declined to indicate provisional measures in the circumstances. There is only one case—the *Anglo-Iranian Oil Co.* case—in which it has indicated provisional measures directed to the merits of the case, and later on preliminary objection proceedings found that it did not have jurisdiction over the merits. This observation relates to the International Court of Justice only. The situation is different where ITLOS has prescribed provisional measures after holding that an Annex VII arbitral tribunal might have jurisdiction, but the arbitral tribunal has held otherwise.

[18] ICJ Rep. 1951, 89.

the Court was confronted with a double challenge. The unwilling respondent was prepared to contest the title of jurisdiction invoked in the application instituting the proceedings. At the same time, it did not take part in the provisional measures proceedings although given the opportunity to do so in accordance with the Rules of Court then in force. This type of situation has since confronted the Court in many of the provisional measures cases that have come before it, and the Court has built up a substantial case-law on the topic. In fact it was not until 1984 that an unwilling respondent who was challenging the title of jurisdiction invoked in the principal claim participated in the provisional measures proceedings before the jurisdiction of the Court had been judicially determined.[19] Sztucki has explained the nature of the problem facing the Court in the following terms:

> The question at stake is not whether or not the Court may act under Article 41 when it (at least for the moment) has no jurisdiction over the merits; nor is the question at stake whether or not that jurisdiction must be definitively established before the Court may act under Article 41—although occasionally the problem was posed in these ways.
>
> [...]
>
> The real issue, as it presents itself against the background of the Court's practice is . . . the question of how much regard must be paid to the prospects of substantive jurisdiction if that jurisdiction is yet to be finally established at the moment when the Court has to decide on interim protection.[20]

The Court's answer has been that it can act under Article 41 if it is satisfied on the basis of the summary pleadings and accelerated deliberation in the proceedings on the request for provisional measures that prima facie it appears that it might have jurisdiction to determine the case brought before it and as placed before it at that stage. By 'jurisdiction' in this context is meant jurisdiction both *ratione personae* and *ratione materiae* over the merits of the claim,[21] as well as jurisdiction to determine whether the provisional measures requested are compatible with the principal claim and do not change the nature of the claim as advanced in the application instituting the proceedings.[22] Conversely, if it is manifest to the Court at that stage that it is without jurisdiction to determine the merits, it will have no jurisdiction to deal with the request for provisional measures, or indeed with any other aspect of the case and it should order the case to be removed from the

19 *Military and Paramilitary Activities in and against Nicaragua* (Provisional Measures) case, ICJ Rep. 1984, 169.

20 J. Sztucki, *Interim Measures in the Hague Court* 221, 222 (Deventer: Kluwer Law and Taxation, 1983).

21 *Application of the Genocide Convention* (Provisional Measures) case, ICJ Rep. 1993, 3, 12 (para. 14).

22 *Arrest Warrant of 11 April 2000* (Provisional Measures) case, ICJ Rep. 2000, 182, 197 (para. 57).

General List.[23] There is also an intermediate situation, where the Court is not satisfied as to the prima facie jurisdiction and therefore is unable to indicate provisional measures, but at the same time the absence of jurisdiction is not manifest, and the proceedings continue. This way of looking at the situation, with a very low threshold inherent in the concept of prima facie jurisdiction, has been developed in the case-law with relatively large majorities and has not been seriously challenged by States. The Court's Rules of 1978 preserve that conception as it had developed up to that time, and Article 290 of the United Nations Convention on the Law of the Sea (*see* § 2.7), with its specific references in paragraphs 1 and 5 to the concept in a wide-ranging and carefully negotiated section on procedures for the binding settlement of disputes arising under the Convention, can be seen as general political endorsement of the process. No purpose is now served by a theoretical discussion of the abstract question of whether this approach is in conformity with the Statute. The process is firmly established.

Accordingly, whenever a request for the indication of provisional measures is brought before the International Court at a time when the Court's jurisdiction to deal with the claim is being challenged, the Court examines whether it has prima facie jurisdiction over the merits of the claim as the basis for its action under Article 41 of the Statute to deal with the request. The Court normally proceeds this way even when it decides that the circumstances do not require it to indicate provisional measures. That is the conception embodied in Article 290 of the Law of the Sea Convention, but it is also implicit in all other cases of provisional measures. This chapter now goes on to examine the competence of two standing international courts to indicate (ICJ) or to prescribe (ITLOS) provisional measures when jurisdiction over the dispute before either of them is not established at the time and, in the case of ITLOS, if it is asked to prescribe provisional measures although the dispute is being submitted to another court or tribunal not yet established when the request for provisional measures is made. The ICJ does this before or no matter whether it has established its own jurisdiction over the merits, if it is satisfied that it prima facie would or could have jurisdiction over the merits.

In the ICJ, the question has only arisen in cases in which it has been seised of the merits, and it can therefore assess the request for provisional measures against the jurisdiction over the merits and against the merits, both of which it will also have to decide. It also has some idea of what the next phase of the case is likely to be—preliminary objections or the merits—and when that phase would be reached, possibly relevant to the issue of urgency (*see* Chapter 5).

[23] This has occurred only twice in Provisional Measures cases—*Legality of Use of Force*, Yugoslavia *v* Spain and Yugoslavia *v* U.S.A. cases. ICJ Rep. 1999, 761, 916.

However, there is no reason why it should not also be requested to indicate provisional measures in a case, such as the *Ambatielos* case,[24] in which it is asked to determine the arbitrability or justiciability of a dispute before another court or tribunal, whether or not constituted at the time of the request for provisional measures. For ITLOS, the question can arise whenever the competent court or tribunal under the Law of the Sea Convention has not been constituted or is not in existence at the time when the request for provisional measures is made. States have given the topic treaty form in Article 290, paragraph 5, of the Convention. This issue has come to the fore three times since the establishment of the Tribunal in 1996, in the *Southern Bluefin Tuna*,[25] the *MOX Plant*,[26] and the *Land Reclamation Activities by Singapore in and around the Straits of Johor*[27] cases, in the last two of which Annex VII and other arbitral proceedings are pending at the time of writing. This is backed by Article 288, paragraph 5, by which in the event of a dispute as to whether a court or tribunal has jurisdiction, the matter shall be settled by decision of that court or tribunal. That reasserts the provisional character of a finding of prima facie jurisdiction in proceedings for the indication of provisional measures.

4.3. INITIAL DEVELOPMENTS IN THE INTERNATIONAL COURT OF JUSTICE

As seen, the issue first arose in the provisional measures phase of the *Anglo-Iranian Oil Co.* case. That requires closer examination, since it lies at the root of later developments. The crisis following the rise to power of Dr Mohammad Mosadegh and his decision to nationalize the Company and its assets in Iran became a major threat to international peace and security, and military and naval preparations were put in hand.[28] On 26 May 1951, the United Kingdom filed an application instituting proceedings against Iran, specifying each country's declaration accepting the compulsory jurisdiction under

[24] *Ambatielos* (Preliminary Objection) case, ICJ Rep. 1952, 28; (Merits), ICJ Rep. 1953, 10. For the arbitral award *see* 12 UNRIAA 87 (1955).

[25] *Southern Bluefin Tuna* (Provisional Measures) cases, ITLOS Rep. 1999, 280; Arbitral Award of 4 August 2000, 119 ILR 508. For early doctrinal views on this, *see* the works of Dumbauld and Hudson in Ch. 2 nn. 58 and 59. For my observations on the ITLOS Order, *see* Sh. Rosenne, 'The International Tribunal for the Law of the Sea: Survey for 1999', 15 *Int'l J. Marine and Coastal L.* 463 (2000).

[26] ITLOS Rep. 2001, 95.

[27] ITLOS Rep. 2003, 10. The Annex VII arbitral tribunal was constituted on 9 October 2003. In accordance with Annex VII, Art. 1, the President of ITLOS appointed three members of the Tribunal, including the President. Statement of President Nelson at the 64th meeting of the General Assembly in its 58th session on 24 November 2003, A/58/PV.64. Also available on the ITLOS website.

[28] For an account of the military preparations that preceded the institution of these proceedings, *see* Sztucki, op. cit. in n. 20, 300.

Article 36, paragraphs 2 and 5, of the Statute (both of which had reservations) as the legal ground upon which the jurisdiction was said to be based. The main claim was for a declaration that the Government of Iran was under a duty to submit the dispute with the Company to arbitration under the provisions of the 1933 Convention with the Company—an anticipation of Article 290, paragraph 5, of the Law of the Sea Convention. The essence of the provisional measures requested was that there should be no interference with the workings of the Company in Iran pending the final judgment of the Court. The Company requested the President of the Court (Guerrero) to exercise his power under the Concession Agreement of 1933 and appoint the President of an arbitral tribunal. These were separate proceedings between the Company and the Iranian Government, in which the President declined to act after the Court had found itself without jurisdiction in the preliminary objection proceedings.[29] Immediately on receipt of notice of the application, Iran informed the Court that in its view the Court had no jurisdiction, but without giving any reasons.[30] On 22 June 1951 the United Kingdom filed a request for the indication of provisional measures of protection. On 29 June Iran sent a message to the Court, explaining more fully why it thought that the Court had no jurisdiction in the case.[31] Iran was not represented at the hearing on this request. A week later, on 5 July, the Court rendered its Order, addressed to both parties, indicating provisional measures. The Court justified its competence to do this in the following passages:

> Whereas it appears from the Application . . . that that Government [United Kingdom] has adopted the cause of a British company and is proceeding in virtue of the right of diplomatic protection;
>
> Whereas the complaint made in the Application is one of an alleged violation of international law by the breach of the agreement for a concession of April 29th, 1933, and by a denial of justice which, according to the Government of the United Kingdom, would follow from the refusal of the Iranian Government to accept arbitration in accordance with that agreement, and whereas it cannot be accepted *a priori* that a claim based on such a complaint falls completely outside the scope of international jurisdiction;
>
> Whereas the considerations stated in the preceding paragraph suffice to empower the Court to entertain the Request for interim measures of protection;

[29] The proceedings with the Company are reproduced in a publication of the Government of Iran entitled *Prime Minister's Reports* (Tehran: 1952). A copy is on file with the author and other copies are available in the UN Library in Geneva, and in the Yale Law School Library. *See* W.M. Reisman, 'The Supervisory Jurisdiction of the International Court of Justice: International Arbitration and International Adjudication', 258 *Recueil* 105 (1997), n. 185.

[30] *Anglo-Iranian Oil Co.* case, Pleadings, 702 (doc. 5).

[31] Ibid. 672, 711 (doc. 20); partly recited in the Court's Order on provisional measures. ICJ Rep. 1951, 89 at 92.

Whereas the indication of such measures in no way prejudges the question of the jurisdiction of the Court to deal with the merits of the case and leaves unaffected the right of the Respondent to submit arguments against such jurisdiction[.][32]

In those paragraphs, while the Court accepted the general thrust of the British argument (which had cited the two passages from Dumbauld and Hudson cited in Chapter 2 notes 58 and 59), the statement that it cannot be accepted a priori that the claim falls completely outside the scope of international jurisdiction is open to question. An international court or tribunal is not interested in whether a claim falls within the scope of 'international jurisdiction'. Its concern is whether the claim falls within its own jurisdiction as invoked. The dissenting opinion of Judges Winiarski and Badawi puts the matter in better perspective:

[T]he Court ought not to indicate interim measures of protection unless its competence, in the event of this being challenged, appears to the Court to be nevertheless reasonably probable. Its opinion on this point should be reached after a summary consideration; it can only be provisional and cannot prejudge its final decision, after the detailed consideration to which the Court will proceed in the course of adjudicating on the question in conformity with all the Rules laid down for its procedure.[33]

The Court has since adopted that approach in dealing with a request for provisional measures when its jurisdiction over the merits is challenged in the provisional measures proceedings.

A year later, after preliminary objection proceedings in which the Court found that it had no jurisdiction in the case, it gave the following explanation:

While the Court derived its power to indicate these provisional measures from the special provisions contained in Article 41 of the Statute, it must now derive its jurisdiction to deal with the merits from the general rules laid down in Article 36 of the Statute. These general rules, which are entirely different from the special provisions of Article 41, are based on the principle that the jurisdiction of the Court to deal with and decide a case on the merits depends on the will of the Parties. Unless the Parties have conferred jurisdiction on the Court in accordance with Article 36, the Court lacks such jurisdiction.[34]

[32] Ibid. 92. That last paragraph has become standard in ICJ orders on provisional measures, referring however to both parties. While it may not be strictly necessary, it serves as a useful reminder to the parties not to read more in the Order than is necessary. It was included by ITLOS in its first Order prescribing provisional measures, in the *Saiga No. 2* case, ITLOS Rep. 1998, 24, but not in its second Order of that kind, in the *Southern Bluefin Tuna* cases, above n. 25, nor in its Order in the *Land Reclamation by Singapore in and around the Straits of Johor* (Provisional Measures) case, ITLOS Rep. 2003, 8 October.

[33] ICJ Rep. 1951, 97. The two Judges reached the provisional conclusion that the Court would be compelled to hold itself without jurisdiction, as in fact occurred the next year. Ibid. 1952, at 93.

[34] *Anglo-Iranian Oil Co.* (Preliminary Objection) case, ICJ Rep. 1952, 93, 102.

The Court concluded its Judgment by saying that since the 1951 Order indicating provisional measures had been made 'pending its final decision' in the proceedings, it followed that the Order 'ceases to be operative upon the delivery of this Judgment and that the Provisional Measures lapse at the same time'.[35]

The reference to 'special provisions of Article 41' is the key to the future developments. Since the Order of 1951 was specific in stating that the provisional measures were indicated 'pending its final decision' it is not certain that the paragraph regarding the suspension of the provisional measures was strictly necessary, especially since there was no operative provision in the Judgment to match it. It can be interpreted as tacitly implying that provisional measures may come to have an independent existence of their own and that their continuation can be contemplated in a case where they were indicated before the proceedings on the merits were suspended, without the Court pronouncing itself upon the merits of the case. By Article 41 of the Statute, the purpose of provisional measures is precisely 'to preserve the respective rights of either party'. If the Court decides that it has no jurisdiction over the merits or that the claim is inadmissible, the respective rights of either party are unaffected, and all that the decision does is to block recourse to the Court for their implementation. That was at a time when there was widespread uncertainty whether an order indicating provisional measures imposed binding obligations on the parties. The passage can be explained in this case by the existence of the independent claim of the Company against the Iranian Government in which the President of the Court was requested to appoint the arbitrators in accordance with the terms of the concession agreement.[36] Now that it is clear that in the International Court of Justice an order indicating provisional measures does impose binding obligations on the parties, it would appear to be more essential that, except where the decision on the provisional measures establishes their duration *ratione temporis*, any later decision in the case, whether a

[35] Ibid. 114. There is no operative clause about the provisional measures. There was a complication in connection with the provisional measures which the Court did not address. After the 1951 Order, the Company instituted proceedings in different countries around the world to secure return of cargoes of oil claimed by or on behalf of the Iranian interests. In those proceedings the Company had invoked the Order as evidence of its title to the oil, and in several of those cases this contention had been accepted. *See* Ch. 6 n. 19.

[36] Regarding this aspect, *see* the *Prime Minister's Reports*, op. cit. n. 29. The Court has included a similar statement in other judgments accepting preliminary objections after an Order indicating provisional measures. *Nuclear Tests* cases, ICJ Rep. 1974, 253 at 272 (para. 61) and 451 at 477 (para. 64). Note also that in the *Request for Examination* case New Zealand, on the basis that the 1974 Judgment was not a final decision, filed what it termed a Further Request for the Indication of Provisional Measures. Here the Court found that the basic request for examination of the situation must be dismissed, and in a separate operative provision found that the further request for the indication of provisional measures must also be dismissed. ICJ Rep. 1995, 288, 306 (para. 67), and 307 (para. 68 (2)).

final decision or not, should clarify its impact on any provisional measures that may have been indicated earlier.

In the *Interhandel* (Interim Protection) case, where jurisdiction was also based on Article 36, paragraph 2, of the Statute, the Court corrected the impression created by the provisional measures Order in *Anglo-Iranian*.[37] It explained that 'by its subject-matter the present dispute falls within the purview of Article 36, paragraph 2,' of the Statute. It repeated in slightly different language the 'without prejudice' provision, but in the circumstances declined to indicate provisional measures. That case shows that even if it is not going to indicate provisional measures, the ICJ will normally first establish its jurisdiction to deal with the request. In principle the Court cannot reach any decision on a request for the indication of provisional measures before it has found that it has jurisdiction to deal with the request.[38] The combination of these two rules has given to each party a wide range of options to air many different contentions in the Court and in that way to 'test the water' as a prelude to the decision on its litigation strategy. It has likewise opened the Court to the institution of contentious proceedings with the prime object of submitting a request for provisional measures of a political character. That is discussed later.[39]

The question next arose in the two *Fisheries Jurisdiction* (Interim Protection) cases brought in 1972 against Iceland. The applicants, the Federal Republic of Germany and the United Kingdom, founded the jurisdiction on a compromissory provision in earlier exchanges of letters said to confer jurisdiction on the Court over issues that arose in those cases. Iceland immediately contested the Court's jurisdiction and did not take part in the

[37] *Interhandel* (Interim Protection) case, ICJ Rep. 1957, 105, 110. Both parties appeared in those proceedings. The Court established prima facie jurisdiction but found that there was no need for it to indicate provisional measures. Judges Wellington Koo, Klaestad (with President Hackworth joining him), and Sir Hersch Lauterpacht (who was the first to use the phrase 'prima facie jurisdiction' in his individual opinion in that case, at p. 117) thought that in this case the Court lacked prima facie jurisdiction, since the American declaration accepting the jurisdiction under that provision of the Statute contained the well-known subjective domestic jurisdiction reservation. Here too the Court was later to find that it was without jurisdiction, but without reference to that reservation. Ibid. 1959, 6. Other cases in which the Court established prima facie jurisdiction and later found that it had no jurisdiction over the merits include the two *Nuclear Tests* cases, ICJ Rep. 1974, 253, 457, and the *Aegean Sea Continental Shelf* case, ICJ Rep. 1978, 3. While it might be rare, it is always possible for the Court to find after full argument that, notwithstanding an earlier finding that prima facie it might have jurisdiction over the merits for provisional measures purposes, yet it does not have jurisdiction over the merits.

[38] This principle is not absolute. In dealing with preliminary objections where the existence of the title of jurisdiction invoked was questioned, the Court overstepped that question and examined whether reservations to that title of jurisdiction would affect the decision. *Aerial Incident of 10 August 1999* (Jurisdiction of the Court) case, ICJ Rep. 2000, 12. It has also done this in dealing with a request for a provisional measures before preliminary objections had been raised. *Aegean Sea Continental Shelf* (Interim Protection) case, ICJ Rep. 1976, 3 at 8 (para. 21).

[39] *See* § 8.10.

proceedings. The Court took the opportunity to restate the law in clearer terms:

> Whereas on a request for provisional measures the Court need not, before indicating them, finally satisfy itself that it has jurisdiction on the merits of the case, yet it ought not to act under Article 41 of the Statute if the absence of jurisdiction on the merits is manifest[.][40]

That is the first use of the word *manifest*, and in the context it clearly means manifest to the Court on a reasonable reading of the relevant text. The Court then in each case examined the title of jurisdiction invoked, to find that it appeared, prima facie, to afford a possible basis on which its jurisdiction might be founded. In a procedural innovation, it required the first set of written pleadings to address the question of jurisdiction, the applicants pleading first.[41] This innovation is far-reaching. It allows the Court to determine by an order that quasi-preliminary objection proceedings should take place, possibly with the applicant pleading first to the jurisdiction, in lieu of the normal preliminary objection proceeding in which the respondent files the objections after the merits have been laid before the Court in the memorial.[42] It also prevents the merits being raised at that stage, beyond what is stated in the instrument instituting the proceedings.

The two *Nuclear Tests* (Interim Protection) cases brought by Australia and by New Zealand against France followed. The proceedings were instituted on 9 May 1973, the applicants simultaneously filing requests for provisional measures. Jurisdiction was based on two titles, the acceptances of the

[40] *Fisheries Jurisdiction* (Interim Protection) cases, ICJ Rep. 1972, 9, 15 (para. 15), 16 (para. 17) and 30, 33 (para. 16), 31 (para. 18). In both cases the Court included the 'without prejudice' clause. Judge Padilla Nervo dissented, partly relying on the dissenting opinion in *Anglo-Iranian Oil. Co.* Ibid. 20 and 37. The Court upheld its jurisdiction in these cases. ICJ Rep. 1973, 3 and 49. These cases were the first to be heard under the revised Rules of 1972. The provisions regarding interim measures were unchanged from the original Rules of 1946. On the ambiguity of the expression 'might be founded' *see* the observation of Judge Schwebel in n. 17.

[41] Although the respondent, Iceland, did not appear in the provisional measures proceedings or otherwise defend its case, the Court did not invoke Art. 53 of the Statute. In the Orders on provisional measures it stated that according to its jurisprudence, the non-appearance of one of the parties cannot by itself constitute an obstacle to the indication of provisional measures, provided the parties have been given an opportunity of presenting their observations on the subject (at pp. 15 (para. 11) and 32 (para. 11)). In the Orders on time-limits and the order of pleading, it referred to the 'circumstances', as justifying its decision. A joint dissenting opinion by Judges Bengzon and Jiménez de Aréchaga objected to that decision partly on the ground that Art. 53 had not been invoked. Ibid. 182, 191. As a technicality, when questions of jurisdiction are to be settled first, the case carries the subtitle *Jurisdiction of the Court*.

[42] This is not an absolute rule. *See Aerial Incident of 3 July 1988* case, ICJ Rep. 1989, 132. Usually in this type of case, on the basis of the arguments raised in the provisional measures proceedings, the Court will require the applicant to file the first written pleading. This procedure has led to a further development, that the parties agree that the issue of jurisdiction be determined separately from the merits, including the order of pleading. This has also been extended to Annex VII arbitrations under the Law of the Sea Convention, for instance in the *Southern Bluefin Tuna* arbitration, 119 ILR 508.

compulsory jurisdiction and the more controversial General Act of 1928 for the Pacific Settlement of International Disputes.[43] Here the respondent, a permanent member of the Security Council, immediately challenged the Court's jurisdiction and took no part in the proceedings. In the hearings, each applicant stated that it was basing its request for provisional measures primarily on Article 41 of the Statute and only subsidiarily on Article 33 of the General Act. The Court refined its explanation regarding its jurisdiction to indicate provisional measures:[44]

> 13. Whereas on a request for provisional measures the Court need not, before indicating them, finally satisfy itself that it has jurisdiction on the merits of the case, and yet ought not to indicate such measures unless the provisions invoked by the Applicant appear, prima facie, to afford a basis on which the jurisdiction of the Court might be founded.

The Court's examination of the material before it regarding jurisdiction led it to the conclusion that the provisions invoked by the applicants 'appear, prima facie, to afford a basis on which the jurisdiction of the Court might be founded'. However, based on the applicants' replies concerning the General Act the Court expressly limited its examination of the request 'only in the context of Article 41 of its Statute'. From there it examined the claims as formulated in the applications and concluded that it could not be assumed a priori that those claims 'fall completely outside the purview of the Court's jurisdiction'; or that the applicant Governments 'may not be able to furnish a legal interest in respect of those claims entitling the Court to admit the Application'. That extends the Court's competence to indicate provisional measures to cases where not only the Court's jurisdiction is challenged, but also the admissibility of the claim on the ground that it does not show a cause of action. The Court accordingly reworded its 'without prejudice' consideration:

[43] 93 LNTS 343; 72 UNTS 101 (Revised General Act). *See further* in Ch. 2 n. 42.

[44] *Nuclear Tests* (Interim Measures) cases, ICJ Rep. 1973, 99 at 101 (para. 13), 102 (para. 17), 103 (paras. 18, 23), 105 (para. 33) and 135, 137 (para. 14), 138 (paras. 18, 19), 140 (para. 24), 142 (para. 34). There were four dissenting opinions to these Orders, by Judges Forster (pp. 111, 148), Gros (pp. 115, 149), Petrén (pp. 124, 159), and Ignacio-Pinto (pp. 128, 163). Although 'paired', New Zealand appointing the same person as judge ad hoc as Australia, the claims and cases were not identical, and in some respects the Orders are not in identical terms. That, however, does not affect the substance of this chapter. The Court never decided the question of its jurisdiction or the admissibility of the claims. It found that by virtue of certain undertakings given by the respondent outside the Court proceedings the claims no longer had any object and that the Court was therefore not called upon to give a decision on them. ICJ Rep. 1974, 253, 457. Nevertheless, the two Judgments left open the possibility of a re-examination of the situation if the basis of the judgment were to be affected by future actions of the respondent. Ibid., at 272 (para. 60) and 477 (para. 63). That laid the basis for the introduction by New Zealand in 1995 of its *Request for an Examination of the Situation in Accordance with Paragraph 63 of the Court's Judgment of 20 December 1974 in the* Nuclear Tests (New Zealand *v* France) *Case*, accompanied by a request for provisional measures. The Court rejected that case. ICJ Rep. 1995, 288.

33. Whereas the decision given in the present proceedings in no way prejudges the question of the jurisdiction of the Court to deal with the merits of the case, or any questions relating to the admissibility of the Application, or relating to the merits themselves, and leaves unaffected the right of the [respondent] Government to submit arguments in respect of those questions[.]

As before, the Court decided that the next phase should address the questions of jurisdiction and admissibility, the applicants filing their written pleadings first.

Those Orders led Judge Jiménez de Aréchaga to clarify underlying issues. He explained his opinion that the Court should not indicate provisional measures without paying due regard to the 'basic question' of its jurisdiction to entertain the merits. 'A request should not be granted if it is clear, even on a prima facie appreciation, that there is no possible basis on which the Court could be competent as to the merits' (pp. 107 and 143). He went on to say—something more controversial—that from a subjective point of view, such an appreciation or estimation cannot be fairly described as a mere preliminary or even cursory examination of the jurisdictional issue. On the contrary, the judge must be satisfied that this basic question of the Court's jurisdiction has received the fullest possible attention which he or she can give to it within the limits of time and of materials available for the purpose. However, those limits of time and of the materials available compel the Court's decision to be preliminary or even cursory, both embodied in the concept of 'prima facie jurisdiction' over the merits. Judge Nagendra Singh (pp. 108 and 145) expressed similar views.

The *Aegean Sea Continental Shelf* (Interim Protection) case was the next occasion for the Court to look into this question. As in the previous cases, the respondent challenged the Court's jurisdiction and did not appear in the provisional measures proceedings. Turkey challenged the jurisdiction on two grounds: that the General Act was no longer in force between Greece and Turkey; and alternatively, even were it in force and applicable, the matters submitted to the Court in the application fell within the terms of a reservation by Greece when it acceded to the General Act in 1931. The Court did not find it necessary to reach a final conclusion at that stage on the continued validity of the General Act and, following the pattern of *Nuclear Tests*, decided to examine the request for interim measures 'only in the context of Article 41 of the Statute'. From this perspective the Court concluded that the alleged breach by Turkey of Greece's exclusive rights did not cause irreparable damage and was capable of reparation by appropriate means, with the consequence that it was unable to find in that alleged breach of Greece's rights such a risk of irreparable prejudice to rights in issue before the Court as might require the exercise of its power under Article 41 of the Statute to indicate provisional measures for their protection.[45] The Court stated that it

[45] For fuller discussion, *see* § 8.7, text to n. 56.

was not called upon to decide any question of jurisdiction to entertain the merits in order to pronounce on the request then before it. Its decision declining the request for provisional measures in no way prejudged any such question or any question relating to the merits, and left unaffected the right of both Governments to submit arguments in respect of any of those questions. At the same time the Court found that it was necessary first to resolve its jurisdiction with respect to the case, and for that reason it could not accede to the respondent's request that the case be removed from the General List. By a separate Order it fixed a date by which Greece was to file the first pleading.[46]

4.4. THE INTERNATIONAL COURT OF JUSTICE SINCE 1978

In 1978 the Court promulgated revised Rules of Court, with changes in the provisions regarding provisional measures (*see* § 3.6). The *U.S. Diplomatic and Consular Staff in Tehran* (Provisional Measures) case (hereafter *Hostages* case) was the first case to be heard under those new Rules. On 4 November 1979 a sequence of events in and around the American Embassy in Tehran began. Those events included the invasion of the embassy premises and the seizure and continued detention of American diplomatic and consular personnel and other Americans on the premises and the diplomatic archives and other property. In November, the United States, which in the meantime had taken economic measures against substantial Iranian assets in the United States, brought the matter before the Security Council, which adopted a presidential statement on 9 November. That statement called for the release of the detained persons without delay. Later in November both Iran and the Secretary-General requested a meeting of the Security Council. On 29 November the United States filed its application instituting proceedings against Iran, basing jurisdiction on the Optional Protocols adopted in connection with the Vienna Conventions on Diplomatic Relations 1961 and on Consular Relations 1963.[47] On the same date, the United States filed a request for the indication of provisional measures. Although worded differently (as is appropriate), both the application and the request asked for the immediate release of the detained persons. In reply to the notification of those instruments, Iran in effect denied the jurisdiction of the Court, and did

[46] *Aegean Sea Continental Shelf* (Interim Protection) case, ICJ Rep. 1976, 3, 42. The Court also considered the question raised by Greece during the hearings whether, under Article 41, the Court had an independent power to indicate interim measures in order to prevent the aggravation or extension of the dispute. also discussed in § 8.7. The Court later found that it had no jurisdiction in this case; ibid. 1978, 3.

[47] 500 UNTS 95, 241; 796 UNTS 261, 487. For the developments in the United Nations *see* *United Nations Yearbook 1979*, 307.

not take part in the proceedings. On 15 December, the Court was unanimous in indicating provisional measures substantially as requested.[48]

The court's approach was first to look into the question whether the provisions invoked in the request for the provisional measures appeared prima facie to afford a basis on which the jurisdiction over the merits might be founded, since the court ought to indicate such measures, unless the provisions invoked by the applicant met that prima facie condition (paragraph 15). For the Court it was 'manifest' from the two Protocols that they furnished such a basis. The Court accordingly found it unnecessary to examine whether jurisdiction might be based on other instruments invoked. The Court also explained why it could not accept Iranian contentions against the exercise of jurisdiction in this phase of the case. The provisional measures requested in large measure followed the main claim in the case and, if granted, and had the provisional measures been binding, might have assumed the character of an interim judgment on part of the claim, so that Iran's compliance with them could have led to the termination of the dispute and relieved the crisis that had developed in the relations between the two countries. Accordingly, the Court made an important statement on the relations between an indication of provisional measures and judgment on the substance of the case:

> [A] request for provisional measures must by its very nature relate to the substance of the case since, as Article 41 expressly states, their object is to preserve the respective right of either party; and whereas in the present case the purpose of the United States request appears to be not to obtain a judgment, interim or final, on the merits of its claims but to preserve the substance of the rights which it claims *pendente lite*. (paragraph 28)

The Court also explained why provisional measures can be unilateral, especially when the adverse party does not appear in the proceedings. Accordingly, the Court did not find in the Iranian letter legal grounds that should lead it to conclude that it ought not to entertain the American request. Examining the circumstances (which were largely matters of common knowledge) the Court had no difficulty in deciding on appropriate measures. The Order contains the usual 'without prejudice' provision. In addition to these legal considerations addressing directly the substance of the request for provisional measures, the Court devoted paragraphs 38 to 44 of its Order

[48] ICJ Rep. 1979, 7. The Court later gave judgment in favour of the United States. Ibid. 1980, 3. The question of damages was outstanding; however, and the case was discontinued only after a series of complicated agreements was reached between the parties and the hostages were released. Ibid. 1981, 45. One outcome was the establishment of the Iran–United States Claims Tribunal, still in existence, to resolve many disputed claims of the citizens of one country against the other as well as some intergovernmental claims. It would be rash to assume, without further historical evidence, what role this combined action of the Court and the Security Council served in resolving this crisis. The United States had powerful economic measures at its disposal against large Iranian assets in the United States, and there is little doubt that economic factors were a major element.

to a series of general pronouncements on the significance of personal inviolability in diplomatic and consular relations between States. While no State is under any obligation to maintain diplomatic or consular relations with another, yet a State cannot fail to recognize the imperative obligations inherent in those relations, codified in the Vienna Conventions of 1961 and 1963.[49] That was the first use by the Court of an order indicating provisional measures for a general pronouncement about basic legal issues raised in the case and to demonstrate direct concern with the welfare of human beings.

The Court accordingly indicated a series of measures to be undertaken by Iran, and it required both parties not to take any action and to ensure that no action is taken which might aggravate the tension between the two countries or render the dispute more difficult of solution.[50] The operative paragraph also introduces something new, what we might term a 'supervisory clause'. The Court decided that until it delivers its final judgment, 'it will keep the matters covered by this Order continuously under review'. The Court gave no explanation, and nothing is known of how the Court kept the matter continuously under review, although of course the case was pending and proceeded to the merits phase.[51] This addition probably reflects two innovations in the 1978 Rules. Article 75, paragraph 1, provides that the Court may at any time decide to examine *proprio motu* whether the circumstances of the case require the indication of provisional measures. We can see this as a sign that the Court intends to exert some control over the implementation of an order indicating provisional measures, and for that purpose may require information on the current circumstances of the case.[52] In addition, the new Article 78, which was not mentioned in the preambular phrase of the Order, would have enabled the Court to request information from the parties on any matter connected with the implementation of that Order.

On 9 April 1984 Nicaragua filed an application instituting proceedings against the United States in the case entitled *Military and Paramilitary Activities in and against Nicaragua*. Many see that case as a turning point in the history of international litigation. Jurisdiction was initially based on the acceptances by each party of the compulsory jurisdiction under Article 36, paragraphs 2 and 5, of the Statute. Nicaragua was alleging a long series of acts said to be in violation of the Charter and of general and customary

[49] The Court also indicated concern at the violation of human rights of the detained persons. *See* § 8.4.

[50] For criticism of United States action found to be in violation of that part of the Order, *see* the Judgment in ICJ Rep. 1980, 3, 41 (para. 93). However, the question of the legality of that impugned action was not before the Court, and accordingly the impugned action had no effect on the Court's decision.

[51] On the obligation to submit reports on compliance with an order on provisional measures, *see* § 7.7.

[52] That was my interpretation at p. 154 of my *Procedure in the International Court: A Commentary on the 1978 Rules of the International Court of Justice* (The Hague: Martinus Nijhoff, 1983).

international law. On the same day Nicaragua filed a request for the indication of provisional measures. The United States immediately replied, *inter alia* objecting to the jurisdiction of the Court on several grounds, one of which contested the very existence of the Nicaraguan declaration (of 1929) as acceptance of the jurisdiction of the present International Court. For the first time since *Interhandel* in this type of case, both parties appeared at the hearing. The issue of jurisdiction was unusual, unique in fact. It related to a single question of fact, namely, whether the depositary, the Secretary-General of the League of Nations, had ever received Nicaragua's ratification of the Protocol of Signature of the Statute of the Permanent Court so that the declaration came within the scope of the transitional provision of Article 36, paragraph 5, of the present Statute. In its Order indicating provisional measures, after describing the history of the instrument of ratification based on the facts then at its disposal, the Court reasserted the prima facie jurisdiction approach going far in outlining the Court's approach to this particular jurisdictional question.[53] It repeated its dictum that in provisional measures proceedings it need not finally satisfy itself that it has jurisdiction on the merits or, as the case may be, that an objection taken to the jurisdiction is well founded. The Court then included the following two paragraphs:

25. Whereas the Court, having given the matter the fullest consideration compatible with the requirements of urgency imposed by a request for the indication of provisional measures, finds that Nicaragua . . . made, on 24 September 1929, following its signature of the Protocol . . . an unconditional Declaration accepting the compulsory jurisdiction of the Permanent Court, in particular without condition as to ratification and without limit of time, but it has not so far been established to the Court's satisfaction that Nicaragua ever deposited an instrument of ratification of that Protocol; whereas however the Court is not convinced, by the arguments so far addressed to it, that the absence of such effective ratification excluded the operation of Article 36, paragraph 5, of the Statute of the present Court, and prevented the transfer to the present Court of the declaration as a result of the consent thereto given by Nicaragua which, having been represented at the San Francisco Conference, signed and ratified the Charter and thereby accepted the Statute in which Article 36, paragraph 5, appears . . . ;
26. Whereas the Court will not now make any final determination of the question of the present validity or invalidity of the declaration of 24 September 1929, and the question whether or not Nicaragua accordingly was or was not, for the purposes of Article 36, paragraph 2, of the Statute of the Court a 'State accepting the same obligation' as the United States of America at the date of the filing of the Application, so as to be able to rely on the United States declaration of 26 August 1946, nor of the question whether, as a result of the [U.S.] declaration of 6 April 1984, the present Application is excluded from the scope of the acceptance by the United States of the compulsory jurisdiction of the Court; whereas however the

[53] ICJ Rep. 1984, 169, 179, 209.

> Court finds that the two declarations do nevertheless appear to afford a basis on which the jurisdiction of the Court might be founded[.]

The Court concluded its recitals with the usual 'without prejudice' clause, and went on to indicate a series of provisional measures. It repeated the supervisory clause introduced in *Hostages* that until it delivered final judgment it would keep the matters covered by the Order 'continuously under review', and ended by deciding that the first pleadings would address the questions of jurisdiction and admissibility, Nicaragua to file its memorial first.[54] There is again no explanation of the 'under review' provision, but as in the *Hostages* case the proceedings in the case were continuing.

Six weeks later Nicaragua requested further provisional measures on the ground that the United States had failed to comply with that Order. The Court considered that the request should await the outcome of the proceedings on jurisdiction and admissibility then pending. Nicaragua did not revert to the matter.[55]

In the *Frontier Dispute between Burkina Faso and Mali* (Provisional Measures) case instituted by special agreement before an ad hoc Chamber of the Court, the Chamber found that its jurisdiction to indicate provisional measures was 'manifestly established'. Following a series of armed actions in the disputed territory, both parties requested an indication of provisional measures. This is the second time that the jurisdiction was seen as 'manifest'. The Chamber revised the wording of the supervisory clause to read: 'pending the final judgment and without prejudice to Article 76 of the Rules, the Chamber will remain seised of the question covered by the present Order'. That is probably a more appropriate formulation.[56] In the *Arbitral Award of 31 July 1988* (Provisional Measures) case between Guinea-Bissau and Senegal (in which both parties appeared in the oral proceedings), jurisdiction, based on the declarations accepting the compulsory jurisdiction, was challenged by Senegal which, however, did not wish to broach the issue of jurisdiction over the main application at that stage. The Court found that the two declarations appeared, prima facie, to afford a basis on which the jurisdiction might be

[54] The parties agreed on the order of pleading in those proceedings. In its Judgment on jurisdiction and admissibility the Court held that it had jurisdiction both under the declarations accepting the compulsory jurisdiction and under another title of jurisdiction that Nicaragua invoked during the proceedings, and that the application was admissible. ICJ Rep. 1974, 392. The United States withdrew from the proceedings after that. The Court finally gave judgment largely in favour of Nicaragua, leaving open the question of damages. Ibid. 1986, 14. While this case was pending the Security Council was also seised of the situation, and adopted resolution 562 (1985), 10 May 1985. During 1984 Nicaragua made several approaches to the Security Council but no meeting was called to deal with the situation there. Nicaragua also tried to invoke Art. 94 of the Charter to secure enforcement of the 1986 Judgment on the merits, but this encountered the American veto. Resolutions were adopted by the General Assembly on the matter. Following a change of regime, Nicaragua discontinued the case. ICJ Rep. 1991, 47.

[55] *See further* in Ch. 7 nn. 53, 54.

[56] *Frontier Dispute* (Burkina Faso/Mali) (Provisional Measures) case, ICJ Rep. 1986, 3.

founded, and it inserted the customary 'without prejudice' clause into its Order.[57]

This brings us to the next major set of cases for the purposes of this examination, the *Lockerbie* cases brought by Libya against the United Kingdom and the United States.[58] They arose out of the destruction of Pan Am flight 103 on 21 December 1988 over the village of Lockerbie in Scotland. Investigations led the two respondents to conclude that the destruction of this civil aircraft was the work of two agents of the Libyan Government.[59] Failing to obtain satisfaction from Libya they brought the matter before the Security Council. On 21 January 1992 the Security Council adopted resolution 731 (1992) urging Libya to provide a full and effective response to requests of the respondent Governments, so as to contribute to the elimination of international terrorism. There was no adequate response to that resolution, and rumours began circulating that the two respondent Governments would propose action in the Security Council under Chapter VII of the Charter, imposing mandatory economic sanctions on Libya. On 3 March 1992 Libya filed two applications instituting these proceedings, founding jurisdiction on the compromissory clause (Article 14, paragraph 1) of the Montreal Convention for the Suppression of Unlawful Acts against the Safety of Civil Aviation of 23 September 1971. On the same day Libya filed two requests for the indication of provisional measures. Libya asked the Court to enjoin each respondent from taking measures calculated to exert coercion on Libya or compel it to surrender the two accused individuals to any jurisdiction outside of Libya; and to ensure that no steps were taken that could prejudice the rights of Libya with respect to the proceedings instituted by Libya's applications—more simply that the respondents should not initiate action in the Security Council under Chapter VII of the Charter. After the hearings were closed and while the Court was deliberating, the Security Council adopted resolution 748 (1992) of 31 March 1992, acting under Chapter VII and imposing mandatory economic sanctions on Libya.

[57] *Arbitral Award of 31 July 1989* (Provisional Measures) case, ICJ Rep. 1990, 62. On the merits the Court found in favour of Senegal, ibid. 1991, 53. For that arbitral award, *see* 20 UNRIAA 119.

[58] *Question of Interpretation and Application of the 1971 Montreal Convention arising from the Aerial Incident at Lockerbie* (Provisional Measures) cases, ICJ Rep. 1992, 3, 114; (Preliminary Objections), ibid. 1998, 9, 115; 149, 152. The two cases were not joined but were heard in common, with Libya making one written and one oral pleading applicable to both cases. For their part, each respondent made its oral pleading in separate sessions of the Court, since in the preliminary objection phase the composition of the Court was different for each case. Judge Oda, at the time Vice-President of the Court, was Acting President for the 1993 phase and Judge Weeramantry for the 1998 phase. For the 1971 Montreal Convention for the Suppression of Unlawful Acts against the Safety of Civil Aviation, *see* 974 UNTS 177.

[59] On 15 March 2002, the Scottish Court sitting in the Netherlands (as part of a compromise between the parties) rejected an appeal by one of those Libyan nationals, the other having been acquitted by the court of first instance. *See* Security Council doc. S/2002/268, 15 March 2002. Following that the cases were discontinued 'with prejudice'. ICJ Rep. 2003, 149, 152.

In its Orders of 14 April 1992 declining to indicate provisional measures, the Court first laid down that in the context of the present proceedings it had to consider the circumstances drawn to its attention as requiring the indication of provisional measures, 'but cannot make definitive findings either of fact or of law on the issues relating to the merits, and the right of the Parties to contest such issues at the stage of the merits must remain unaffected by the Court's decision'. It went on to state that at the stage of provisional measures, it considered that the obligation of the parties as members of the United Nations under Article 25 of the Charter extended to the decision contained in resolution 748, and that, in accordance with Article 103 of the Charter, the obligations of the parties in that respect prevailed over their obligations under any other international agreement, including the Montreal Convention.[60] The Court went further, and considered that without at that stage determining 'definitively' the legal effect of the Security Council resolution, the rights claimed by Libya under the Montreal Convention 'cannot now be regarded as appropriate for protection by the indication of provisional measures'. In addition, an indication of the measures requested by Libya would be likely to impair the rights which prima facie were to be enjoyed by each respondent by virtue of that resolution of the Security Council. Ending its reasoning with the usual 'without prejudice' clause, the Court found that the circumstances were not such as to require an indication of provisional measures. Notable in those two Orders is the absence of any statement that the applicants had established a prima facie case of jurisdiction over the merits. Acting President Oda commented on this. He thought there did not seem to exist any convincing ground for asserting that the Court's jurisdiction was so obviously lacking.[61]

Those Orders attracted powerful dissents and criticism both in the Court and from the academic community. The main ground for those criticisms was that the Court should have reviewed the compatibility with the Charter of the action of the Security Council, including the propriety and even legality of its adopting resolution 748 while the Court was deliberating. This is not the place to examine that criticism. It is enough to point out that proceedings for provisional measures have developed their own characteristics. Their dominant features are the Court's marked unwillingness and limited competence to go into the merits any more than is necessary for the immediate decision, and the repeatedly asserted provisional character of any finding of fact or of law contained in the decision on provisional measures. On the central issue of

[60] By Art. 103 of the Charter, 'In the event of a conflict between the obligations of the Members of the United Nations under the present Charter and their obligations under any other international agreement, the obligations under the present Charter shall prevail.' This applies to obligations arising from a judgment and now to obligations arising from provisional measures indicated by the ICJ.

[61] ICJ Rep. 1992 at 18 and 130.

review of the actions of the Security Council, in its 1998 Judgments on preliminary objections the Court, while upholding its jurisdiction under the Montreal Convention, rejected general objections to the admissibility. However, on the major issue of the effect of the Security Council resolutions it held that the objection did not, in the circumstances, have an exclusively preliminary character. The Court could consider that objection when it reached the merits. However, the dispute was settled, the sanctions were lifted and the cases were thereupon discontinued.

That is the first instance in which a case has been brought before the Court with a request for provisional measures expressly aimed at preventing the imposition of mandatory sanctions by the Security Council. Despite its cautious language (appropriate to an Order on provisional measures), the Court has shown that it will not encourage using the provisional measures procedure for that purpose.

The Court confirmed that position in the next case to be considered, the *Application of the Convention on the Prevention and Punishment of the Crime of Genocide* (Provisional Measures) case brought by Bosnia-Herzegovina (hereafter *Bosnia*) against Yugoslavia [Serbia & Montenegro].[62] The situation arising out of the disintegration of the former Socialist Federal Republic of Yugoslavia (SFR) has been on the active agenda of the Security Council since 1991, as a threat to international peace and security. In resolution 713 (1991) of 25 September 1991, the Security Council, acting under Chapter VII of the Charter, imposed a general and complete embargo on all deliveries of weapons and military equipment to Yugoslavia. The Security Council reaffirmed that embargo in resolution 724 (1991) of 15 December. At that time the term *Yugoslavia* designated the whole territory of the former Socialist Federal Republic. The independence of the secessionist States had not yet been recognized or confirmed.

On 20 March 1993 Bosnia filed an application instituting proceedings against Yugoslavia [Serbia & Montenegro], alleging a series of violations of the Genocide Convention and other violations of international law, and basing jurisdiction on the compromissory clause (Article IX) of the Genocide

[62] *Case concerning the Application of the Convention on the Prevention and Punishment of the Crime of Genocide* (Provisional Measures), ICJ Rep. 1993, 3; (Further Provisional Measures), ibid. 325; (Preliminary Objections), ibid. 1996 (II), 595; (Counter-claims), ibid. 1997, 243; (Withdrawal of Counter-claims), ibid. 2001, 572. The case on the merits is ready for hearing and pending at the time of writing. Neither side appointed a judge ad hoc for the first provisional measures phase. The author must disclose an interest, as counsel for Yugoslavia in the provisional measures phases. On 24 April 2001 the Federal Republic of Yugoslavia [Serbia & Montenegro] filed a request for the revision of the preliminary objection Judgment. The Court found that this application was inadmissible. ICJ Rep. 2003, 7. This case must be distinguished from another case of the same name brought by Croatia against Yugoslavia [Serbia & Montenegro], ICJ Rep. 1999, 1015. For the Genocide Convention in the International Tribunal for the Former Yugoslavia (ICTY), *see Prosecutor* v *Krstić*, in the Trial Chamber, Case IT-98-33-T (2 August 2001), Appeals Chamber, Case IT-98-33-A (19 April 2004).

Convention.[63] On the same date Bosnia filed a request for provisional measures. The measures requested covered a wide range of activities. They included a request for the respondent to cease and desist from all acts of genocide, from providing any type of support to any group engaged in or planning military or paramilitary activities against the Government of Bosnia (a reference to the Republika Srpska), that Yugoslavia must cease and desist from all types of military or paramilitary activities against Bosnia and from any other use or threat of force in its relations with Bosnia, that under current circumstances the Government of Bosnia had the right to seek and receive support from other states in order to defend its people, including by means of immediately obtaining military weapons, equipment, and supplies. In addition it claimed that Bosnia had the right to request the immediate assistance of any State to come to its defence, including by means of immediately providing weapons etc., and that under the current circumstances any State had the right to come to the immediate defence of Bosnia including by means of immediately providing weapons etc. Those last two requests were designed to challenge the application of the Security Council embargo to what had in the meantime become an independent State and a member of the United Nations, Bosnia-Herzegovina.

The Court first clarified the scope of its jurisdiction to indicate provisional measures by specifying that the concept of prima facie jurisdiction 'embraces jurisdiction both *ratione personae* and *ratione materiae*, even though, inasmuch as almost all States are today parties to the Statute of the Court, it is in general only the latter which requires to be considered'. The Court therefore first considered its jurisdiction *ratione personae*, and concluded that if Bosnia and Yugoslavia were both parties to the Genocide Convention, disputes to which Article IX applies 'are in any event prima facie within the jurisdiction *ratione personae* of the Court'. Parenthetically, this clarification could be useful for ITLOS, since its jurisdiction, and more so that of the Seabed Disputes Chamber, is based on different rules from those applying in the ICJ.

From there the Court went on to examine its jurisdiction *ratione materiae*. That raised complicated questions of State succession. The Court reached the conclusion that whereas Article IX of the Convention, to which both States were parties, appeared to afford a basis on which the jurisdiction of the Court might be founded to the extent that the subject-matter of the dispute related to the interpretation, application, or fulfilment of the Genocide Convention (the words used in Article IX of the Genocide Convention), including disputes relating to the responsibility of a State for genocide or for any of the other acts renumerated in Article III of the Convention (that is, the ancillary crimes of aiding etc. the commission of the principal crime), it did not go

[63] Convention on the Prevention and Punishment of the Crime of Genocide, 1948, 78 UNTS 277.

beyond that. Considering the extent of the claims in the application and the wide range of the measures requested, this presaged considerable scaling down of the scope of the case *ratione materiae*. The Court confirmed this in the following passage:

> 35. Whereas the Court, having established the existence of a basis on which the jurisdiction might be founded, ought not to indicate measures for the protection of any disputed rights other than those which might ultimately form the basis of a judgment in the exercise of that jurisdiction; whereas accordingly the Court will confine its examination of the measures requested, and of the grounds asserted for the request for such measures, to those which fall within the scope of the Genocide Convention[.]

The Court also again revised the without prejudice reservation in its Order. It explained that it could not make definitive findings of fact or of imputability, and that the right of each party to dispute the facts alleged against it, to challenge the attribution to it of responsibility for those facts, and to submit arguments in respect of the merits, must remain unaffected by the Court's decision (paragraph 44). In the proceedings Bosnia introduced another new possible title of jurisdiction. After examination the Court found that it could not regard that as constituting a prima facie basis of jurisdiction, and that it must proceed on the basis only that it has prima facie jurisdiction, both *ratione personae* and *ratione materiae*, under Article IX of the Genocide Convention.

On 27 July 1993 Bosnia filed a second request for provisional measures. It formulated many of the measures requested in terms of the Genocide Convention. Others, however, were more general. Yugoslavia was to desist from all efforts to partition, dismember, annex, or incorporate the sovereign territory of Bosnia; the Government of Bosnia must have the means to prevent the commission of acts of genocide; the contracting parties to the Genocide Convention were obliged to prevent the commission of acts of genocide; the Government of Bosnia must have the means to defend the State 'from any forms of genocide and partition and dismemberment by means of genocide.' Requests relating to the arms embargo were also formulated in terms relating to the Genocide Convention; and the UN Peace-keeping Force in Bosnia (UNPROFOR) was required to do all in its power to ensure the flow of humanitarian relief supplies to the Bosnian people through the Bosnian city of Tuzla.

In its Order of 13 September 1993 the Court repeated its previous findings regarding the scope of its jurisdiction in this case.[64] Additional possible titles of jurisdiction were introduced in this phase, but the Court did not see in them a possible basis for a finding of prima facie jurisdiction. The applicant also claimed that the Court's jurisdiction was grounded in the customary and

[64] ICJ Rep. 1993, 325.

conventional international law of war and international humanitarian law. Here the Court replied that the applicant had not brought to its notice any provision conferring upon the Court jurisdiction to deal with a dispute between the parties concerning matters to which those texts relate. Accordingly, 'such jurisdiction is not prima facie established' (paragraph 33). The Court made no further findings concerning the topic here being examined. In its 1996 Judgment on preliminary objections, the Court confirmed all those earlier findings regarding its jurisdiction in this case. These cases are useful clarifications of what is embraced within the concept of 'jurisdiction' in provisional measures proceedings, and of the relationship between measures indicated and the Court's provisional findings on its jurisdiction over the merits.

The next relevant cases are those brought in 1999 by Yugoslavia [Serbia & Montenegro] against ten States then members of NATO. They arose out of the military actions taken by NATO against Serbia in relation to the Kosovo crisis of that time. They go under the name of *Legality of Use of Force* cases.[65] The aerial bombardment of Serbia by NATO forces began on 24 March and ended on 9 June 1999. On 26 April Yugoslavia deposited a declaration accepting the compulsory jurisdiction for all disputes arising or which may arise after the signature of that Declaration [25 April], with regard to the situations or facts subsequent to this signature. On 29 April Yugoslavia [Serbia & Montenegro] filed the ten applications instituting these proceedings, simultaneously requesting the indication of provisional measures, namely, an immediate cessation of the acts of use of force against Yugoslavia.

For present purposes the cases fall into three groups. In all of them, Article IX of the Genocide Convention was invoked as a title of jurisdiction.[66] In the cases against Belgium, Canada, the Netherlands, Portugal, Spain, and the United Kingdom, jurisdiction was also based on their declarations accepting the compulsory jurisdiction. However, the declarations of Spain and the United Kingdom excluded disputes in regard to which the other party

[65] *Legality of Use of Force* Yugoslavia, cases, n. 12. Those cases were not joined but were heard in common in the sense of the *Lockerbie* cases, n. 58. Yugoslavia made a single pleading for all ten cases. However, the composition of the Court varied. Belgium, Canada, Italy and Spain each appointed a judge ad hoc. Portugal waived its right to do so. Nationals of France, Germany, the Netherlands, the United Kingdom, and the United States of America were among the members of the Court. Yugoslavia appointed a single judge ad hoc for all ten cases. Declarations, separate opinions, or dissenting opinions were appended by Vice-President Weeramantry and Judges Oda, Shi, Koroma, Vereschchetin, Higgins, Parra-Aranguren, and Kooijmans and Judges ad hoc Gaja and Kreĉa. Most Judges appended their opinions to the Order against Belgium, with cross-references and necessary adaptations in the other cases. Judge ad hoc Kreĉa appended his dissenting opinion to each Order. Judge Weeramantry was Acting President for all these cases. For the preliminary objections, all the respondent States were held to be in the same interest and no judges ad hoc were accepted.

[66] *See* n. 63.

or parties had accepted the compulsory jurisdiction of the Court less than twelve months prior to the filing of the application instituting the proceedings—reservations applicable in the present cases. In all the cases, Yugoslavia invoked the *forum prorogatum* jurisdiction as set out in Article 38, paragraph 5, of the Rules of Court (the invitation was not accepted by any of the named respondents).[67] Additional titles of jurisdiction were invoked during the oral proceedings in the cases against Belgium and the Netherlands. Clearly this set a complicated jurisdictional problem before the Court.

As is a matter of common knowledge, the chief protagonist and principal participant in the bombardment of Serbia was the air force contingent of the United States. For that reason, the case against the United States assumed an importance far beyond that of the other named respondents.

The United States and Spain each had ratified the Genocide Convention with a reservation to Article IX. Spain's reservation was simply to the whole of Article IX. That of the United States was more complicated, namely, that 'before any dispute to which the United States is a party may be submitted to the jurisdiction of the International Court of Justice under Article IX, the specific consent on the United States is required in each case'.[68] Notwithstanding that on the face of things, the absence of jurisdiction in the cases against Spain and the United States was manifest, the Court transmitted the applications and requests to those two States, both of which decided to appear in the hearings scheduled for the requests for provisional measures. By that action the Court did not apply the reservations automatically but required the respondents to invoke them specifically. In the case against Spain the Court had no difficulty in finding that the declarations under Article 36, paragraph 2, 'manifestly cannot constitute a basis of jurisdiction in the present case, even prima facie' (paragraph 25). Likewise, because of the reservation, not prohibited by the Genocide Convention, Article IX 'manifestly does not constitute a basis of jurisdiction in the present case, even prima facie' (paragraph 33). Spain also refused a *forum prorogatum* invitation. All that led the Court to declare that it was 'quite clear that in the absence of consent by Spain, given pursuant to Article 38, paragraph 5, of the Rules, the Court cannot exercise jurisdiction in the present case, even prima facie' (paragraph 34). Accordingly, it rejected the request for provisional measures (Judges Shi and Vereschchetin voting negative), and ordered the case to be removed from the General List (Judges Vereschchetin and Parra-Aranguren and Judge ad hoc Kreĉa voting negative). This was the first instance of such action on provisional measures proceedings since the establishment of the Permanent Court in 1921. The Order in the case against the

[67] *See* n. 7.

[68] For the text of these reservations, *see* Multilateral Treaties Deposited with the Secretary General: Status as at 31 December 2003, vol. I, Ch. IV.1 (doc. ST/LEG/SER.E/22 (vol. I)), and corresponding later issues.

United States was similar, without a passage about the compulsory jurisdiction that would have been inapplicable, and the operative clause was similar, with Judge ad hoc Kreĉa voting negative on the decision to reject the request for provisional measures.

The repeated use of the word *manifest* in those two Orders, and the painstaking way in which the Court reached its conclusions, should be noted. In fact, one may wonder why the Court even entered those two cases in the General List, given the precise language of Article 38, paragraph 5, of the Rules. A possible, but not fully convincing explanation is that the question whether lack of jurisdiction is or is not 'manifest' cannot always be treated as an administrative matter but may have to be established judicially. The complete rejection of the case against the United States reduced the general importance of the other cases. However, the remaining eight were not withdrawn, and the Court was left to deal with them. Preliminary objections have been raised in each case, and at the time of writing are pending.[69]

Regarding the Genocide Convention, the Court first established in each of the remaining cases that both parties were parties to the Convention without reservation. It then went on to find that Article IX of the Genocide Convention appeared to constitute a basis on which the jurisdiction of the Court might be founded 'to the extent that the dispute relates to the "interpretation, application or fulfilment"' of the Convention, including disputes 'relating to the responsibility of a State for genocide or for any of the other acts enumerated in Article III' of the Convention. Analysing the relevant provisions of the Convention the Court found that it was not in a position to find at that stage of the proceedings that the impugned acts were 'capable of coming within the provisions of the Convention invoked by Yugoslavia and accordingly cannot constitute a basis on which the jurisdiction of the Court could prima facie be founded in this case'.[70] While therefore this prevented the Court from indicating provisional measures on the basis of the Genocide Convention, it was not the Court's last word on the matter, and the Court accordingly left the further proceedings open.

In the cases against Belgium, Canada, the Netherlands, Portugal, and the United Kingdom, in which Yugoslavia invoked the compulsory jurisdiction alongside the Genocide Convention, the declaration of the United Kingdom had a reservation similar to that of Spain. The Court used similar reasoning to hold that its declaration 'manifestly cannot constitute a basis of jurisdiction in the present case, even prima facie' (paragraph 25), leaving open its jurisdiction

[69] ICJ Rep. 1999 (11) 988 (Belgium) and following to p. 1010 for the other cases fixing the original time limits, and ICJ Rep. 2000 149 (Belgium) to p. 171 for the other cases, fixing the time limits for the preliminary objections proceedings. Those hearings were held in April 2004 and judgments are awaited as this book goes to press.

[70] Order against Belgium, paras. 34 to 41 and equivalent paragraphs in the Orders against the other respondents except Spain and the United States.

under other titles invoked. In the other cases it had to consider the Yugoslav double temporal reservation. For present purposes it is sufficient to take the case against Belgium, the other cases following it with the necessary changes.

The Court's approach was to examine whether the dispute before the Court 'arose' before or after 25 April 1999 (paragraph 6). For this purpose it found that the essence of the application was directed against the bombing of Yugoslavia, to which the Court was asked to put an end. That had begun on 24 March and had been conducted continuously over a period extending beyond 25 April. The Court had no doubt that a legal dispute between Yugoslavia and the NATO member States arose 'well before 25 April 1999 concerning the legality of those bombings as such, taken as a whole' (paragraph 28). That dispute had persisted since 25 April. That fact was not such as to alter the date on which the dispute arose, and each individual air attack could not have given rise to a separate subsequent dispute (paragraph 29). After referring to the condition of reciprocity in the compulsory jurisdiction, the Court reached the conclusion that the declarations made under Article 36, paragraph 2, of the Statute 'do not constitute a basis on which the jurisdiction of the Court could prima facie be founded in this case' (paragraph 30). This is the first occasion on which the Court examined in detail the operation of a temporal exclusion clause in provisional measures proceedings. Previously any such examination had been a matter for preliminary objection proceedings, and was occasionally deferred to the merits.

As for the Genocide Convention, the Court repeated its observation in the cases against Spain and the United States (paragraph 41). On the further title of jurisdiction invoked in the second round of oral argument in the cases against Belgium and the Netherlands, the Court found that action at such a late stage 'seriously jeopardizes the principle of procedural fairness and the sound administration of justice'. In consequence it could not, for the purpose of deciding on provisional measures, take the new title of jurisdiction into consideration (paragraph 44). The Court concluded with the following:

45. Whereas the Court has found above that it had no prima facie jurisdiction to entertain Yugoslavia's Application, either on the basis of Article 36, paragraph 2, of the Statute or of Article IX of the Genocide Convention; and whereas it has taken the view that it cannot, at this stage of the proceedings, take account of the additional basis of jurisdiction invoked by Yugoslavia; and whereas it follows that the Court cannot indicate any provisional measure whatsoever in order to protect the rights claimed by Yugoslavia in its Application;

46. Whereas, however, the findings reached by the Court in the present proceedings in no way prejudge the question of the jurisdiction of the Court to deal with the merits of the case or any question relating to the admissibility of the Application, or relating to the merits themselves; and whereas they leave unaffected the right of the Governments of Yugoslavia and Belgium to submit arguments in respect of those questions[.]

In the three remaining cases, those against France, Germany, and Italy, where Yugoslavia invoked the *forum prorogatum* of Article 38, paragraph 5, of the Rules, the reasoning regarding the Genocide Convention is the same. In the absence of consent given pursuant to Article 38, paragraph 5, the Court 'cannot exercise jurisdiction in the present case, even prima facie' (case against France, paragraph 31). The Court repeated paragraphs 45 and 46 of the Order against Belgium, and added, in the cases against France and Italy, that it could not accede to their requests to remove the cases from the General List, since the lack of jurisdiction was not manifest. The Court wisely declined to consider whether various resolutions of the Security Council and the General Assembly concerning the status of Yugoslavia as a member of the United Nations and a party to the Statute affected its prima facie jurisdiction (paragraphs 31 to 33). Had it not done so it would have walked into a political minefield.[71]

In the operative clause in all these cases the Court, by twelve votes to three (Judges Shi and Vereschchetin and Judge ad hoc Kreĉa), rejected the requests for provisional measures, and by fourteen votes to one (Judge Oda) reserved the subsequent procedure for further decision.[72]

In each of these cases, including those against Spain and the United States, the Court opened its Order with a general statement of its deep concern with the human tragedy, the loss of life, and the enormous suffering in Kosovo, and its profound concern with the use of force in Yugoslavia which raised 'very serious issues of international law'. The Court continued that it was 'mindful of the purposes and principles of the United Nations Charter and of its own responsibilities in the maintenance of peace and security under the Charter and the Statute of the Court', and it emphasized that all parties appearing before it must act in conformity with their obligations under the Charter and other rules of international law, including humanitarian law.[73]

[71] Cf. R. Etinski, 'The Role of the Legal Adviser in Considering the Legality of Decisions of International Organizations', United Nations, Office of Legal Affairs, *Collection of Essays by Legal Advisers of States, Legal Advisers of International Organizations and Practitioners in the field of International Law*, United Nations Sales No. E/F/S/99.V.13, 1999, 243. Etinski was the Yugoslav agent in these cases. By resolution 55/12, 1 November 2000, the present Federal Republic of Yugoslavia was admitted into the United Nations. After the Court had dismissed as inadmissible Serbia's request for the revision of the preliminary objection Judgment in the original *Genocide Convention* case brought by Bosnia-Herzegovina, the different cases are proceeding. On the inadmissibility of the request for the revision of the Judgment on preliminary objections, *see* n. 62.

[72] At a meeting with the President, where the respondents wished the questions of jurisdiction and admissibility to be determined separately, Yugoslavia insisted on filing a memorial on the merits, leaving the respondents free to raise preliminary objections in the normal way. The Acting President (Weeramantry) acceded to that request and fixed time-limits in the eight remaining cases for a memorial and counter-memorial. ICJ Rep. 1999 (II) 988, 991, 994, 997, 1000, 1003, 1006, 1009. Preliminary objections were raised and are pending at the time of writing; *see* n. 69.

[73] Case against Belgium, paras. 15 to 19, and the corresponding paras. in the other Orders.

It also concluded its Orders with a statement indicating in a general way certain legal considerations that were applicable regardless of whether the Court had any jurisdiction, as follows:[74]

30. Whereas there is a fundamental distinction between the question of the acceptance by a State of the Court's jurisdiction and the compatibility of particular acts with international law; the former requires consent; the latter question can only be reached when the Court deals with the merits after having established its jurisdiction and having heard full legal arguments by both parties;
31. Whereas, whether or not States accept the jurisdiction of the Court, they remain in any event responsible for acts attributable to them that violate international law, including humanitarian law; whereas any disputes relating to the legality of such acts are required to be resolved by peaceful means, the choice of which, pursuant to Article 33 of the Charter, is left to the parties;
32. Whereas in this context the parties should take care not to aggravate or extend the dispute;
33. Whereas, when such a dispute gives rise to a threat to the peace, breach of the peace or act of aggression, the Security Council has special responsibilities under Chapter VII of the Charter[.]

The inclusion of those paragraphs in Orders declining to indicate provisional measures is about as far as the Court could go, and even that is open to criticism, at all events as regards cases which the same Order removes a case from the General List. That this was clearly discussed in the Court is seen in the following paragraph from the Declaration of Judge Koroma:

[T]he Court, as the principal judicial organ of the United Nations, whose primary raison d'être remains the preservation of international peace and security, is under a positive obligation to contribute to the maintenance of international peace and security and to provide a judicial framework for the resolution of a legal dispute, especially one which not only threatens international peace and security but also involves enormous human suffering and continuing loss of life as well as the disintegration of normal society. Given the prevalence of these circumstances in this dispute, the Court has decided, rightly in my view, not to remain silent.[75]

In the *Armed Activities on the Territory of the Congo* (Uganda) (Provisional Measures) case, the Democratic Republic of the Congo (hereafter *Congo*) had filed on 23 June 1999 three applications instituting proceedings against Burundi, Rwanda, and Uganda. Jurisdiction in the case against Uganda was based on the declarations accepting the compulsory jurisdiction. In the other two cases, it was based on a compromissory clause in a treaty. In October the Court fixed 21 July 2000 and 21 April 2001 for the filing of the memorial and counter-memorial of Uganda. On 16 June 2000, the Security Council, which

[74] That is taken from the Order in the case against the United States at p. 925, and it appears in all the other Orders.

[75] Ibid. 930. For further discussion, *see* text to Ch. 8 n. 78.

had been seised of the situation in the Great Lakes region of Africa since early 1999, acting under Chapter VII of the Charter adopted resolution 1304 (2000), calling for a cessation of hostilities throughout the territory of the Congo, and demanding that Uganda and Rwanda withdraw all their armed forces from the territory of the Congo, with various ancillary requirements.

On 19 June 2000, before the memorial was filed, Congo requested an indication of provisional measures in the case against Uganda, but not in the other two cases. The measures requested went beyond those ordered by the Security Council in resolution 1304. This was the first instance of a request for provisional measures immediately after the Security Council had acted under Chapter VII and called for measures to meet the crisis. In the hearings, Uganda contended that the request for provisional measures was inadmissible. The Court had received no pleadings on any question of jurisdiction or admissibility, and none was due until the date fixed for the filing of the counter-memorial, in 2001. In its Order of 1 July 2000, the Court limited itself to stating that the declarations accepting the compulsory jurisdiction constituted a prima facie basis upon which the jurisdiction might be founded.[76] It indicated provisional measures (using the word *must* and not the more usual word *should* in the English text of the Order), substantially following the Security Council resolution. The Order ended with the usual 'without prejudice' clause, but did not include any supervisory provision.

In the *Arrest Warrant of 11 April 2000* (Provisional Measures) case, where the jurisdiction was apparently based on the acceptances of the compulsory jurisdiction, the Court introduced two new formulas.[77] On the issue of jurisdiction to indicate provisional measures it said:

> 67. Whereas, when the Court has before it a request for the indication of provisional measures, it has no need, before deciding whether or not to indicate such measures, to satisfy itself beyond doubt that it has jurisdiction on the merits of the case, but whereas it cannot nevertheless indicate those measures unless the provisions invoked appear prima facie to constitute a basis on which the jurisdiction could be founded[.]

The use of the word *could* in that passage may reflect the criticism of the word *might* in the corresponding passage in the earlier orders. In the operative clause (paragraph 78 (2)), the Court found that 'the circumstances, as they now present themselves, are not such as to require the exercise of its

[76] *Armed Activities on the Territory of the Congo* (Provisional Measures) case, ICJ Rep. 2000, 111. On this case, *see* L. Savagodo, 'Case concerning Armed Activities on the Territory of the Congo (Democratic Republic of the Congo *v* Uganda): The Court's Provisional Measures Order of 1 July 2000', 72 BYIL 357 (2001).

[77] *Arrest Warrant of 11 April 2000* (Provisional Measures), ICJ Rep. 2000, 182. The application instituting these proceedings did not cite the Congo's declaration accepting the jurisdiction. The Congo only referred to that instrument in the second round of the oral proceedings, ibid. at 193 (para. 42).

power ... to indicate provisional measures'. From the terms of the Order it would appear that the meaning of this obscure phrase could be that should circumstances change, the request for provisional measures could be renewed. Prima facie jurisdiction would appear to be exercisable even when the Court has doubt about the possibility of its jurisdiction over the merits but not when the Court finds that the circumstances do not justify provisional measures, a very low threshold.

In the *Armed Activities on the Territory of the Congo* (Rwanda) (New Application: 2000) (Provisional Measures) case, the Court included the following statement in its Order:[78]

57. Whereas the Court, under its Statute, does not automatically have jurisdiction over legal disputes between States parties to that Statute or between other States entitled to appear before the Court; whereas the Court has repeatedly stated that one of the fundamental principles of its Statute is that it cannot decide a dispute between States without the consent of those States to its jurisdiction; and whereas the Court therefore has jurisdiction only between States parties to a dispute who not only have access to the Court but also have accepted the jurisdiction of the Court, either in a general form or for the individual dispute concerned (*Legality of Use of Force (Yugoslavia [Serbia & Montenegro]* v *Belgium), Provisional Measures, ICJ Reports 1999 (I),* p. 132, para. 20).
58. Whereas on a request for provisional measures the Court need not, before deciding whether or not to indicate them, finally satisfy itself that it has jurisdiction on the merits of the case, yet it ought not to indicate such measures unless the provisions invoked by the applicant appear, prima facie, to afford a basis on which the jurisdiction of the Court might be established; whereas moreover, once the Court has established the existence of such a basis for jurisdiction, it should not however indicate measures for the protection of any disputed rights other than those which might ultimately form the basis of a judgment in exercise of that jurisdiction (*Application of the Convention on the Prevention and Punishment of the Crime of Genocide, Provisional Measures, Order of 8 April 1993, ICJ Reports 1993, p.* 19, para. 35)[.]

The Court then examined a long series of contentions regarding jurisdiction advanced by the Congo and reached the conclusion that taken together, the Court did not in the present case have the prima facie jurisdiction necessary to indicate those provisional measures requested by the Congo (paragraph 89). The Court continued with the passage from paragraph 90 of the Order.[79]

In the *Avena and other Mexican Nationals* (Provisional Measures) case, the respondent did not make an issue of whether the Court possesses prima facie jurisdiction 'although this is without prejudice to its right to contest the

[78] ICJ Rep. 2002, 219, 241, 249.
[79] *See* n. 117 below.

Court's jurisdiction at the appropriate stage later'. In view of that, the Court considered that, prima facie, it had jurisdiction under the title of jurisdiction invoked 'to hear the case'.[80] In the merits phase the respondent raised a series of pleas in bar which were dismissed. Regarding the provisional measures, the Court said:

> 152. By its Order of 5 February 2003 the Court . . . indicated by way of provisional measure that 'the United States of America shall take all measures necessary to ensure that [three Mexican nationals] are not executed pending final judgment in these proceedings . . . The Order of 5 February 2003, according to its terms and to Article 41 of the Statute, was effective pending final judgment, and the obligations of the United States in that respect are, with effect from the date of the present Judgment, replaced by those declared in this Judgment'.[81]

The Judgment then imposed specific obligations on the United States in respect of those three Mexican nationals.

In the *Certain Criminal Proceedings in France* case, the proceedings were instituted as a *forum prorogatum* case under Article 38, paragraph 5, of the Rules, the first example of this.[82] The application was filed in the Registry on 9 December 2002, and with it the request for the indication of provisional measures. It was forwarded to the respondent, France. On 8 April 2003 France, in a letter received in the Registry on 11 April, consented to the jurisdiction of the Court to entertain the application pursuant to Article 38, paragraph 5, of the Rules. The case was then entered in the General List and the usual statutory notification to the Secretary-General of the United Nations was made. No other action by the Registrar or by the President is recorded in the Order of 17 June, beyond fixing a date for the opening of the oral proceedings.[83] With regard to jurisdiction, the Court repeated its usual statement regarding the requirement of prima facie jurisdiction (paragraph 20) and added:

> 21. Whereas in the present case the Applicant did not in its Application invoke any provisions relied on as affording a basis on which the jurisdiction of the Court might be established, but proposed to found the jurisdiction of the Court upon a consent thereto yet to be given by France, as contemplated by Article 38, paragraph 5, of the Rules of Court; whereas by a letter dated 8 April 2003 from the Minister for Foreign Affairs of France, France consented explicitly to the jurisdiction of the Court to entertain the Application on the basis of that text[.]

[80] ICJ Rep. 2003, 77, 87 (paras. 41, 42). For the Judgment on the merits *see* ICJ Rep. 2004, 31 March.

[81] ICJ Rep. 2004, 31 March, para. 152.

[82] ICJ Rep. 2003, 102, 106 (para. 21). On this form of jurisdiction, see nn. 5, 7.

[83] The President of the Court, Judge Shi, in his statement to the General Assembly in its 58th session, commented on this: since France was free to disregard the application, the fact that it chose to accept jurisdiction and to appear and defend the case is an encouraging tribute to the value of judicial proceedings as a means of pacific settlement of disputes. A/58/PV.50, 4 and on the Court's website. This attitude stands in marked contrast to France's attitude in the 1970s following the *Nuclear Tests* cases.

4.5. CONCLUSIONS REGARDING THE INTERNATIONAL COURT OF JUSTICE

What conclusions can we draw from this survey?

Clearly, the existence of jurisdiction over the merits, both *ratione personae* and *ratione materiae* and its absence can each be 'manifest' to the Court, although there is a difference between the two. For purposes of provisional measures proceedings, jurisdiction also includes admissibility, meaning primarily that the request meets the requirements of Article 41 of the Statute and corresponds to the rights claimed in the principal proceedings, not admissibility for the purpose of the decision on the merits. The absence of jurisdiction will be manifest if this is evident from a perusal of the documents adduced as the legal grounds on which the jurisdiction of the Court is said to be based, in the words of Article 38, paragraph 2, of the Rules of Court. On the other hand, if the proceedings are regularly instituted the Court's prima facie jurisdiction to indicate provisional measures has to be established from such judicial examination of the title of jurisdiction and of the objections to it that is feasible in the short time available within which the decision on the provisional measures has to be made. The manifestness is established from the document instituting the proceedings or, if the request for the provisional measures comes later, from all the relevant pleadings. When in such a case the absence of jurisdiction is obviously 'manifest', the Court cannot indicate provisional measures on the basis of that particular title of jurisdiction or indeed take any other action in relation to the case, except (depending on other possible titles of jurisdiction) have it removed from the General List if it has been entered on it. Even then, the Court may, if appropriate, give some general indication of the principal legal issues in the case and of the behaviour expected of the parties. However, if the prima facie jurisdiction is not established but there is no manifest absence of jurisdiction, the case remains on the General List, any finding of this nature in provisional measures proceedings being without prejudice to the definitive decision on jurisdiction or admissibility to be reached after the usual written and oral argument. In instances in which the existence of a regularly filed case is in question the Court, acting under Article 48 of the Statute, can arrange for special pre-judicatory proceedings, written and perhaps also oral, of the question whether it has been seised of any case at all, and no provisional measures (if requested) can be considered until that question is decided.[84]

The concept of prima facie jurisdiction means little more than the Court's appreciation from the proceedings to date, that it appears that the Court might or could have jurisdiction over the merits and that the absence of that

[84] *Request for Examination of the Situation in accordance with Paragraph 63 of the Court's Judgment of 20 December 1974 in the Nuclear Tests (New Zealand* v *France)* Case, ICJ Rep. 1995, 288. On pre-judicatory proceedings, *see Law and Practice*, vol. II, 905.

jurisdiction is not manifest. Although ambiguous (and perhaps deliberately so), that is sufficient for the Court to be able to deal with a request for provisional measures of protection. It is a low threshold, nothing more than a hypothesis. The Court's findings in provisional measures proceedings, whatever the extent of the arguments on the matter, are provisional. They imply no more than that the applicant has presented an arguable case for jurisdiction over the merits, enough for the Court to be in a position to deal with the request for provisional measures, and in due course and without reference to the earlier decision to decide whether it can deal with the merits. At the same time, as was obvious in the *Military and Paramilitary Activities in and against Nicaragua* (Provisional Measures) case, the decision on the request for provisional measures can give a hint of the Court's thinking on the question of jurisdiction.[85] As the *Application of the Genocide Convention* case shows, any paring down of the scope of the jurisdiction for the purposes of a decision on provisional measures will probably carry through to the next stage of the case. In any later stage, the Court will have before it full written and oral argument that the time pressures in provisional measures proceedings did not enable the parties to produce.[86] The prima facie jurisdiction finding is thus without prejudice to the Court's formal decision reached after full argument.

One can go further. The provisional finding is irrelevant for the definitive decision on the question of jurisdiction, whether that definitive decision is rendered by the Court or by another court or tribunal. That was indicated by the passage from the *Anglo-Iranian Oil Co.* Judgment.[87] By 'full argument' the Court seems to mean written and oral argument following the requirements of the Statute and the Rules of Court, the parties being free to adduce whatever contentions of fact and of law they deem appropriate, no matter how they argued the matter in the proceedings for the provisional measures. It can take several forms: formal preliminary objection proceedings; formal proceedings limited to the questions of the Court's jurisdiction on the merits and if necessary on the admissibility of the claim; or if there is a plea in bar not submitted as a preliminary objection, following normal procedures on the merits.[88] The cases also show that this concept of prima facie jurisdiction

[85] The Court is aware of this. The President of the Court (Shi), in his statement at the 58th session of the General Assembly (above n. 83) mentioned that the Court had noted the increasing tendency of parties to use requests for the indication of provisional measures as an opportunity to provide an early outline of their case on the merits, and was therefore looking into ways of emphasizing—and indeed requiring—that in hearings on such requests parties should focus on the legal conditions for the indication of provisional measures. A/59/PV.50 p. 5, and on the Court's website.

[86] This was brought out in para. 37 of the Award of the Arbitral Tribunal in the *Southern Bluefin Tuna* case. 119 ILR 508, 529. And *see* the quotation from that Award in Ch. 2 n. 61.

[87] *See* n. 32.

[88] On that kind of plea not involving the suspension of the proceedings on the merits, made after an appropriate reservation in the proceedings on a request for provisional measures, *see* the *Avena and other Mexican Nationals* case, ICJ Rep. 2004, 31 March (para. 24).

can make serious inroads into the traditional consensual basis of the Court's jurisdiction, especially when, as occurred in *Anglo-Iranian* (and perhaps to some extent in *Nuclear Tests*), the Court should later decline to decide the merits of the case. That possibility must impose an attitude of caution on any court or tribunal deciding to exercise its own jurisdiction based on an appreciation prima facie of its jurisdiction on the merits or that of another tribunal. At the same time, it is a notable fact that most of the cases have been decided with a substantial majority of the judges participating in the case, and there has been only one instance in which after indicating provisional measures on the basis of prima facie jurisdiction the ICJ in normal preliminary objection proceedings has declined to entertain the case.

4.6. THE UN CONVENTION ON THE LAW OF THE SEA AND THE INTERNATIONAL TRIBUNAL FOR THE LAW OF THE SEA

The provisions of the UN Convention on the Law of the Sea relating to the settlement of disputes are radically different, and more regulated than the relatively unsystematic character of the general law of the settlement of disputes. The compulsory jurisdiction is in principle limited to disputes concerning the interpretation or application of the Law of the Sea Convention or a related treaty. The Convention regulates the settlement of disputes principally in Part XV (Articles 279 to 299) as *lex generalis*, with special provision for the settlement of disputes relating to activities in the international seabed Area set out in Part XI, Section 5 (Articles 186 to 191) of the Convention.[89] Article 279 lays down the obligation to settle disputes concerning the interpretation or application of the Convention by peaceful means in accordance with Article 2, paragraph 3, of the United Nations Charter, and to that end to seek a solution by the means indicated in Article 33, paragraph 1, of the Charter. That was an integral part of the negotiation which led to the Convention.

From that starting point Part XV, section 1 (Articles 279 to 285), contains a series of general rules, of which the most important, from the point of view of jurisdiction, is Article 280. That provides that nothing in Part XV impairs the right of any States Parties to agree at any time to settle a dispute between them concerning the interpretation or application of the Convention by any peaceful means of their choice. It is followed by Article 281, according to which the procedures provided for in Part XV apply only where no settlement has been reached by recourse to such means and the agreement between the parties does not exclude any further procedure. Article 282 provides that

[89] On Part XV, *see* in general the Virginia *Commentary* (Ch. 2 n. 52), vol. V, 3. On Part XI, section 5, *see* ibid. vol. VI at 595.

if States Parties which are parties to a dispute concerning the interpretation or application of the Convention have agreed, through a general, regional, or bilateral agreement or otherwise, that such dispute shall at the request of any party to the dispute, be submitted to a procedure that entails a binding decision, that procedure shall apply in lieu of the procedures provided for in this Part, unless the parties to the dispute otherwise agree.[90] Article 283 requires the parties to a dispute to proceed expeditiously to an exchange of views regarding its settlement by negotiation or other peaceful manner.

Where no settlement has been reached by recourse to section 1, section 2 (Articles 286 to 296) comes into play. Accordingly, by Article 286 the dispute shall be submitted at the request of any party to the court or tribunal having jurisdiction under section 2. This is a complicated matter regulated in principle by Article 287 which envisages four distinct courts or tribunals which a party to a dispute is free to choose as its compulsory dispute settlement procedure. In the event that the parties have each chosen a different procedure, or neither of them has made a choice, arbitration under Annex VII becomes obligatory.[91] Article 288 deals with the jurisdiction of all the courts and tribunals that could have jurisdiction under Part XV, section 2, to render decisions that are binding on the parties for the settlement of disputes. Article 288 (which in the case of the ICJ and any other standing court or tribunal, including ITLOS, which might become involved, would be subject to the constituent instrument of that court or tribunal) raises a number of issues. Entitled *Jurisdiction*, it provides:

1. A court or tribunal referred to in Article 287 shall have jurisdiction over any dispute concerning the interpretation or application of this Convention which is submitted to it in accordance with this Part.
2. A court or tribunal referred to in Article 287 shall also have jurisdiction over any dispute concerning the interpretation or application of an international agreement related to the purposes of this Convention, which is submitted to it in accordance with the agreement.[92]
3. The Seabed Disputes Chamber of the International Tribunal for the Law of the Sea established in accordance with Annex VI, and any other chamber or arbitral

[90] This provision is frequently interpreted as covering the jurisdiction of the ICJ when both parties have made a declaration under Art. 36, para. 2, of the Statute and neither side invokes reservations that could obstruct the Court's action on the merits of the case.

[91] This is based on the so-called Riphagen compromise, adopted early in the Conference. On that compromise, *see* Sh. Rosenne, 'UNCLOS III – The Montreux (Riphagen) Compromise', *Realism in Law-Making, Essays on International Law in Honour of Willem Riphagen* 169 (Dordrecht: Martinus Nijhoff, 1986). The choice available under Art. 287 is between the ICJ, ITLOS, arbitration under Annex VII, and special arbitration under Annex VIII. The first two are standing tribunals. Arbitrations under the Annexes are ad hoc, each Annex containing provisions for an appointing authority to appoint arbitrators, to prevent frustration of the obligation to arbitrate. The first Annex VII arbitrations not preceded by provisional measures in ITLOS are the pending cases between Barbados/Trinidad and Tobago, and between Guyana/Suriname under the presidency of Judges Schwebel and Nelson.

[92] *See* § 2.10.

tribunal referred to in Part XI, section 5, shall have jurisdiction in any matter which is submitted to it in accordance therewith.
4. In the event of a dispute as to whether a court or tribunal has jurisdiction, the matter shall be settled by decision of that court or tribunal.

Section 3 (Articles 297 to 299) of Part XV contains limitations and exceptions to the applicability of section 2. This balances Article 309 which prohibits reservations to the Convention.

Article 290 (*see* § 2.7) is in section 2. A major difference between Article 41 of the Statute of the International Court of Justice and Article 290 of the Convention, is that Article 290, paragraph 6, requires the parties to the dispute to 'comply promptly with any provisional measures prescribed under this Article'. Article 41 is silent as to compliance with any provisional measures indicated under it, and as seen (*see* § 2.5) the question whether such orders had binding force was not settled until the *LaGrand* Judgment of the ICJ in 2001. Another difference between the two provisions is that there is nothing in Article 290 corresponding to Article 41, paragraph 2, of the ICJ Statute. However, by Article 4, paragraph 1 (*b*) (ii), of the Agreement on Co-operation and Relationship between the United Nations and ITLOS the Registrar is to transmit to the United Nations information and documentation relating, *inter alia*, to applications submitted to ITLOS in accordance with Article 290 of the Convention.[93] This is in addition to the transmission of the information to the States Parties under Annex VI, Article 24, paragraph 3, of the Convention. The Registrar does this as a matter of routine, by transmitting the relevant information to the Secretary-General of the United Nations.

In appearance Article 290 is fuller than Article 41 of the Statute of the International Court of Justice. Nevertheless, except for paragraphs 5 and 6, it does little more than reproduce in codified form the law developed by the International Court as the Law of the Sea Conference saw it at the time. The prima facie jurisdiction in paragraphs 1 and 5 is the same low threshold jurisdiction limited to disputes under the Convention that the International Court requires to exercise its provisional measures jurisdiction, and that does not call for further comment here. Paragraph 5 goes further. It gives ITLOS a residual power to prescribe provisional measures of protection in a case in which the competent procedure for the binding settlement of a dispute relating to the application or interpretation of that Convention is arbitration under either Annex VII or Annex VIII (neither of which contains any provision corresponding to Annex VI, Article 25), and the request for provisional

[93] *ITLOS Yearbook 1996–97*, 178. Approved by the General Assembly in resolution 52/251, 15 September 1998, and by the Meeting of States Parties in 1998, *see* docs. SPLOS 27 and SPLOS 31, reproduced in Netherlands Institute for the Law of the Sea, 13 *International Organizations and the Law of the Sea: Documentary Yearbook 1997*, 231, 235 (Ch. IV); 14 id. 1998, 418, 430 (paras. 67, 68).

measures is made before the States concerned have established the arbitral tribunal. Until the arbitral tribunal is created, any court or tribunal agreed upon by the parties or, failing such agreement, ITLOS may prescribe, modify or revoke provisional measures of protection if it considers that prima facie the tribunal which is to be constituted would have jurisdiction over the merits and that the urgency of the situation so requires. Once constituted, the tribunal to which the dispute has been submitted may modify, revoke or affirm those provisional measures, acting in conformity with paragraphs 1 to 4.[94]

In so far as Article 290 refers to the prima facie jurisdiction of ITLOS or of the competent court or tribunal, broadly speaking it incorporates the general law as developed by the ICJ regarding its jurisdiction to indicate provisional measures. ITLOS has had no difficulty in following that jurisprudence, both when acting under paragraph 1[95] and when acting under paragraph 5 of that article.[96] The applicants have always alleged breach of one or more of the provisions of the Convention whatever other allegations have been made, and provided that the Tribunal is satisfied that other conditions of the Convention have been met, it will regard itself or the Annex VII arbitration as having prima facie jurisdiction. That is sufficient to enable it to prescribe provisional measures. The Tribunal does this even if there is a dispute between the parties whether the competent court or tribunal has jurisdiction over the merits, as has occurred in all the provisional measures cases to date mentioned. Without directly citing any authority from the International Court, the Tribunal has left that question for determination by the competent court or tribunal. That is in accordance with Article 288, paragraph 4, of the Convention, that in the event of a dispute as to whether a court or tribunal has jurisdiction, 'the matter shall be settled by decision of *that* [emphasis supplied] court or tribunal'.

In consequence of these provisions of the Convention, any court or tribunal having jurisdiction under the Convention, and especially ITLOS with its residual jurisdiction, may be required to satisfy itself that the preconditions of the Convention for the mainline jurisdiction have been met before it

[94] The first request for the prescription of provisional measures to come before ITLOS was initially based on Art. 290, para. 5. However, during the proceedings the parties agreed to transfer the merits of the case to ITLOS, and the request for provisional measures became an incidental proceeding under Art. 290, para. 1. The *Saiga (No. 2)* (Provisional Measures) case, ITLOS Rep. 1998, 10. The *Southern Bluefin Tuna* cases thus became the first to be determined entirely in application of Art. 290, para. 5. ITLOS Rep. 1999, 280. It has since been followed by the *MOX Plant* and *Land Reclamation by Singapore in and around the Straits of Johor* cases, ITLOS Rep. 2001, 95 and 2003, 10. In both those cases Annex VII arbitrations are pending.

[95] The *Saiga No. 2* (Provisional Measures) case, ITLOS Rep. 1998, 24.

[96] The *Southern Bluefin Tuna* (Provisional Measures) cases (joined), *MOX Plant* (Provisional Measures) case, the *Land Reclamation by Singapore in and around the Straits of Johor* (Provisional Measures) case. *See* n. 94.

reaches the question of its prima facie jurisdiction to deal with a request for provisional measures. Any decision of that kind in provisional measures proceedings is provisional, and does not bind the court or tribunal seised of the merits. By implication the Seabed Disputes Chamber has similar powers in cases over which it has exclusive jurisdiction. If there is no other court or tribunal with jurisdiction to prescribe provisional measures, ITLOS (or in appropriate cases the Seabed Disputes Chamber) has compulsory jurisdiction to prescribe provisional measures pending the constitution of the arbitral tribunal. Since in those circumstances ITLOS is not seised of the merits of the case, Article 89, paragraph 4, of the Rules of the Tribunal requires a special procedure for the institution of proceedings for provisional measures under paragraph 5 (see Chapter 7, text to note 8). That is designed to give ITLOS the first opportunity for a judicial examination of the claim, although its conclusions are provisional and are not binding on the court or tribunal seised of the principal claim. Moreover, unlike the position in the International Court, the reasoning of ITLOS on prima facie jurisdiction cannot be seen as a hint of the possible decision of the arbitral tribunal after full pleadings. In the resolution on the judicial practice of the Tribunal, the Tribunal envisages short and somewhat rigid time-limits for different stages of the deliberation, and these can be reduced for cases of provisional measures.[97]

In the *Saiga (No. 2)* (Provisional Measures) case the parties were in disagreement whether ITLOS had jurisdiction, notwithstanding that they had agreed to submit the dispute to that Tribunal, and they also agreed that in so doing the Tribunal in a single phase should deal with all aspects of the case including Guinea's objection to the jurisdiction (paragraph 28).[98] In its Order of 11 March 1998 ITLOS followed the practice of the International Court. It held that before prescribing provisional measures it needed to be satisfied that the provisions invoked by the applicant appeared prima facie to afford a basis on which the jurisdiction of the Tribunal might be founded, and that the provision invoked by the applicant did prima facie afford such a basis (paragraphs 29, 30).

The Tribunal proceeded similarly in the *Southern Bluefin Tuna* (Provisional Measures) cases. ITLOS had no difficulty in reaching the low threshold required for the exercise of its power to prescribe provisional measures, finding that the arbitral tribunal would prima facie have jurisdiction over the disputes.[99] It would have acted rashly had it taken any other position at that

[97] *See* the resolution on the internal judicial practice of the Tribunal, ITLOS, *Basic Texts 1998*, 1999, 70. The Appendix indicates the time elapsed for each request for provisional measures in both the ICJ and ITLOS.

[98] ITLOS Rep. 1998, 24, 37 (paras. 25 to 30).

[99] ITLOS Rep. 1999, 280, 295 (para. 62). The Arbitral Tribunal decided that it was without jurisdiction to rule on the merits of the dispute. 119 ILR 508.

stage of the proceedings. The Tribunal also clarified some other specific issues concerning its jurisdiction, arising out of other provisions of the Convention. Thus, Article 281, paragraph 1, provides:

1. If the States Parties which are parties to a dispute concerning the interpretation or application of this Convention have agreed to seek settlement of the dispute by a peaceful means of their own choice, the procedures provided for in this Part [Part XV] apply only where no settlement has been reached by recourse to such means and the agreement between the parties does not exclude any further proceedings.

The Tribunal interpreted that provision to the effect that a State Party is not obliged to pursue procedures under Part XV, section 1 [Articles 279 to 285, general provisions regarding the settlement of disputes] of the Convention when it concludes that the possibilities of settlement have been exhausted.[100]

In the *Southern Bluefin Tuna* (Provisional Measures) cases, the jurisdiction of ITLOS was first challenged on the ground that the disputes were scientific rather than legal, so that the condition of Article 288, paragraph 1, was not fulfilled. The Tribunal found that 'the differences between the parties also concern points of law'. It proceeded to cite the early Judgment of the Permanent Court in the *Mavrommatis Palestine Concessions* case[101] for the definition of 'dispute', and added that it must be shown that the claim of one party is positively opposed by the other.[102] In the *Land Reclamation by Singapore in and around the Straits of Johor* (Provisional Measures) case, the Tribunal observed that Article 283 only requires an expeditious exchange of views regarding the settlement of the dispute by negotiation or other peaceful means, and that the obligation to proceed expeditiously to an exchange of views applies equally to both parties to the dispute.[103] In the same case the Tribunal followed the ICJ in holding that neither in the Charter nor otherwise in international law is any general rule to be found to the effect that the exhaustion of diplomatic negotiations constitutes a precondition for a matter to be referred to the Court.[104]

The *MOX Plant* (Provisional Measures) case is more paradoxical. Article 290, paragraph 5, of the Law of the Sea Convention explicitly mentions 'the urgency of the situation' as one of the requirements for the prescription of provisional measures under that provision. In this respect, paragraph 5 differs from paragraph 1, which does not specifically mention urgency

[100] ITLOS Rep. 1999, at 295 (para. 60); followed in the *MOX Plant* (Provisional Measures) case, ibid. 2001, at 107 (para. 60); *Land Reclamation by Singapore in and around the Straits of Johor* (Provisional Measures) case, ibid. 2003, 10, 19 (para. 45).

[101] PCIJ, Ser. A 2 (1925), 11. This definition has been slightly revised by the present ICJ in the *East Timor* case, ICJ Rep. 1995, 90, 99 (para. 22).

[102] *South West Africa* (Preliminary Objections) cases, ICJ Rep. 1962, 319, 328.

[103] ITLOS Rep. 2003, Order of 8 October 2003 (paras. 37, 38).

[104] Ibid. (para. 52), quoting the *Land and Maritime Boundary between Cameroon and Nigeria* (Preliminary Objections) case, ICJ Rep. 1998, 275, 303 (para. 56).

(although, as will be seen in Chapter 5, urgency as a matter of substance is inherent in the conception of provisional measures of protection pending the final decision in a case). In its Order ITLOS, after a long examination of the case as then before it, reached the conclusion that 'in the circumstances, the Tribunal does not find that the urgency of the situation required the prescription of the provisional measures requested by Ireland, in the short period before the constitution of the Annex VII arbitral tribunal'. This suggests that urgency in paragraph 5 has a special meaning, related to the anticipated time to elapse before the constitution of the arbitral tribunal. Nevertheless, the Tribunal went on to introduce entirely new considerations (which had not been argued by the parties, nor had the Tribunal indicated to them that it would like to hear argument on the question) based on the duty to co-operate in the protection of the marine environment under the relevant part of the Convention. It referred to Article 89, paragraph 5, of the Rules, allowing the Tribunal to prescribe measures different in whole or in part from those requested—a doubtful interpretation of that Rule in the circumstances. On that basis, the Tribunal prescribed a series of measures amounting to little more than that the parties, already in arbitration over the dispute, should negotiate ways and means to prevent pollution of the Irish Sea from the operation of the plant.[105] An obligation to negotiate or to consult is not very substantial and, as has been pointed out, such an obligation in a binding order for provisional measures is not easy to monitor, measure, or enforce.[106] Negotiation under compulsion, however mild and formal, is not the best way to conduct international business, and a treaty that emerges from it might be void under Article 51 or 52 of the Vienna Convention on the Law of Treaties.

The Annex VII arbitral tribunal also had to consider this question.[107] In its Order No. 3 of 24 June 2003 suspending the proceedings and dealing with Ireland's request for the prescription of provisional measures the Arbitral Tribunal, whose jurisdiction had been challenged but not yet decided, first had to consider whether it had prima facie jurisdiction over the dispute as submitted to it. On this it said:

[105] *Dispute concerning Access to Information under Article 9 of the OSPAR Convention*, available on the website of the Permanent Court of Arbitration, Final Award of 2 July 2003. *See* M. Fitzmaurice, 'The Ospar Award', 18 *Int'l J. Marine and Coastal L.* 541 (2003). That was separate from the Annex VII arbitration, which took place after the ITLOS proceedings.

[106] Statement of Mr Bill Mansfield, who had been counsel for New Zealand in the *Southern Bluefin Tuna* case, New Zealand Ministry of Foreign Affairs and Trade, Seapol Inter-Regional Conference (Bangkok, 21–23 March 2001), Session 3A, at 2; also in his Letter to the Editor, 16 *Int'l J. Marine and Coastal L.*, 363 (2001).

[107] Order No. 3, 24 June 2003 (Ch. 3 n. 46) paras. 14, 15. In para. 17 of that Order the Tribunal concluded that none of the jurisdictional issues that had been raised casts doubt on its prima facie jurisdiction. For the Orders and proceedings in this case *see* the website of the Permanent Court of Arbitration.

> 14. ... ITLOS found, in its Order, that 'the Annex VII Tribunal would *prima facie* have jurisdiction over the dispute'...The Tribunal sees no reason to disagree with the finding that *prima facie* it has jurisdiction. Ireland and the United Kingdom are both parties to the [Law of the Sea] Convention; the arbitral tribunal has been duly constituted in accordance with Part XV of the Convention and Annex VII to the Convention; it is apparent that Ireland has presented its claims on the basis of various provisions of the Convention; the Parties agree that there is a dispute concerning the MOX plant; that dispute clearly concerns the interpretation and application of the Convention (in that the Parties have adopted different legal position on that matter); and there is nothing which manifestly and in terms excludes the Tribunal's jurisdiction.

It went on to explain that before proceeding to any final decision on the merits, it must satisfy itself that it has jurisdiction in a definitive sense. Moreover, it continued, even to proceed to hear argument on the merits the Tribunal needs to be satisfied at least that there are no substantial doubts as to its jurisdiction.

The Arbitral Tribunal then turned to Ireland's request for the prescription of further provisional measures. It dealt with the question of its jurisdiction to hear that request:

> 41. For the reasons previously explained, the Tribunal considers that *prima facie* it has jurisdiction over the dispute, which has been duly submitted to it by Ireland in accordance with Part XV of the Convention. Accordingly, pursuant to Article 290, paragraph 1, of the Convention, the Tribunal may prescribe 'any provisional measures which it considers appropriate in the circumstances to preserve the respective rights of the parties to the dispute or to prevent serious harm to the marine environment, pending the final decision.' Although the language of Article 290 is not in all respects identical to that of Article 41 of the Statute of the International Court of Justice, the Tribunal considers that it should have regard to the law and practice of that Court, as well as to the law and practice of ITLOS, in considering provisional measures. Furthermore, it considers that Ireland, as the Party requesting provisional measures, bears the burden of establishing that the circumstances are such as to justify the measures sought.

In the circumstances it found that Ireland had not established that any harm which may be caused to the marine environment by virtue of the operation of the MOX plant, pending the determination of the case on the merits, met the threshold test of serious harm (paragraph 55). It also was not satisfied that in the present circumstances there was an urgent and serious risk of irreparable harm to Ireland's rights which would justify it in prescribing provisional measures relating to discharge from the MOX plant (paragraph 62). At the same time it confirmed the ITLOS Order as regards intergovernmental notification and co-operation, without making any further order at that stage. It decided that each party was to submit to the Tribunal and to the other party an initial report and information on compliance with the provisional order affirmed, and the recommendations in that respect made by the Arbitral Tribunal, on 12 September 2003 and subject to any further order of the Tribunal, not later than 17 November 2003 a further report and information on compliance. The Tribunal would keep under review the possible need for further measures in this connection. This was confirmed and new dates for reporting were set in the Tribunal's Order No. 4, 14 November 2003.

The last sentence of Article 288, paragraph 1 ('dispute . . . which is submitted to it in accordance with this Part') has also been discussed by the Tribunal. In the *Southern Bluefin Tuna* (Provisional Measures) cases, where this issue first appeared, the Tribunal decided that the fact that another Convention applied between the parties does not preclude recourse to the procedures of Part XV, section 2, of the Convention.[108]

In the *Saiga No. 2* (Provisional Measures) case, where the parties disagreed whether the exception of Article 297, paragraph 1 (in section 3 of Part XV) applied, the Court in the provisional measures phase deferred that question to the merits in the passage cited at note 98.[109]

The question arises whether the obligation of compliance that Article 290, paragraph 6, of the Convention imposes on the parties to the dispute has any effect on the issue of prima facie jurisdiction. A similar question arose in the International Court when the General Act was invoked, but the Court had been able to deal with the provisional measures without referring to that aspect. In the *LaGrand* case the question was put in a different way. The Court asked whether Article 94 of the Charter precluded attributing binding effect to that Court's indicating provisional measures.[110] The Court reached a negative conclusion on that question, and *a fortiori* ITLOS was in due course also able to answer the question in the negative.[111]

The provisional measures cases so far determined by ITLOS show that this provision does not affect the manner in which ITLOS will assess its prima facie jurisdiction to prescribe provisional measures when the merits of the dispute are to be decided by an Annex VII arbitral tribunal. On the other hand, in cases under paragraph 5 it might impose on ITLOS an attitude of caution regarding the requirement that the parties report to the Tribunal on

[108] Above n. 91 at 294 (para. 55). The Order in the *MOX Plant* case is to the same effect, in paras. 48 and following.

[109] The objection was not repeated in the merits phase and accordingly the Tribunal unanimously found that it had jurisdiction over the dispute as submitted to it. *Saiga No. 2* case, ITLOS Rep. 1999, 10, 31, 69 (paras. 44, 45, 183(1)).

[110] Art. 94, para. 1, imposes on each member of the United Nations an undertaking to comply with the Court's decision in any case to which it is a party. Para. 2 provides that if any party to a case fails to perform the obligations incumbent upon it under a judgment rendered by a Court, the other party may have recourse to the Security Council.

[111] *LaGrand* case, ICJ Rep. 2001, 466, 505 (para. 108).

their compliance with the Order. That requirement derives from the Tribunal's Rules (Article 95), not from the Convention.

The suggestion has been made that the time has come to consider whether an applicant for provisional measures should, as in some municipal systems, provide a guarantee in the application that if the measures sought are granted, but discontinued if the substantive matter is decided in the respondent's favour, to pay damages incurred and costs to the respondents.[112] This is a new instance of a suggestion to import domestic law analogies into the structure of international litigation. Provisional measures in international litigation have as their essential purpose to prevent any unilateral action by one party from frustrating a possible decision in favour of the other party, and are closely related to the basic principle of international litigation, that the consent *ad litem* of all parties to the dispute is essential before any international court or tribunal can act. What could be appropriate in a municipal court with compulsory jurisdiction is not easily transferred into the international sphere.

4.7. REMOVING A CASE FROM THE LIST

An exception to the rule that all findings of fact and of law in provisional measures cases are provisional is where the Court finds that the absence of jurisdiction over the merits is so manifest that not only the Court cannot indicate any provisional measures, but it goes further and orders the case to be removed from the list, in that way putting an end to those proceedings. This question first arose in the provisional measures phase of the *Military and Paramilitary Activities in and against Nicaragua* case.[113] Immediately on receipt of the notification of the institution of these proceedings, the United States informed the Court of its firm conviction that the Court was without jurisdiction to deal with the application and requested the Court to remove the case from the list. This issue was argued between the parties in the hearings, leading the Court to pronounce itself on this issue:

> 21. Whereas the Court undoubtedly possesses, and has in the past exercised, a power summarily to remove a case from the General List in circumstances in which the Applicant—while inviting the State named as Respondent to accept the jurisdiction *ad hoc*—itself concedes that there is no subsisting title of jurisdiction; whereas however in the present case the Applicant has indicated a subsisting title of jurisdiction . . . ; whereas the question is thus not whether a jurisdictional instrument exists, but whether Nicaragua . . . can claim to be a 'State accepting the same

[112] Judge Lucky, in his separate opinion in the *Land Reclamation by Singapore in and around the Straits of Johor* (Provisional Measures) (Malaysia *v* Singapore) case. ITLOS Rep. 2003, 10, 59 at 64 (para. 64).

[113] ICJ Rep. 1984, 169, 178 (para. 21).

> obligation' within the meaning of Article 36, paragraph 2, of the Statute, so as to invoke the United States declaration notwithstanding the fact that, as it appears, no instrument of ratification by Nicaragua of the Protocol of Signature of the Statute of the Permanent Court was ever received by the League of Nations; whereas the Court considers that where the contentions of the parties disclose a 'dispute as to whether the Court has jurisdiction' in accordance with Article 36, paragraph 6, of the Statute, 'the matter shall be settled by the decision of the Court', that is to say by a judicial decision stating the reasons on which it is based and rendered after fully hearing the parties; whereas therefore the Court is unable to accede to the request of the United States of America summarily to remove the case from the list[.]

The question arose again in a different form in the provisional measures phase of the *Arrest Warrant of 11 April 2000* case.[114] Here, in the second round of the hearings, Belgium argued that because of a change in the circumstances the case as set out in the application had become moot and should therefore be removed from the list. The Court accepted that 'mootness of the Application is one of the grounds to remove a case from its List without further consideration'.[115] However, the Congo had retained its original claims, and that led the Court to conclude that 'the application has not at the present time been deprived of its object' so that the Court 'cannot therefore accede to Belgium's request for the case to be removed from the List at the present stage of the proceedings'.

In the *Armed Activities on the Territory of the Congo* (Rwanda, New Application: 2000) (Provisional Measures) case[116] Rwanda argued that none of the jurisdictional grounds advanced by the Congo offered any prospect whatever of jurisdiction on the merits, and that 'that would be reason enough for the Court to remove the case from its List'. The Court found that none of the titles of jurisdiction invoked by the Congo conferred on the Court the prima facie jurisdiction necessary to indicate the provisional measures requested. Nevertheless—reflecting the provisional nature of those findings—the Court went on:[117]

> 90. Whereas, however, the findings reached by the Court in the present proceedings in no way prejudge the question of the jurisdiction of the Court to deal with the merits of the case or any questions relating to the admissibility of the Application, or relating to the merits themselves; and whereas they leave unaffected the right of the Governments of the Congo and of Rwanda to submit their arguments in respect of those questions;
>
> 91. Whereas in the absence of a manifest lack of jurisdiction, the Court cannot grant Rwanda's request that the case be removed from the List[.]

114 ICJ Rep. 2000, 182, 197 (para. 56). On the merits the Court found the application admissible, and held against Belgium. Ibid. 2002, 3.

115 Ibid. 197 (para. 55).

116 Ibid. 219.

117 Ibid. 249 (paras. 90, 91).

On the other hand, when in proceedings for provisional measures the Court is satisfied that the absence of jurisdiction over the merits is manifest, it will order the case to be removed from the list. The Court has explained this as follows:[118]

> 35. Whereas it follows from what has been said above that the Court manifestly lacks jurisdiction to entertain Yugoslavia's Application; whereas it cannot therefore indicate any provisional measures whatsoever in order to protect the rights invoked therein; and whereas, within a system of consensual jurisdiction, to maintain on the General List a case upon which it appears certain that the Court will not be able to adjudicate on the merits would most assuredly not contribute to the sound administration of justice[.]

These extracts from the different Orders in provisional measures proceedings bring out the exceptional nature of this form of decision and the strictness with which the Court will accept a contention that the case should at that stage be removed from the General List.

[118] *Legality of Use of Force* (Yugoslavia *v* Spain) (Provisional Measures) case, ICJ Rep. 1999 (II), 761, 773 (para. 35). Similarly in the case against the United States of America, ibid. 916, 925 (para. 29).

5

Urgency

5.1. URGENCY IN THE CIRCUMSTANCES

Urgency as such is not mentioned in Article 41 of the Statute of the International Court of Justice, or in Article 290, paragraph 1, of the Law of the Sea Convention. However, it can be said to be implied when Article 41 empowers the Court to indicate provisional measures if it 'considers that the circumstances so require', and in Article 290, paragraph 1, which uses the expression 'under the circumstances' without more ado. Its first appearance in treaty form is in paragraph 5 of that Article, where the 'urgency of the situation' is specifically mentioned as one of the requirements for the prescription of provisional measures by ITLOS when the merits of the dispute are being submitted to arbitration under Annex VII or Annex VIII and the arbitral tribunal has not yet been constituted. The formal introduction of urgency into the law of provisional measures was made by the Judges of the International Court of Justice and followed by the Judges of ITLOS. They have always examined the circumstances in which the request was made to find whether the urgency of the matter justified the ordering of provisional measures. Urgency is also implicit in the requirement that in the circumstances immediate action is necessary to protect the rights being claimed (of both parties), something that cannot wait until the final decision in the case. The state of the proceedings when the request is made, and the estimated period likely to elapse before the decision of the court or tribunal on the principal claim, is thus also an element relevant to the determination of the urgency of the matter. In this connection, urgency has become linked to the gravity of the harm sought to be avoided by a provisional measure. Only if the Court finds that the potential damage would be irreparable, will urgency come to the forefront.

The expression 'final judgment' is frequently encountered in this context, for instance in Article 76, paragraph 1, of the ICJ Rules of Court. That is incorrect and possibly misleading. The final decision might be a judgment on preliminary objections which simply declares that the court or tribunal seised of the case has no jurisdiction over it, or that the claim is inadmissible. It can also be a decision to remove the case from the General List. Neither of these affects the claim itself, and notwithstanding the judicial decision, other means can be found to settle the dispute, for instance renewed negotiation. The judgment on the merits may not be the final decision in the case, as, for example, when damages are claimed and have to be assessed by the court or tribunal in further proceedings. In those circumstances, if provisional measures have been indicated, they will probably be replaced by or absorbed in the judgment on the merits while the proceedings on the assessment of damages continue. That occurred in the *U.S. Diplomatic and Consular Staff in Tehran* case, where the Judgment on the merits in favour of the applicant (similar to the order on provisional measures) envisaged further proceedings to settle the form and amount of reparation due unless the parties reached agreement on that, and the final decision, on the discontinuance of the case following an agreement of the parties, was only rendered in 1981.[1] The case might be withdrawn before a decision on the merits, in which case the final decision would be in the form of an order, and other circumstances can be conceived in which the final decision is not necessarily in the form of a judgment. That error is not repeated either in the Law of the Sea Convention (Article 290 and Annex VI) or in the Rules of the Tribunal.

In the law relating to provisional measures, both in the International Court of Justice and in ITLOS, urgency appears in two forms and with two meanings. Urgency is a matter of procedure, relevant to the convening of the Court or Tribunal if not in session when the request is made. Urgency is a matter of substance among the circumstances justifying provisional measures. It is probably the most important of those circumstances. The International Court has explained that since provisional measures are indicated pending its final decision on the merits, they are only justified if there is urgency in the sense that action prejudicial to the rights of either party is likely to be taken before that final decision is given. In that connection it has cited the dictum of the Permanent Court in the *South-Eastern Greenland* case to the effect that no action taken *pendente lite* by a State engaged with another State in a dispute before the Court can have any effect whatsoever as regards the legal situation which the Court is called upon to decide and such action cannot improve its legal position vis-à-vis that other State.[2] The substantive implication of urgency is to ensure that. Consequently both the Rules of Court and the Rules of the Tribunal contain appropriate but not identical provisions to ensure the urgent handling by the ICJ or by ITLOS of all requests for provisional measures submitted to them.

As a matter of procedure the first mention of urgency in connection with provisional measures appeared in Article 57, paragraph 1, of the Rules of the Permanent Court of 1931. That was an immediate reaction to observations made in the 1929 Committee of Jurists.[3] It took the form of a directive to the President on the procedure for dealing with a request. The Permanent Court

[1] ICJ Rep. 1980, 3; ibid. 1981, 45.

[2] *Passage through the Great Belt* (Provisional Measures) case, ICJ Rep. 1999, 12, 17 (para. 17), 19 (para. 32). For the *Legal Status of the South-Eastern Territory of Greenland* case, *see* PCIJ Ser. A/B 48 (1932) at 287.

[3] *See* § 2.3.

then laid down that the decision on an application for provisional measures 'shall be treated as a matter of urgency'. In the *South-Eastern Greenland* case, the Court reached a decision while organizing the oral proceedings, stating that for the purpose of those proceedings it could admit the Judges ad hoc duly appointed by the Parties, 'having regard to the fact that in this case the presence of judges ad hoc is not inconsistent with the urgent nature of interim measures of protection'.[4] That passage indicates an assimilation of the urgency of the procedure with the substantive urgency justifying the indication of provisional measures. Article 61, paragraph 2, of that Court's Rules of 1936 slightly revised the formulation, and provided that the decision on a request shall be treated as a matter of urgency. There was no further mention of urgency in either of its two aspects in the following jurisprudence of the Permanent Court. The text of Article 61, paragraph 2, was retained as Article 61, paragraph 2, of the present Court's Rules of 1946, renumbered as Article 66, paragraph 2, of the Rules of 1972.

The current (1978) Rules approach the matter differently. Article 74, paragraph 2, provides that the Court shall be convened immediately for the purpose of proceeding to a decision on the request 'as a matter of urgency'. That has to be read in conjunction with two other provisions. Article 54, paragraph 2, on fixing the date for the opening of oral proceedings, recognizes that Article 74 grants priority to oral proceedings on a request for provisional measures. Both those provisions deal with the procedural aspect, and Article 74 has sometimes led to a suspension of the oral proceedings or of the deliberations in another case pending before the Court at the time the request was filed. Article 73, paragraph 2, requires that a request for provisional measures shall specify the reasons for it, and 'the possible consequences if it is not granted'. That introduces substantive considerations, dependent upon all the circumstances of the request. The Court has not as yet made any pronouncement on that aspect.[5] The Appendix shows little consistency with regard to the period of time elapsing between the filing of the formal request for an indication of provisional measures, the date for the oral proceedings on that request, and the order, although on the whole clearly the procedure is accelerated in light of the circumstances as known to the Court, and normally one can expect a decision within four to six weeks of the filing of the request for provisional measures. In ITLOS the period is shorter and consequently the reasoning more summary and provisional. Article 11 of the Tribunal's Resolution on its Internal Judicial Practice provides that deliberations concerning applications for provisional measures and applications for the prompt release of a vessel or crew are conducted in

[4] PCIJ Ser. A/B 48 (1932) 277, 280, *and see* Ch. 7 text to n. 34.

[5] The matter was discussed in ITLOS in the *Land Reclamation by Singapore in and around the Straits of Johor* (Provisional Measures) case, ITLOS Rep. 2003, 8 October (paras. 60 ff.).

accordance with the principles and procedures set out in the Resolution, 'taking account of the nature and urgency of the case'.[6]

5.2. THE INTERNATIONAL COURT OF JUSTICE

As a matter of substance, the International Court of Justice has rarely mentioned urgency by name, preferring to recite the circumstances which have led it to exercise or not its power under Article 41. Thus, in the *Interhandel* (Interim Protection) case, it accepted an undertaking by the United States that it would not 'at the present time' be taking any action of the type of which Switzerland was complaining.[7] As a result it did not appear to the Court that the circumstances required the indication of the provisional measures requested. Urgency was not mentioned in that Order, but clearly the Court's decision was based on the fact that there was no urgency to justify action under Article 41.

In the *Nuclear Tests* (Interim Protection) cases, the Court analysed the claims of Australia and New Zealand.[8] It concluded that those allegations gave substance to the applicants' contention that there was an immediate possibility of a further atmospheric nuclear test being carried out by France in the Pacific and that the possibility should not be excluded that damage to the two applicants might be shown to be caused by the deposit on their territory of radioactive fallout resulting from such tests and to be irreparable. In those circumstances, the Court was satisfied that it should indicate provisional measures of protection 'in order to preserve the right claimed by Australia/New Zealand in the present litigation in respect of the deposit of radio-active fall-out' in their territory. The Court continued that 'the circumstances of the case do not appear to require the indication of interim

[6] Resolution on the Internal Judicial Practice of the Tribunal adopted on 31 October 1997, *Basic Texts* 70 (The Hague: Kluwer Law International, 1999). There is no equivalent provision in the Resolution concerning the Internal Judicial Practice of the Court adopted by the ICJ on 12 April 1978. Acts and Documents relating to the Organization of the Court, No. 5, *Charter of the United Nations, Statute and Rules of Court and Other Documents* 164 (1989). The Court has taken steps to accelerate proceedings for provisional measures. In a statement at the 52/36th meeting of the General Assembly on 27 October 1997, the President of the Court (Schwebel) noted that it had been the practice of the Court to dispense with the Judges' written notes in the case of urgent requests for provisional measures. A/54/PV.36, 5, reproduced in ICJ Yearbook 1997–98, 288 at 294. For a complaint that 'time constraints' imposed by the Court prevented a Judge from making a complete explanation of his disagreement with the judgment, *see* the separate opinion of Judge Parra-Aranguren in the *Avena and other Mexican Nationals* case, ICJ Rep. 2004, 31 March (para. 1).

[7] ICJ Rep. 1957, 105. Later the Court held that the application was inadmissible on ground of non-exhaustion of local remedies. Ibid. 1959, 6.

[8] ICJ Rep. 1973, 99, 135. In the *Passage through the Great Belt* (Provisional Measures) case, the Court repeatedly found that the object of the request was not urgent. ICJ Rep. 1991, 12 *passim*.

measures of protection in respect of other rights claimed ... in the Application'. This indicates that as a concept implicit in the requirement for provisional measures, urgency is construed strictly and in direct connection with the rights claimed.

In the *Trial of Pakistani Prisoners of War* (Interim Protection) case, in which the date for the hearings was postponed several times at the request of the parties, Pakistan informed the Court during the hearings that negotiations would be taking place in the near future in which the issues that were the subject of the principal application would be under discussion.[9] Pakistan asked the Court to postpone further consideration of its request for provisional measures, and to fix time-limits for the written pleadings in the case. Commenting on this, the Court said:

> 13. Whereas it is of the essence of a request for interim measures of protection that it asks for a decision by the Court as a matter of urgency; as is expressly recognized by the Court in Article 66, paragraph 2, of its Rules of Court;
> 14. Whereas the fact that the Government of Pakistan now asks the Court to postpone further consideration of its request... signifies that the Court no longer has before it a request for interim measures which is to be treated as a matter of urgency; and whereas the Court is not therefore called upon to pronounce upon the said request[.]

That too seems to refer as much to the procedural as to any substantive aspects of urgency in this context.

As a matter of substance, in the *Military and Paramilitary Activities in and against Nicaragua* (Provisional Measures) case, the Court, dealing with an issue of its principal jurisdiction over the merits as a prerequisite to its finding of prima facie jurisdiction to indicate provisional measures, stated that it had given the matter of its jurisdiction 'the fullest consideration compatible with the requirement of urgency imposed by a request for the indication of provisional measures'.[10]

In the *Passage through the Great Belt* (Provisional Measures) case, the Court's jurisdiction to decide the merits was not contested and there was no dispute over the existence of the applicant's rights, only over their nature and extent.[11] Such a disputed right may be protected by the indication of provisional measures under Article 41 of the Statute if the Court 'considers that circumstances so require'. The Court went on to reiterate that provisional measures under Article 41 are indicated 'pending the final decision' of the Court on the merits of the case, and are therefore only justified if there is urgency in the sense that action prejudicial to the rights of either party is

[9] ICJ Rep. 1973, 328, 330. The Court in the same order fixed time-limits for the first round of written pleadings, limited to the question of jurisdiction.

[10] ICJ Rep. 1984, at 179 (para. 25).

[11] ICJ Rep. 1991, 12; ibid. 1992, 348.

likely to be taken before such final decision is given. Examining the situation as placed before it, the Court found that it could not in interlocutory proceedings suppose that interference with the right claimed by the applicant might be justified in certain circumstances, but in the light of assurances given by the respondent, the Court found that it had not been shown that the right claimed would be infringed by construction work during the pendency of the proceedings. The Court confirmed the ruling in *South-Eastern Greenland* to the effect that no action taken *pendente lite* by a State engaged in a dispute before the Court with another State can have any effect whatever as regards the legal situation upon which the Court is called to decide. At the same time it gave a warning to each party. To the respondent, Denmark, it suggested consideration of the impact which a judgment upholding the claim could have upon the implementation of the Great Belt Project, and to decide whether or to what extent it should accordingly delay or modify the project. As for the applicant, Finland, it should decide whether or not to promote reconsideration of ways of enabling drill ships and oil rigs to pass through the Danish Straits in the event that the Court should decide that the project would not infringe any rights appertaining to Finland. Reaffirming the well-known dictum from the *Free Zones of Upper Savoy and the District of Gex* case that the judicial settlement of disputes is simply an alternative to the direct and friendly settlement of a dispute,[12] the Court gave a very direct indication to both parties that they should settle the dispute:

> 35. Whereas ... pending a decision of the Court on the merits, any negotiation between the Parties with a view to achieving a direct and friendly settlement is to be welcomed[.]

Following negotiations, a settlement was reached and the case was discontinued.

The three capital punishment cases are in a category of their own, and are discussed in § 8.5.

In the *Armed Activities on the Territory of the Congo* (Uganda) (Provisional Measures) case, the Application instituting the proceedings was filed on 23 June 1999, and a year later, on 29 June 2000, Congo filed its request for the indication of provisional measures.[13] The Court stressed that provisional measures 'are only justified if there is urgency' (paragraph 39). It found from the information at its disposal that provisional measures must be indicated as a matter of urgency and that the situation was not affected by the fact that the request for provisional measures was not filed simultaneously with the application instituting the proceedings (paragraphs 41, 42). In the operative clauses of that Order, the Court used the word 'forthwith' (*immédiatement*). In the *Arrest Warrant of 11 April 2000* (Provisional Measures) case, the

12 PCIJ Ser. A 22 (1929) at 13.
13 ICJ Rep. 2000, 111.

Court confirmed that provisional measures are justified 'solely if there is urgency'. It found that in the circumstances of that case, that degree of urgency was not reached.[14]

In the *Certain Criminal Proceedings in France* (Provisional Measures) case, the Court consolidated its fundamental doctrine of the place of urgency in the law relating to provisional measures:[15]

> 22. Whereas the power of the Court to indicate provisional measures under Article 41 of the Statute of the Court has as its object to preserve the respective rights of the parties pending the decision of the Court, and presupposes that irreparable prejudice should not be caused to rights which are the subject of the dispute in judicial proceedings; whereas it follows that the Court must concern itself with the preservation by such measures of the rights which may subsequently be adjudged by the Court to belong either to the Applicant or to the Respondent; and whereas such measures are justified solely if there is urgency[.]

The Court found that the first question to be decided at that stage of the case was whether the criminal proceedings pending in France entailed a risk of irreparable prejudice to Congo's right to respect by France of the immunities of the Head of State 'such as to require, as a matter of urgency, the indication of provisional measures' (paragraph 30). Examining the facts as then before it, it reached the conclusion that 'there is at the present time no risk of irreparable prejudice, so as to justify the indication of provisional measures as a matter of urgency' (paragraph 35). For that and for other reasons it found that the circumstances 'as they now present themselves to the Court' were not such as to require the exercise of its power under Article 41 of the Statute to indicate provisional measures.[16]

5.3. THE INTERNATIONAL TRIBUNAL FOR THE LAW OF THE SEA

As we have seen, urgency is mentioned specifically only in Article 290, paragraph 5, of the Law of the Sea Convention (and not in paragraph 1), and for ITLOS it is regulated in Articles 89 to 95 of the Rules of the Tribunal. Provisional measures prescribed by the Tribunal, the Seabed Disputes Chamber or (to less extent) the Chamber of Summary Procedure under paragraph 5, remain in force until modified or revoked by the court or tribunal to which the merits of the case are assigned (and not until the final decision, as in paragraph 1). At the time of the proceedings in ITLOS for the prescription of provisional measures, except where ITLOS is seised of the

[14] ICJ Rep. 2000, 182, 291 (paras. 69 and 72).
[15] ICJ Rep. 2003, 102, 107 (para. 22).
[16] Ibid. (para. 41). *See also* the dissenting opinion of Judge ad hoc de Cara for a long analysis of the concept of urgency.

merits (under paragraph 1), it would normally not be known when the court or tribunal to which the case is being submitted would most likely be in a position to act, and from that, how long the provisional measures as prescribed by ITLOS would remain in force. This raises a question of the meaning of 'urgency' in that type of situation: does it mean that the situation is such that the prescription of provisional measures is urgent whatever their duration, or does it mean that the urgency for the prescription of the measures has a limited temporal purpose, pending the establishment of the competent court or tribunal, which can, if so requested, take the matter up and then act under Article 290, paragraph 1?

This question first arose in that form in the ITLOS proceedings in the *Southern Bluefin Tuna* (Provisional Measures) case. There, on 15 July 1999 Australia and New Zealand sent to Japan the formal notifications required to introduce Annex VII arbitration proceedings, reserving the right to seek provisional measures in accordance with Article 290. Two weeks later (as required by Article 290, paragraph 5), on 30 July they filed in ITLOS their requests for the prescription of provisional measures. In its Order, ITLOS quoted paragraph 5 to the effect that 'provisional measures may be prescribed pending the constitution of the arbitral tribunal if the Tribunal considers that the urgency of the situation so requires' (paragraph 63).[17] It continued in paragraph 64 that it must therefore decide 'whether provisional measures are required pending the constitution of the arbitral tribunal', which, once constituted, may modify or revoke or affirm any provisional measures prescribed by the Tribunal (paragraph 65). After examining the contentions of the parties, the Tribunal concluded:

> 80. *Considering* that, although the Tribunal cannot conclusively assess the scientific evidence presented by the parties, it finds that measures should be taken as a matter of urgency to preserve the rights of the parties and to avert further deterioration of the southern bluefin tuna stock[.]

It accordingly prescribed provisional measures 'pending a decision of the arbitral tribunal'. Formally those measures were directed to all parties. However, the Tribunal noted that Japan had given a commitment regarding its 1999 experimental fishing programme but had made no commitment regarding any experimental fishing programmes after that year. It also called on the parties to resume meaningful negotiations on future catches. The Tribunal therefore couched its Order in general terms applying to all annual catches pending the decision of the Arbitral Tribunal.

In his separate opinion, Judge Laing referred to this as 'procedural urgency', and he quoted the passage from the Virginia *Commentary* mentioned above (Chapter 2, note 62).[18] Judge Treves also pointed out that the urgency

[17] ITLOS Rep. 1999, 280. [18] Ibid. 305, 307.

of paragraph 5 has to be commensurate with the fact that the Tribunal has been requested to grant provisional measures pending the constitution of the arbitral tribunal which once constituted would be able to modify, revoke, or affirm them, and to prescribe provisional measures of its own. He accordingly thought that the requirement of urgency is stricter when the Tribunal is acting under paragraph 5 than when it is acting under paragraph 1.[19] He continued:

> In particular, there is no 'urgency' under paragraph 5 if the measures requested could, without prejudice to the rights to be protected, be granted by the arbitral tribunal once constituted. As regards the moment up to which it is needed that the measures be complied with, the only urgency which is relevant is that of paragraph 1 of article 290. The measures are supposed to apply 'pending the final decision' and this expression should be read as meaning up to the moment in which a judgment on the merits has been rendered. Of course, in the case of measures requested under paragraph 5, this applies to the judgment on the merits by the arbitral tribunal. In both cases the measures may be revoked or modified before the final decision on the merits respectively by the court or tribunal competent under paragraph 1, or by the arbitral tribunal competent under paragraph 5.
>
> 5. Closely linked to the temporal dimension of the requirement of urgency is what may be called its qualitative dimension. The Convention envisages it in paragraph 1 of article 290 by stating that the court or tribunal must consider the measures 'appropriate under the circumstances to preserve the respective rights of the parties to the dispute or to prevent serious harm to the marine environment'. That the International Court of Justice sees the need to preserve the respective rights of the parties a requirement of 'irreparable damage' or 'irreparable harm' is well known.

The members of the Annex VII Arbitral Tribunal were appointed in due course, and on 19 January 2000, the parties met with the President of the Tribunal (Judge Schwebel) at The Hague. At that meeting the parties agreed that the Arbitral Tribunal should first decide on preliminary objections raised by Japan, and they fixed a schedule for the filing of appropriate pleadings. In the arbitration proceedings, neither side requested any modification of the provisional measures prescribed by ITLOS, nor did the Tribunal raise the matter, so they remained in force until the end of the arbitration proceedings, on 4 August 2000.

In ITLOS the question of urgency under Article 290, paragraph 5, arose again in the *Land Reclamation by Singapore in and around the Straits of Johor* (Provisional Measures) case. Malaysia instituted the Annex VII arbitration proceedings on 4 July 2003 and at the same time invited Singapore voluntarily to take some provisional measures. On 5 September 2003 Malaysia instituted provisional measures proceedings in ITLOS. Its request related

[19] Ibid. 316, 317.

to two different areas in the vicinity of the maritime boundary between the two countries. In the course of the proceedings in ITLOS, Singapore contended that as the arbitral tribunal was to be constituted not later than 9 October 2003, there was no need to prescribe provisional measures given the short period of time remaining before that date. ITLOS rejected that argument.[20] It pointed out (paragraph 67) that there was nothing in Article 290 of the Convention to suggest that the measures it prescribes must be confined to the period ending with the composition of the arbitral tribunal. ITLOS explained:

> 68. . . . the said period is not necessarily determinative for the assessment of the urgency of the situation or the period during which the prescribed measures are applicable and that the urgency of the situation must be assessed taking into account the period during which the Annex VII arbitral tribunal is not yet in a position to 'modify, revoke or affirm those provisional measures'[.][21]

It went on to point out that the provisional measures it prescribes may remain applicable beyond that period.

ITLOS then examined the situation as presented to it. It found that the evidence produced by Malaysia

> does not show that there is a situation of urgency or that there is a risk that the rights it claims with respect to an area of territorial sea would suffer irreversible damage pending consideration of the merits of the case by the Annex VII arbitral tribunal (paragraph 72).

Therefore, the Tribunal did not consider it appropriate in the circumstances to prescribe provisional measures with respect to the land reclamation by Singapore in the sector of Tuss.

With regard to other disputed areas, during the hearings Singapore gave a number of undertakings which Malaysia found provided 'some further clarifications' on three relevant requested measures. Malaysia was prepared to accept those assurances 'if the Tribunal made them a matter of formal judicial record' (paragraph 79). ITLOS placed them on record (paragraph 81) and went on to consider the requests in light of that. Both parties had

[20] This date apparently follows from Annex VII, Art. 3, concerning the dates for the composition of the arbitral tribunal by agreement between the parties or by the appointing authority—the President of ITLOS. The tribunal was formed on 9 October 2003.

[21] In fact an Annex VII arbitral tribunal can be in a position to deal with a request for provisional measure from the moment of its composition. The *Southern Bluefin Tuna* Annex arbitral tribunal worked without any rules of procedure, procedural issues being settled ad hoc by agreement between the parties and the President of the Tribunal. An arbitral tribunal can always adopt temporarily the relevant optional rules for the different kinds of arbitration prepared in 1996 by the Permanent Court of Arbitration, in the same way that ITLOS adopted temporarily the provisional rules of the tribunal prepared by the Preparatory Commission, before it adopted its own version of those rules. For the optional rules of the Permanent Court of Arbitration, *see* Ch. 1 n. 26.

made various commitments relevant to that, and the Tribunal placed those commitments on record (paragraph 88). It recalled that both parties were under the obligation not to create an irremediable situation and in particular not to frustrate the purpose of the study that they had agreed would be undertaken by a group of independent experts (paragraph 90). It also recalled that the two countries shared the same marine environment in and around the Straits of Johor—an important reminder of the mutual duties of States that share a single strait.[22] It found that it could not be excluded that, in the particular circumstances of the case, the land reclamation works might have adverse effects on the marine environment, and that the hearing had shown a change in the attitude of the parties resulting in the commitments which the Tribunal had put on record. '[I]t is urgent to build on the commitments made to ensure prompt and effective cooperation [*sic*] of the parties in the implementation of their commitments.' On that basis ITLOS prescribed a series of provisional measures 'pending a decision by the Annex VII arbitral tribunal'.

Although there is no doubt that in taking this decision the Tribunal was careful to limit its observations to the situation that confronted it, namely a dispute over the maritime boundaries in a strait, the importance of this decision goes beyond that. Urgency in a case coming under Article 290, paragraph 5, is determined solely by the circumstances that the Tribunal had before it when making the decision, and in those circumstances the unknown future date when the Annex VII tribunal will be constituted is of no relevance. The time-limits that Annex VII lays down (designed to prevent frustration of the obligation to have recourse to Annex VII arbitration) are only applicable in the absence of the agreement of the parties on the composition of the Annex VII (or any other) arbitral tribunal, and they can reach that agreement at any time they like. They are not relevant so long as the parties are negotiating about that and about anything else to do with the dispute. On the other hand, provisional measures prescribed under Article 290, paragraph 5, remain in force until any decision on them is made by the arbitral tribunal, and as the arbitral tribunal that decided the *Southern Bluefin Tuna* cases well demonstrated, the decision of the arbitral tribunal may build on the provisional measures and in that way lay the foundation for a negotiated settlement of the dispute. This element was brought to the notice of ITLOS.

[22] Malaysia was claiming violation by Singapore of Art. 123 of the Convention, on co-operation of States bordering on enclosed or semi-enclosed seas. While the Convention deals with straits used for international navigation (Arts. 34 to 45), the mutual duties and responsibilities of States whose coasts share a single strait, whether or not it is used for international navigation, come within the scope of Art. 123.

5.4. ANNEX VII ARBITRATION

In the *Southern Bluefin Tuna* case the ITLOS Order was not the end of the matter and it was to play an important part in the Annex VII arbitration. The Arbitral Tribunal quoted all the main findings of ITLOS, and concluded: 'In any event, the ITLOS holdings upheld no more than the jurisdiction prima facie of this Tribunal. It remains for it to decide whether it has jurisdiction to decide upon the merits of the dispute.'[23] After the Arbitral Tribunal found that it had no jurisdiction to determine the dispute, it turned to the question of the ITLOS Order on provisional measures:

> 66. In view of this Tribunal's conclusion that it lacks jurisdiction to deal with the merits of the dispute, and in view of the terms of Article 290(5) of UNCLOS [the Convention] providing that, 'Once constituted, the tribunal to which the dispute has been submitted may modify, revoke or affirm those provisional measures . . . ', the Order of the International Tribunal for the Law of the Sea of August 27, 1999, prescribing provisional measures shall cease to have effect as of the date of the signing of this Award.[24]

The Award then went on to indicate the position of the parties in regard to the effects of their conduct in compliance with the Order. This aspect is discussed later.[25]

The *MOX Plant* (Provisional Measures) case introduces a new element.[26] This was a complicated case, and the dispute was already subject to arbitration proceedings instituted by Ireland under the Oslo/Paris Convention for the Protection of the Marine Environment of the North-East Atlantic of 1992.[27] On 25 October 2001 Ireland submitted its Notification and Statement of Claim instituting arbitral proceedings under Annex VII of the Law of the Sea Convention, and on 9 November 2001 Ireland filed with ITLOS its request for the prescription of interim measures in accordance with Article 290, paragraph 5, of the Convention. ITLOS issued its Order on 3 December.[28] Ignoring the statement in the Award in *Southern Bluefin Tuna* about the parallelism of treaty obligations for the settlement of disputes, ITLOS found that the Annex VII arbitral tribunal would prima facie have jurisdiction over the dispute (paragraph 62). In the next paragraph it recited Article 290, paragraph 1, to the effect that it may prescribe provisional measures to

23 Award of 4 August 2000, 119 ILR 508, 530 (para. 37).

24 Ibid. 554 (para. 66). The date of the signing of an award is not necessarily the date of its direct communication to or receipt by the parties. Not all States are equipped to accept modern advanced electronic communications. A more precise formula, based on Universal Standard Time (UST or GMT) would be preferable.

25 *See* Ch. 6, text to n. 25.

26 ITLOS Rep. 2001, 95.

27 *Law of the Sea Bulletin* No. 23 (1993) 32. For particulars of the *Dispute concerning Access to Information under Article 9 of the OSPAR Convention* arbitration, which was administered through the Permanent Court of Arbitration, *see* Ch. 3 n. 46.

28 *Dispute concerning the MOX Plant, International Movements of Radioactive Materials, and the Protection of the Irish Sea*, Order No. 3, 24 June 2003, *see* Ch. 3 n. 46.

preserve the respective rights of the parties to the dispute or to prevent serious harm to the marine environment. ITLOS then returned to paragraph 5, which it interpreted as follows:

64. *Considering* that, according to article 290, paragraph 5, of the Convention, provisional measures may be prescribed pending the constitution of the Annex VII arbitral tribunal if the Tribunal considers that the urgency of the situation so requires in the sense that action prejudicial to the rights of either party or causing serious harm to the marine environment is likely to be taken before the constitution of the Annex VII arbitral tribunal;
65. *Considering* that the Tribunal must, therefore, decide whether provisional measures are required pending the constitution of the Annex VII arbitral tribunal[.]

During the hearings the United Kingdom gave certain undertakings relevant to this aspect, which the Tribunal placed on record and continued:

81. *Considering* that, in the circumstances of this case, the Tribunal does not find that the urgency of the situation requires the prescription of the provisional measures requested by Ireland, in the short period before the constitution of the Annex VII arbitral tribunal[.]

One might have thought that this would be the end of the matter. However, ITLOS continued to deal with the problem of the prevention of pollution of the marine environment. On that basis it proceeded to prescribe a series of provisional measures consisting of obligations on both parties to exchange information and to monitor the effects of the operation of the MOX plant. Those measures were prescribed 'pending a decision by the Annex VII arbitral tribunal'. Here the Tribunal applied paragraph 1 of Article 290, notwithstanding that paragraph 5 has separate criteria for the prescription of provisional measures in the circumstances to which that paragraph applies. Commenting on this in his separate opinion, Judge Treves made the following remark:

7. It is regrettable that the Tribunal has not been more explicit in giving the reasons for deciding not to prescribe the measures requested by Ireland, in particular the measure concerning the suspension of the authorisation of the MOX plant or the prevention with immediate effect of its operation. Paragraph 81 mentions the lack of urgency 'in the short period before the constitution of the Annex VII arbitral tribunal'. From the fact that, according to the reasons given for the measure prescribed, justification for such measure lies in the need to preserve rights arising from the general duty of cooperation in the prevention of pollution, it would seem that the Tribunal drew a distinction between the substantive right invoked by Ireland not to be polluted or exposed to a risk of pollution because of the commissioning of the MOX plant and rights of a procedural character relating to cooperation and information. While the Tribunal did not find the requirement of urgency to be satisfied as far as the former right was concerned, it implicitly considered it as satisfied as regards the latter rights.[29]

[29] Ibid. 137, 139 (para. 7).

This decision shows that the Tribunal has accepted the temporal limitation of the urgency provision of paragraph 5, as suggested in the opinions of Judges Laing and Treves in *Southern Bluefin Tuna* (Provisional Measures). The provisional measures prescribed do not address directly any question of the protection of the marine environment of the Irish Sea, which could have provided some justification for this action. They are limited to some secondary procedural actions that, with two arbitrations pending, could not have any real effect on the situation.

In the Annex VII arbitration, both the ITLOS Order and the question of urgency were prominent when the Arbitral Tribunal turned to Ireland's request for further provisional measures. For that Tribunal, this request fell under Article 290, paragraph 1, of the Convention (paragraph 39). On the issue of urgency, it included the following in its Order No. 3:

> 58. International judicial practice confirms that a general requirement for the prescription of provisional measures to protect the rights of the Parties is that there needs to be a showing both of urgency and of irreparable harm to the claimed rights . . .
>
> 59. The Tribunal notes that ITLOS was requested by way of provisional measures to order that the MOX plant not be approved or commissioned. This ITLOS declined to do, although it did prescribe a different provisional measure focusing on improved co-operation between the Parties and the provision of information.
>
> 60. The Tribunal further notes that in the period since it was constituted, Ireland could have sought a modification of the ITLOS order if it had been dissatisfied with its operation, or it could have sought additional provisional measures if evidence available to it had indicated an urgent need for them in terms of the criteria of article 290, paragraph 1.

In the circumstances the Arbitral Tribunal was not satisfied that there was an urgent and serious risk of irreparable harm to Ireland's claimed rights, which would have justified it in prescribing provisional measures relating to the discharges from the MOX plant (paragraph 62).

On the question of co-operation between the parties in relation to the preservation of the marine environment of the Irish Sea, the Arbitral Tribunal observed that the matter had been dealt with to some extent at least in the ITLOS Order. Both parties accepted that that Order was still in force and binding upon them. Moreover, Ireland was not seeking any modification of the ITLOS Order as such, as distinct from an order requiring further measures of co-operation and exchange of information. Here the Tribunal, while satisfied that as required by the ITLOS Order there had been an increased measure of co-operation and consultation, it was nevertheless concerned that it may not always have been as timely or effective as it could have been, and it made an appropriate recommendation (paragraphs 65 to 67).

6

Duration of Provisional Measures

6.1. TIME FOR REQUESTING PROVISIONAL MEASURES

Neither Article 41 of the Statute of the International Court of Justice nor Article 290 of the Convention on the Law of the Sea contains any clear statement of the period of time within which provisional measures may be indicated. This gap is completed by Article 73, paragraph 1, of the ICJ Rules and Article 89, paragraph 1, of the ITLOS Rules.

For the ICJ, a request for the indication of provisional measures may be made by a party 'at any time during the course of the proceedings in the case in connection with which the request is made'. The word 'party' in this context refers to a State recognized by the Court as a party to the case in question. If for any reason the Court does not recognize a State as a party to that case, that State cannot submit a request for provisional measures, nor conversely can it be a respondent to such a request.[1] The expression *during the course of the proceedings in the case in connection with which the request is made* means the period of time commencing at the moment on which a party files a valid document instituting the proceedings in the Registry and the case is entered in the General List, and ending with the final decision of the Court terminating the proceedings and removing the case from the General List.[2] That final decision is any decision, in whatever form, that terminates the case however and wherever it was instituted, even if it does not dispose of the merits of the case or otherwise settle the dispute. Neither before nor after that space of time is *during the course of the proceedings in the case in connection with which* the request was made. This has to be stressed. Although a judgment is final and without appeal, it is nevertheless open to proceedings for interpretation (with no time-limit) and revision (for a period of ten years). Any such proceeding, whether instituted by special agreement or by

[1] There has been one instance in which a State respondent to a claim has argued that until the Court had decided on its jurisdiction, there was no 'case' and it was not a party. That was contended by France in the *Nuclear Tests* cases in 1973. The Court rejected that contention.

[2] In the *Legal Status of the South-Eastern Territory of Greenland* case the Permanent Court stated that it is 'in principle arguable' that the power to indicate provisional measures exists only in respect of a dispute already submitted to it, but refrained from going further into that question after finding that the dispute had been regularly submitted. PCIJ Ser. A/B 48 (1932) at 283. Here the request for interim measures was included in and formed part of the application instituting the proceedings. PCIJ Ser. C 69 (1932) at 10, 15. In the *Request for Examination of the Situation in accordance with Paragraph 63 of the Court's Judgment of 20 December 1974 in the* Nuclear Tests (New Zealand *v* France) *Case* and the *Certain Criminal Proceedings in France* case, no action was taken on the requests for provisional measures until the cases had been entered in the General List.

application, is technically regarded as a new case, and does not lead to the reopening of the earlier case. The possibility of such proceedings taking place has no effect on the period of time during which a request for provisional measures may be filed. The position was stated very clearly by ITLOS in the *Land Reclamation by Singapore in and around the Straits of Johor* (Provisional Measures) case. As a matter of procedure the Tribunal established that while its jurisdiction to prescribe provisional measures is limited *ratione temporis* to the period that elapses with the constitution of the arbitral tribunal, there is no limit to the duration of any prescribed measures which 'may remain applicable beyond that period'.[3]

A request may be made while the proceedings on the merits are suspended as a consequence of the filing of a preliminary objection, as in the *Land and Maritime Boundary between Cameroon and Nigeria* (Provisional Measures) case in the International Court or for any other cause as in the *MOX Plant* Annex VII arbitration.[4] The condition is that the rights to be protected have been clearly presented to the Court before the suspension of the proceedings on the merits. In that case two paragraphs in the Court's Order indicating provisional measures are relevant:

> 31. Whereas the Court, which has taken note of the opinion expressed by the Agent of Nigeria with respect to its prima facie jurisdiction, is of the view that the preliminary objections raised by that State are not such as to exclude that jurisdiction; whereas the Court, in fact, considers that the declarations made by the Parties in accordance with Article 36, paragraph 2, of the Statute constitute a prima facie basis upon which its jurisdiction in the present case might be founded;

And:

> 33. Whereas, without ruling on the question whether, faced with a request for the indication of provisional measures, the Court must, before deciding whether or not to indicate such measures, ensure that the Application of which it is seised is admissible prima facie, it considers that, in this case, the consolidated Application of Cameroon does not appear prima facie to be inadmissible in the light of the preliminary objections raised by Nigeria[.]

In 1978 the ICJ introduced formally, in Article 38, paragraph 5, of the revised Rules of Court, the concept of the *forum prorogatum* allowing the consent *ad litem* to the case to be given after the application has been filed.[5] A similar provision appears in Article 54, paragraph 5, of the ITLOS Rules. In addition, Article 14 of the ICJ Instructions for the Registry provides:

[3] ITLOS Rep. 2003, 8 October (paras. 67, 69).

[4] ICJ Rep. 1996 (I), 13, 21 (paras. 31, 33). The request for provisional measures in the *Prince von Pless* case was filed after the Court had decided to join preliminary objections to the merits. PCIJ Ser. A/B 54 (1933). On the *MOX Plant* arbitration, *see* Ch. 3 n. 46.

[5] *See* Ch. 4 n. 4.

Any failure to conform to the directions of the Statute or Rules which may be noted by him [the Registrar] in a document instituting proceedings or in a pleading, will be brought by him to the notice of the party or person from whom the document emanates.[6]

There has been at least one instance in which the Registrar has found that the document instituting the proceedings did not conform to the provisions of the Statute or the Rules. In that case, he simply informed the author of the document of the deficiency.[7] The *Certain Criminal Proceedings in France* (Provisional Measures) case was the first instance of a *forum prorogatum* case in the ICJ in which provisional measures were requested.[8]

Article 41 clearly allows either party to request provisional measures at any time during the pendency of the proceedings. There is no reason why in response to a request for provisional measures the adverse party should not itself request provisional measures. That would not be regarded as a counter-claim and would not attract any other consequences adverse to that State. The Court confirmed that holding in its later decisions on the requests for provisional measures and in its Judgment on preliminary objections in the *Application of the Genocide Convention* case.[9]

In ITLOS the position is more complicated. Article 89, paragraph 1, of the Rules referring to requests made under Article 290, paragraph 1, of the Convention, follows Article 73, paragraph 1, of the ICJ Rules. When the request is made under Article 290, paragraph 5, the time element is different, since Article 290, paragraph 5 of the Convention and following it Article 89, paragraph 2, of the ITLOS Rules impose a temporal requirement that is applicable to requests for provisional measures in those cases. If the parties have so agreed, either party may request provisional measures at any time. Otherwise a party may make such a request at any time after two weeks from the notification to the other party of a request for provisional measures, if the parties have not agreed that such measures may be prescribed by another court or tribunal.

If the final decision is a judgment by which the Court finds that it has no jurisdiction or that the claim is inadmissible, or an order directing the removal of the case from the General List, the course of the proceedings in the Court comes to an end. The claim, however, remains outstanding and the

[6] Sh. Rosenne (ed.), *Documents on the International Court of Justice/Document relatifs à la Cour internationale de Justice* 453 (Dordrecht: Martinus Nijhoff, 1974). There is no similar instruction *expressis verbis* in the ITLOS Instructions for the Registry of 17 March 2000 (available on the Tribunal's website).

[7] *See* the incident involving an attempt in 1994 by Yugoslavia to institute proceedings against States members of NATO, *Law and Practice*, vol. III, 1223.

[8] *Certain Criminal Proceedings in France* (Provisional Measures) case, ICJ Rep. 2003, 102 (paras. 1 to 7).

[9] *Application of the Convention in the Prevention and Punishment of the Crime of Genocide* case, ICJ Rep. 1993, 3, 325; ibid. 1996 (II), 595, 620 (para. 40).

parties are free to renew their efforts to settle their dispute by negotiating it away. In some cases in the ICJ, the judgment on the merits may declare that an international wrongful act has been committed and that reparation is due, the amount and any other details to be settled by the Court unless the parties agree between themselves.[10]

In ITLOS the same rule would apply when the provisional measures are prescribed under Article 290, paragraph 1, of the Law of the Sea Convention. Where they are prescribed under paragraph 5 of that Article, the course of the proceedings in ITLOS comes to an end with the establishment of the relevant arbitral tribunal which then, subject to any provision in its constituent instrument, would have power to prescribe provisional measures under Article 290, paragraph 1, and under paragraph 5 to confirm, amend, or revoke provisional measures that ITLOS had prescribed.

The judgment on the merits is not necessarily the final judgment signifying the end of the proceedings. In some circumstances the title of jurisdiction may also be relevant in determining whether the judgment on the merits is the end of the matter. The *Gabčíkovo–Nagymaros Project* case, brought on the basis of a special agreement between the parties, supplies an important illustration of this. The Judgment on the merits answered some of the questions posed in the special agreement, and required action by each party to implement it. It also indicated where compensation was due and how a settlement of accounts was to be effected.[11] The special agreement also provided that if the parties were unable to reach agreement on executing the Judgment within six months, either party might request the Court to render an 'additional judgment' to determine the modalities for executing the Judgment. On 3 September 1998 Slovakia filed a request for an additional Judgment. In October of that year the President (Schwebel) met with the representatives of the parties, and it was decided that Hungary would file a written statement of its position on that request. That statement was duly filed. To the time of writing, no further action has been taken by the Court on the case, which remains on the General List. The Court has, however,

[10] This occurred in the Permanent Court in the long-drawn-out proceedings between Germany and Poland over the *Chorzów Factory*. Instances of this in the present Court include the *Corfu Channel* case, when the final Judgment determining the reparation due followed further proceedings after the Judgment on the merits; the *U.S. Diplomatic and Consular Staff in Tehran* case, which was terminated after the parties had concluded the Algiers Agreement of 1981 (1 *Iran–U.S. Claims Tribunal Reports 1981–1982* 3 [Cambridge: Grotius Publications, 1983], one of the provisions of which was an undertaking by the U.S. Government to withdraw all claims against Iran then pending in the International Court); and the *Military and Paramilitary Activities in and against Nicaragua* case, where proceedings for the determination of the reparation due were under way when the proceedings were discontinued. *See* on these cases, ICJ Rep. 1949, 244; ibid. 1981, 45; ibid. 1986, 14; ibid. 1991, 47. In the second and third of those cases, at the request of the applicant State provisional measures had been indicated in the initial stage, and the measures indicated became absorbed in or replaced by the Judgments on the merits, in each case in favour of the applicant State.

[11] ICJ Rep. 1997, 7.

reported to the General Assembly that the parties have resumed negotiations and have informed the Court on a regular basis of their progress.[12] In these circumstances, the 1997 Judgment is not a final decision, and the proceedings have not yet run their course.

6.2. ENTRY INTO FORCE OF PROVISIONAL MEASURES

Neither the Statute nor the Convention, nor the respective Rules, contains any indication of when an order indicating or prescribing provisional measures enters into force or becomes operative. Article 94, paragraph 2, of the ICJ Rules and Article 124, paragraph 2, of the ITLOS Rules provide that a judgment becomes binding on the parties on the day of the reading (an imprecise term[13]). The general presumption is that this rule is also applicable to orders made by the Court and the Tribunal, including orders indicating provisional measures of protection, unless otherwise provided in the order.

If an order on provisional measures requires immediate action by one or other party, obviously reasonable allowance must be made for its terms to reach the capital concerned—given modern communications this would not have to be very long, but account should be taken of any time difference between The Hague and that capital. Only Article 73, paragraph 2, of the ICJ Rules and Article 94 of the ITLOS Rules introduce a time element for the entry into force, and that in a roundabout way: 'Pending the final decision, notice of the measures suggested shall forthwith be given to the parties and to the Security Council' (ICJ) and 'Any provisional measures prescribed by the Tribunal or any modification or revocation thereof shall forthwith be notified to the parties and to such other States Parties as the Tribunal considers appropriate' (ITLOS). In both cases the Rules amplify this provision. Article 77 of the ICJ Rules states in an impersonal way that any measures indicated by the Court and any decision revoking or modifying provisional measures 'shall forthwith be communicated to the Secretary-General of the United Nations for transmission to the Security Council in pursuance of Article 41, paragraph 2, of the Statute'.[14] The word 'forthwith' too is imprecise when it comes to so serious a matter as the entry into force of a binding order on

[12] ICJ Report of the International Court of Justice 1 August 2002–31 July 2003 UNGAOR 58th session, Supp. 4. (A/58/4), para. 136 (a fuller account of this is given in previous reports).

[13] This may not be the appropriate description of time in the context of universal jurisdiction extending all around the globe. The word 'day' can mean more than a period of 24 hours and, if one of the parties is the other side of the international dateline (as in the *Southern Bluefin Tuna* cases), even the date may be different for different parties. The international dateline is customarily taken as the 180th meridian east of Greenwich, London, with local adjustments.

[14] By virtue of Art. 26, para. 1 (*a*), of the Rules, the Registrar is responsible for effecting this communication. For a discussion of the meaning of 'without delay' *see Avena and other Mexican Nationals* case, ICJ Rep. 2004, 31 March (paras. 75 ff.). For a discussion of reasonable time for the execution of a decision of the court, *see* A. Azar, *L'exéution des décisions de La Cour internationale de Justice* 242 (Brussels: Brylant, 2003).

provisional measures, and it also must be given a reasonable interpretation, taking into account the working practices in the office of the Registrar and of the capitals. Article 94 of the ITLOS Rules parallels this. As in the ICJ, this communication is the responsibility of the Registrar by Article 36, paragraph 1 (*a*), of the Rules.[15] This is reinforced by Article 4, paragraph 1 (*b*) (ii), of the Agreement on Co-operation and Relationship between the United Nations and the Tribunal.[16] By that provision, the Registrar is to transmit to the United Nations all documentation relating to applications submitted to ITLOS in accordance with Article 290 of the Convention. In that way the period of time within which provisional measures may be indicated is established through the actions of the Registry. The agents or their representatives would probably be in the Court or the Tribunal if the order indicating provisional measures is read in open court, but that order has to be transmitted to the agents' capitals where it might arrive well out of normal working hours. If a State party is not present in the Court or Tribunal when the Order is read, or if the Order is not read in open Court, the Registry has to communicate it to the address which each State supplies to the Registry for communications from the Court, normally its embassy at The Hague or some nearby capital, or some other appropriate diplomatic mission, or the Foreign Ministry itself. In the case of ITLOS, that would be the embassy in Berlin or the consulate at Hamburg.

6.3. THE TERMINATION OF PROVISIONAL MEASURES

Unless the court or tribunal should specify otherwise when ordering provisional measures, such an order remains in force until either it is changed or cancelled by the competent court or tribunal or until the final decision on the merits or other definitive decision of the court or tribunal.[17] The ICJ has stressed this particularly when it has later found that it could not entertain the case. Thus, in the *Anglo-Iranian Oil Co.* case, it included a statement that

[15] In the Order prescribing provisional measures in the *Southern Bluefin Tuna* cases, the Tribunal decided that the provisional measures prescribed in that Order should forthwith be notified by the Registrar through appropriate means to States Parties to the Convention participating in the fishery for southern bluefin tuna. However, it is doubtful if it is within the responsibilities of the Registrar to determine to what States such an order should be transmitted. Art. 290, para. 4, states clearly that the tribunal shall give that notice, the implication being that ITLOS should decide on those States.

[16] *ITLOS Yearbook 1996–97*, 178, *see* Ch. 4 n. 93.

[17] As examples of provisional measures being indicated for a fixed period of time, see the initial Orders indicating provisional measures in the *Fisheries Jurisdiction* cases, ICJ Rep. 1972, 12, 49. On the expiry of that period, new Orders were issued, to remain in force until final judgment. ICJ Rep. 1973, 302, 313. The existence of an order does not prevent the conclusion of an interim agreement designed to prevent further incidents. (Merits), ICJ Rep. 1974, at 18 (para. 38).

since its 1951 Order indicating provisional measures of protection had been made 'pending its final decision in the proceedings', it followed that the Order ceased to be operative upon the delivery of the Judgment and that the provisional measures lapsed at the same time.[18] The intention behind that last phrase is not clear. If the order ceased to be operative, it would follow that the measures would cease to be in force at the same time. This case firmly establishes the separation of the jurisdiction to indicate provisional measures from jurisdiction over the merits, with the technical consequence that provisional measures can remain in force so long as the Court is seised of the case. This leaves open the question of the legal position of any third State or other entity which might have taken action in conformity with what it considered to be the legal position under the provisional measures, the lapse of which is prospective and not retroactive according to the Court.[19] Nevertheless, the fact that important provisional measures were indicated in the case and that later the Court held itself to be without jurisdiction over the application has troubled both the Court and publicists.

In the two *Nuclear Tests* Judgments the Court simply repeated the formula of the *Anglo-Iranian Oil Co.* case and stated that the Orders ceased to be operative upon the delivery of the Judgments and that the provisional measures lapsed at the same time. In the *U.S. Diplomatic and Consular Staff in Tehran* case, the Court's Judgment on the merits in effect replaced the provisional measures indicated earlier. Consequently, there was no need for that Judgment to contain any statement regarding the provisional measures which technically lapsed when it was delivered.[20] In the *Avena and other Mexican Nationals* case the Court pointed out that its Order indicating provisional measures was 'effective pending final judgment in these proceedings'. It went on to state formally that the obligations of the United States under that Order were, with effect from the date of the Judgment on the merits, 'replaced by those declared in the judgment'. The Court then went on to recall that in the Judgment it had rejected Mexico's submission regarding

[18] ICJ Rep. 1952, at 124; *Nuclear Tests* cases, ICJ Rep. 1974, at 272 (para. 61) and 477 (para. 64).

[19] For decisions by different national courts concerning property said to belong to the Anglo-Iranian Oil Company, rendered in the period between the indication of provisional measures in 1951 and the final judgment of the Court in 1952 (declining jurisdiction), *see Law and Practice*, vol. I, 225, n. 47. The provisional measures Order was frequently accepted as evidence of the title of the Anglo-Iranian Oil Company to the consignments in question. For other instances of internal litigation in which an Order indicating provisional measures was relevant, *see* ibid. 226 n. 48.

[20] However, the Judgment on the merits was not the final judgment in the case, since it anticipated further proceedings to settle the form and amount of reparation to which the United States was entitled under that Judgment. For the Order, *see* ICJ Rep. 1979, 7; for the Judgment on the merits, *see* ibid. 1980, 3. That Judgment criticizes the United States for action that was not compatible with the provisional measures Order. However, as there was no claim before the Court about that, the Court's findings were not affected by that incident; ibid. 43 (paras. 93, 94). The case was later discontinued. ICJ Rep. 1981, 45.

restitutio in integrum and laid down other obligations of the United States in respect of established breaches of international law. The Court considered that in those cases it was for the United States to find an appropriate remedy having regard to different provisions of the Judgment that were relevant.[21] This was the first substantive case after *LaGrand* in which the Court had to consider the relationship between the obligations deriving from an order on preliminary objections with those deriving from the substantive findings on the merits, which replaced the provisional measures.

In its Judgment upholding jurisdiction in the *Military and Paramilitary Activities in and against Nicaragua* (Preliminary Objections) case, the Court concluded:

> 112. In its ... Order of 10 May 1984, the Court indicated provisional measures 'pending its final decision in the proceedings instituted on 9 April 1984 by the Republic of Nicaragua against the United States of America'. It follows that the Order of 10 May 1984, and the provisional measures indicated therein, remain operative [*continueront d'avoir effet*] until the delivery of the final judgment in the present case.[22]

The Judgment on the merits in that case contains a long passage about the provisional measures.[23] The Court noted that no complaint had been made of any further action of the kind mentioned in the first provisional measure ordered, cessation of any action restricting, blocking, or endangering access to or from Nicaraguan ports (paragraph 286). It then referred to Nicaragua's complaint of the failure of the United States to comply with the order (paragraph 287).[24] It went on to re-emphasize a long passage from the provisional measures Order concerning respect for Nicaragua's right to sovereignty and independence (paragraph 288), and in paragraph 289 the Court stated:

> 289. Furthermore, the Court would draw attention to the further measures indicated in the Order, namely that the Parties 'should each of them ensure that no action of any kind is taken which might aggravate or extend the dispute submitted to the Court' and 'should each of them ensure that no action is taken which might prejudice the rights of the other Party in respect of the carrying out of whatever decision the Court might render in this case'.

[21] ICJ Rep. 2004, 31 March (para. 152).
[22] ICJ Rep. 1984, 392, 442 (para. 112).
[23] ICJ Rep. 1986, 14, 143 (paras. 286 to 291). In its memorial on compensation, Nicaragua picked this up and contended that a statement in the Judgment on the merits recalling a finding in the provisional measures Order constituted a circumstance relevant to the determination of reparation for moral damage. *See* the Pleadings in that case, vol. 5 at 332 (paras. 427, 428). The issue of compensation was never decided by the Court, the parties having in the meantime discontinued the proceedings.
[24] Discussed in § 7.5.

When the Court finds that the situation requires that measures of this kind should be taken, it is incumbent on each party to take the Court's indications seriously into account, and not to direct its conduct solely by what it believes to be its rights. Particularly is this so in a situation of armed conflict where no reparation can efface the results of conduct which the Court may rule to have been contrary to international law.

Those last two cases illustrate the imprecision in the phrase 'final judgment' used in Article 76, paragraph 1, of the Rules of Court. No similar statement appears in the Judgment rejecting the preliminary objections and upholding the Court's jurisdiction and the admissibility of the application in the *Application of the Genocide Convention* (Preliminary Objections) case.

All the preceding statements were made before the Judgment in *LaGrand*, when there were still controversy and uncertainty whether orders indicating provisional measures were binding.

ITLOS has not yet had occasion to pronounce itself on this aspect. However, the Annex VII arbitral tribunal that decided the *Southern Bluefin Tuna* dispute made an important statement of general application.[25] After recalling that in view of its conclusion that it lacked jurisdiction to deal with the merits of the dispute the ITLOS Order would cease 'to have effect as of the date of the signing of this Award', it continued:

67. However, revocation of the Order prescribing provisional measures does not mean that the Parties may disregard the effects of that Order or their own decisions made in conformity with it. The Order and those decisions—and the recourse to ITLOS that gave rise to them—as well as the consequential proceedings before this Tribunal, have had an impact not merely in the suspension of Japan's unilateral experimental fishing program during the period that the Order was in force, but on the perspectives and actions of the Parties.

[...]

69. Counsel for Australia pointed out that the ITLOS Order already had played a significant role in encouraging the Parties to make progress on the issue of third-party fishing. The Agents of Australia and of New Zealand declared that progress in settling the dispute between the Parties had been made.

This indicates that carefully crafted provisional measures prescribed by ITLOS may have an implication for the future actions of the parties and lay the basis for the final solution of the dispute, even when the arbitral tribunal does not have jurisdiction over the dispute. There is no reason why this notion should not be given a wider application, in that way making the

[25] 119 ILR 508, 554. *And see* B. Mansfield, 'Letter to the Editor: The Southern Bluefin Tuna Arbitration: Comments on Professor Barbara Kwiatkowska's article', 16 *Int'l J. Marine and Coastal L.* 361, 363 (2001). For Kwiatkowska's article 'The *Australia and New Zealand* v *Japan (Jurisdiction and Admissibility)* Award of the first Law of the Sea Annex VII Arbitral Tribunal', *see* ibid. 239.

provisional measures proceedings an important element in the general procedures available to States for the pacific settlement of their international disputes.

If the final decision determines the merits of the claim, it will in the nature of things override provisional measures designed to preserve the respective rights of either party pending that decision. But if the final decision does not relate to the merits, for instance if it holds that the court or tribunal is without jurisdiction or that the claim is inadmissible, that may not put an end to the claim or to the dispute, and any decision regarding provisional measures will not be directly relevant to the future disposition of the dispute, although it may affect future diplomatic actions to bring the dispute to an end. In this kind of case the International Court has developed the practice of stating in an order indicting provisional measures how long they are intended to be in force, and later of stating in its final decision what are the consequences for any provisional measures indicated previously. This was first employed in the *Anglo-Iranian Oil Co.* case.[26]

In ITLOS, there is no experience yet regarding the termination of orders made under Article 290, paragraph 1. As regards orders made under paragraph 5, the Tribunal's power to prescribe, amend, or revoke provisional measures comes to an end with the completion of the constitution of the arbitral tribunal, whether under Annex VII or VIII, or under any other provision agreed by the parties. That leaves unaffected any order previously made by ITLOS, which remains in force unless and until the arbitral tribunal takes it up.

[26] ICJ Rep. 1952, 93, 114.

7

Procedure

7.1. THE INSTITUTION OF PROVISIONAL MEASURES PROCEEDINGS

As a matter of procedure, a request for provisional measures gives rise to proceedings that are independent of the principal proceedings on the merits of the claim. With the exception of a decision to remove the case from the list (*see* § 4.7), all findings of fact and of law and all decisions in connection with provisional measures are provisional and do not directly affect the merits of the case, or any related incidental question of jurisdiction or admissibility. The party requesting the provisional measures is in the formal position of applicant and in the oral proceedings is the first to address the court or tribunal. That party is not necessarily the applicant in the principal case, or even when the case is instituted by the filing of a special agreement, when technically both parties are simultaneously in the position of applicant and respondent. That party requesting the provisional measures has to establish that the circumstances justify the ordering of provisional measures. This does not prevent the other party from also suggesting other provisional measures if it considers that the circumstances so warrant, and the burden of justifying that request falls on that other party. Even when the decision on the request for provisional measures is binding, that too is provisional and temporary, and there is no element of finality or *res judicata* in the decision.

In the International Court of Justice proceedings for the indication of provisional measures are commenced unilaterally by the filing of a written request (*demande en indication de mesures conservatoires par écrit*) in a case that is already pending before the Court. The request should specify the reasons therefor, the possible consequences if it is not granted, and the measures requested.[1] A request may be filed together with the instrument instituting the proceedings or at any time thereafter, and it is irrelevant that the jurisdiction of the Court or the admissibility of the claim might be in issue. The request may even be annexed to or be included in the application instituting the proceedings.[2] Any State party to the principal litigation may request provisional measures to protect any rights which it is claiming. This option is not available to a non-party intervener.

[1] Rules of Court, Art. 73.

[2] This occurred in the *Certain Criminal Proceedings in France* (Provisional Measures) case, ICJ Rep. 2003, 102, 103 (para. 4).

There is no other way in which a claim for provisional measures can be introduced in the International Court. In the Preliminary Objections phase of the *Right of Passage over Indian Territory* case, Portugal added to its submissions a statement requesting the Court to recall to the parties the universally admitted principle that they should facilitate the accomplishment of the Court's task by abstaining from any measure capable of exercising a prejudicial effect in regard to the execution of its decisions or which might bring about either an aggravation or an extension of the dispute. However, Portugal expressly disclaimed any intention of invoking the provisions of Article 41. On this, the Court stated that it did not consider, in the circumstances of the case, that it should comply with the Portuguese request.[3]

In ITLOS, the normal procedure, when the dispute is submitted to ITLOS and provisional measures are requested under Article 290, paragraph 1, of the Law of the Sea Convention, is for the interested party to submit a written request for the prescription of provisional measures (*une demande par écrit en prescription de mesures conservatoires*) at any time during the course of those proceedings.[4] Article 290, paragraph 1, also provides that provisional measures may be requested to prevent serious harm to the marine environment pending the final decision. As seen (§ 2.7), that is a major extension of the concept of provisional measures. As in the ICJ, the request shall specify the measure requested, the reasons therefor, and the possible consequences if it is not granted,[5] for the preservation of the respective rights of the parties or for the prevention of serious harm to the marine environment.[6] By Article 291 (and subject to Article 288) only States Parties to the Convention, a term that includes regional organisations of integration (as defined in Article 1, paragraph 2, and Annex IX), have access to the Tribunal.

In cases under Article 290, paragraph 5, that is where the dispute is being submitted to an arbitral tribunal not yet constituted, the procedure is different. This is not limited to an arbitral tribunal established under Annex VII or Annex VIII of the Convention. Many of the other treaties and agreements related to the purposes of the Law of the Sea Convention contain provisions for the binding settlement of disputes arising under those agreements by a specially constituted arbitral tribunal. Since in those circumstances ITLOS is not seised of the merits of the case, Article 89, paragraph 4, of the Rules of the Tribunal supplies the link to that other court or tribunal. It requires that a request for the prescription of provisional measures under Article

[3] *Right of Passage over Indian Territory* (Preliminary Objections) case, ICJ Rep. 1957, 125, 152.

[4] Rules of the Tribunal, Art. 89, para. 1.

[5] In the *Land Reclamation by Singapore in and around the Straits of Johor* (Provisional Measures) case, Singapore objected that the request for provisional measures was inadmissible as it did not meet this requirement. ITLOS overruled that objection and declared the request admissible. ITLOS Rep. 2003, 8 October (para. 63).

[6] Rules, Art. 89, para. 3.

290, paragraph 5, shall also indicate the legal grounds upon which the arbitral tribunal which is to be constituted would[7] have jurisdiction and the urgency of the situation. A certified copy of the notification or other document instituting the proceeding before the arbitral tribunal is to be annexed to the request.[8] That gives ITLOS the first opportunity for a judicial examination of the claim, although its conclusions are provisional and are not binding on the court or tribunal seised of the principal claim. Moreover, unlike the position in the ICJ, the reasoning of ITLOS on prima facie jurisdiction cannot be seen as a hint of the possible decision of the arbitral tribunal after full pleadings. In the resolution on the judicial practice of the Tribunal, the Tribunal envisages short and somewhat rigid time-limits for different stages of the deliberation, and these can be reduced for cases of provisional measures.[9] All the requests for provisional measures so far submitted to the Tribunal have been originally based on paragraph 5.[10] Once the arbitral tribunal has been constituted, provisional measures prescribed by ITLOS remain in force until the arbitral tribunal decides otherwise, but any new request for provisional measures or for further provisional measures, or for modification of provisional measures previously prescribed by ITLOS, is submitted directly to the arbitral tribunal under Article 290, paragraph 1 (subject to its rules of procedure, if any).

In the case of arbitration under Annex VII or of special arbitration under Annex VIII of the Convention (recourse to which may be compulsory), subject to any rules that the arbitral tribunal may have adopted, proceedings are instituted by written notification addressed to the other party or parties to the dispute, the notification being accompanied by a statement of the claim and the grounds on which it is based.[11]

In the Annex VII arbitration in the *MOX Plant* case, after the Arbitral Tribunal had announced its intention to suspend the proceedings pending possible action in the European Court of Justice, Ireland submitted a request for further provisional measures 'to preserve Ireland's rights under the United Nations Convention on the Law of the Sea and to prevent harm to the marine environment'.[12] In its Order No. 3 of 24 June 2003,[13] the Arbitral Tribunal had this to say:

[7] This is another variant of 'might' and 'could' in this context.

[8] Rules, Art. 89, para. 4.

[9] *See* the resolution on the internal judicial practice of the Tribunal, ITLOS, *Basic Texts 1998* 70 (The Hague: Kluwer Law International, 1999). The Appendix indicates the time elapsed for each request for provisional measures in both the ICJ and ITLOS.

[10] In the first of these cases, the *Saiga No. 2* case, in the course of the provisional measures proceedings the parties agreed to submit the dispute to the Tribunal, and the case was transferred from para. 5 to para. 1 of Art. 290. ITLOS Rep. 1998, 10.

[11] Annex VII, Art. 1; Annex VIII, Art. 1. This document accordingly has to be annexed to the request for the prescription of provisional measures.

[12] *See* § 5.4.

[13] *See* above Ch. 3 n. 46. Order No. 3, 24 June 2003, Suspension of Proceedings on Jurisdiction and Merits and Request for Further Provisional Measures, para. 40. In Order No. 4,

40. To the extent this may be relevant, the Tribunal considers that there has been a change in the circumstances in which ITLOS prescribed its provisional measure. First, this Tribunal has now been constituted. Furthermore, following the suspension of the proceedings, the time that will elapse before the Tribunal can reach a decision on the merits is likely to be greater than was expected when ITLOS made its Order. In the view of the Tribunal, the longer delay in reaching a final decision on the merits of the dispute constitutes a change in the circumstances that would, if necessary, warrant modification of the provisional measure prescribed by ITLOS in accordance with Article 290, paragraph 5, of the Convention.

The Tribunal pointed out that for it the relevant period during which any provisional measures it prescribed could be in force was 'pending the final decision' and that harm which may be caused thereafter was a matter to be considered in the context of the case on the merits (paragraph 52). Examining the question of serious harm to the marine environment as required by Article 290, paragraph 1, of the Convention, the Tribunal, in the present state of the evidence, did not consider that Ireland had established that any harm which may be caused to the marine environment pending the determination of the case on the merits 'meets this threshold test' (paragraph 55). On the question of the protection of the rights of the parties, the Tribunal was not satisfied that in the circumstances there was urgent and serious risk of irreparable harm to Ireland's claimed rights to justify it in prescribing provisional measures relating to discharges from the MOX plant (paragraph 62). In the operative clause of the Order the Arbitral Tribunal affirmed the provisional measure prescribed by ITLOS, rejected part of Ireland's request for further provisional measures, and decided that no further order was required as to co-operation and the provision of information at that stage. It also made some recommendations to the parties regarding co-operation and co-ordination.

In the ICJ the request should be structured in accordance with Article 73, paragraph 2, of the Rules. The request is given the same circulation as an application introducing proceedings required under Article 40 of the Statute, that is through the Secretary-General to all the members of the United Nations and to any other State entitled to appear before the Court.[14] In ITLOS, by Annex VI, Article 24, the Registrar is to notify all States Parties to

Further suspension of Proceedings on Jurisdiction and Merits, 14 November 2003, the Arbitral Tribunal decided that further proceedings in the case should remain suspended until the European Court of Justice had given judgment or the Tribunal otherwise determines, and it confirmed the provisional measures prescribed in Order No. 3. Available on the PCA and the ECJ's websites.

[14] Exceptionally, if, owing to the length of the application introducing the proceedings and the short time available before the hearing when provisional measures are requested the Registry is unable to prepare the usual bilingual text for circulation, the Registrar simply informs the States concerned of the filing of the application and of the request. This is now the normal practice whenever oral proceedings take place before the Registry can complete the Court's translation of the documents into the other official language, required for its formal circulation.

the Convention of the institution of any proceedings before the Tribunal, and that includes applications for the prescription of provisional measures under Article 290, paragraph 5. By Article 4, paragraph 1 (*b*) (ii), of the Agreement on Co-operation and Relationship between the United Nations and the International Tribunal for the Law of the Sea, the Registrar is to transmit to the United Nations information and documentation relating to the work of the Tribunal, including documentation relating to pleadings, oral proceedings, orders, judgments, and other communications and documentation, and that extends specifically to those relating to applications submitted to the Tribunal in accordance with Articles 290 and 292 (on the prompt release of vessels) of the Convention.[15] In fact both the ICJ and ITLOS give wide publicity to the institution of any form of proceedings before them, through press releases frequently circulated through the internet and e-mail, although this is not a satisfactory or reliable substitute for hard copies of important messages and texts.

Hitherto in other arbitration proceedings between States, provisional measures have been rare unless the tribunal is authorised to render interim decisions. As seen in § 1.4, the Hague Conventions of 1899 and 1907 make no provision for this, although the different sets of optional rules adopted by the Permanent Court of Arbitration at the end of the twentieth century repair that omission.

If neither the ICJ nor ITLOS is sitting when the request is made, it is to be convened forthwith for the purpose of deciding on the request 'as a matter of urgency' and the President is to fix a date for a hearing which will afford all parties an opportunity of being represented at it.[16] In the two cases concerning the *Interpretation and Application of the 1971 Montreal Convention* the Acting President (Oda) fixed the date for the hearings having regard to the wishes of the parties. In the *Application of the Genocide Convention* (Further Provisional Measures) case, the President (Sir Robert Jennings) acceded to a request by the respondent to fix a date for the hearing that would enable it adequately to prepare its response. He rejected appeals by the applicant to reconsider that date and also an amended request by the applicant 'for an immediate order without hearing pursuant to Article 75, paragraph 1', of the Rules. The reason was that the President followed an earlier decision of the Court on the first request for an indication of provisional measures, to

[15] On that Agreement, *see* Ch. 4 n. 93. *And see* the Guidelines concerning the preparation and presentation of cases before the Tribunal, ITLOS, *Basic Texts 1998* (n. 9), 78.

[16] Presumably the Registrar will formally convene the Court or Tribunal, no doubt in consultation with the President. The ICJ Rules, Art. 74, para. 3, and the ITLOS Rules, Art. 90, paras. 2 and 3, use impersonal language as regards the convening of the Court, but refer to the President specifically in connection with the fixing of the date of the hearing. It is not clear whether that means the President of the Court in all circumstances, or the President of the Bench should the President of the Court be unable to act as President of that Bench, or to sit in the case.

the effect that the Court did not consider that the question arose of the exercise of its powers under Article 75, paragraph 1, of the Rules of Court.

7.2. THE PROCEEDINGS

By requiring the Court to 'receive and take into consideration any observations that may be presented to it before the closure of the oral proceedings', Article 74, paragraph 3, of the ICJ Rules and Article 90, paragraph 3, of the ITLOS Rules relax the formality of written proceedings in provisional measures cases and place the emphasis on the hearing. There is accordingly no provision requiring opportunity to be given to the adverse party to submit written observations on the request, but nothing to prevent it. That is also compatible with the major change regarding the institution of proceedings by application introduced in Article 38, paragraph 5, of the 1978 ICJ Rules and Article 54, paragraph 5, of the ITLOS Rules, incorporating into international litigation procedure the so-called *forum prorogatum* jurisdiction.[17]

The formula of Article 74, paragraph 3, of the ICJ Rules and of Article 90, paragraph 3, of the ITLOS Rules performs several functions. It envisages the situation in which the circumstances of the case require quick action by the Court, leaving little or no time for formal written observations by the adverse party. It also takes account of the situation where the respondent to the case as a whole or to the request for provisional measure has not 'appeared' when the proceedings on the request are being held, and has made its position known to the Court or the Tribunal in some other way. In the *Application of the Genocide Convention* (Further Provisional Measures) case, the Court accepted several written statements submitted by the applicant up to and even during the oral proceedings. While the Court found it difficult to reconcile this with an orderly progress of the procedure before the Court and with respect for the principle of equality of the parties, it considered that because of paragraph 3, and taking into account the urgency of the situation and other circumstances, it could receive the documents in question as 'observations', 'to the extent that they related to the requests for the indication of provisional measures'.[18] Paragraph 3 also corresponds to suggestions that the Court's power to indicate provisional measures should be exercised in a way that is more closely integrated with its jurisdiction over the merits. In practice, the adverse party may file written observations which are, naturally, transmitted to the other party. The Court has always accepted the communications sent to it when exercising its jurisdiction to indicate provisional measures.[19]

[17] *See* Ch. 4 n. 5. [18] ICJ Rep. 1993, 336 (para. 21).

[19] The two *Fisheries Jurisdiction* cases, the *Aegean Sea Continental Shelf* case (in which provisional measures were declined and the Court later found that it was without jurisdiction), and the *U.S. Diplomatic and Consular Staff in Tehran* case.

The hearing in proceedings for provisional measures follows the normal rules for hearings applicable in the court or tribunal seised of the request. Current practice in both the ICJ and ITLOS is to allow equal but little time to each side.[20] Often the oral proceedings afford the parties the one opportunity to present any substantive pleading, even if only in outline and as a provisional statement of that party's legal position. The party making the request is given the opportunity for an oral reply which may be followed by an oral rejoinder. It follows that in proceedings for provisional measures the oral phase is the more important. After the oral proceedings are closed, the deliberations are accelerated.[21]

It is the constant practice and case-law of the ICJ that the non-appearance of the respondent to the request for the indication of provisional measures cannot by itself constitute an obstacle to the indication of provisional measures, provided that the parties have been given an opportunity of presenting their observations on the subject. The ICJ does not apply Article 53 of its Statute if any of the parties does not appear before the Court or fails to defend its case. On the other hand, it will take into account any written observations which that party may have sent to the Court following receipt of the initial application instituting the proceedings.[22] Since Annex VI, Article 28, of the Law of the Sea Convention follows Article 53 of the Statute of the ICJ, it may be assumed that ITLOS will follow the same practice.

Practice is not consistent as regards the notifications required under Article 63, paragraph 2, of the Statute of the ICJ when provisional measures are requested in a case where the construction of a multilateral treaty is in question (except where the notice has already been circulated as a matter of routine before the request for provisional measures was filed). In the *Nuclear Tests* cases notice of the institution of the proceedings was sent to the parties to the General Act for the Pacific Settlement of Disputes after the orders indicating provisional measures were made, but early in the jurisdiction and admissibility phase.[23] In the *Trial of Pakistani Prisoners of War* case it appears that in the Court the majority 'even opposed considering the question of notification in respect of the Genocide Convention before the Court had pronounced on the request . . . for the indication of provisional measures of protection'.[24] In the *U.S. Diplomatic and Consular Staff in*

[20] On the requirement of *succinctness, see* Practice Direction VI. By Practice Direction XI parties in their oral pleadings should limit themselves to what is relevant to the criteria for provisional measures as indicated in the statute, rules, and jurisprudence of the court. They should not enter into the merits of the case beyond what is strictly necessary for that purpose.

[21] On the acceleration of the deliberations in provisional measures proceedings, *see* Ch. 5 n. 6.

[22] *See* Ch. 3 n. 29. A good illustration of this is the *Anglo-Iranian Oil Co.* (Interim Protection) case, ICJ Rep. 1951, 89.

[23] II Pleadings 384 (doc. 99). This was the subject of adverse comment by Judge Petrén in his dissenting opinions to the Orders. ICJ Rep. 1973, 125, 160.

[24] Separate opinion of Judge Petrén, ICJ Rep. 1973, 35. Here too the notification was sent when the proceedings on jurisdiction were in progress. Pleadings 166 (doc. 55).

Tehran (Provisional Measures) case the notification under Article 63 was sent to the parties to the Vienna Conventions on Diplomatic and on Consular Relations of 1961 and 1963 after the request for provisional measures was filed, and before the hearings.[25] In the *Military and Paramilitary Activities in and against Nicaragua* case, there is no record of any specific notification having been sent, but the normal general notification of the filing of the application was sent to all States entitled to appear before the Court.[26] No notification was made in the *Passage through the Great Belt* case, where jurisdiction was partly based on the Optional Protocol of Signature concerning the Compulsory Settlement of Disputes adopted by the First United Nations Conference on the Law of the Sea of 1958, and the subject-matter of the dispute related both to the Copenhagen Convention of 1857 on the Abolition of the Sound Dues and the 1958 Convention on the Territorial Sea and Contiguous Zone.[27] In the *LaGrand* and *Avena and other Mexican Nationals* cases, the notification required by Article 63 of the Statute was duly sent to all States parties to the Vienna Convention on Consular Relations of 1963 and the accompanying Optional Protocol on the Settlement of Disputes after the proceedings on provisional measures.[28]

On the other hand, in the *Question of the Interpretation and Application of the 1971 Montreal Convention arising from the Aerial Incident at Lockerbie* cases, Article 63, paragraph 2, of the Statute was applied in relation to the parties to the Montreal Convention of 1971 before the hearings on the requests for provisional measures. In addition, in accordance with Article 69, paragraph 3, of the Rules, the International Civil Aviation Organization was given the formal notification required by Article 34, paragraph 3, of the Statute.[29] Similarly, in the *Application of the Genocide Convention* case, the request for provisional measures was circulated in accordance with Article 40 of the Statute and notice was given to the States parties to the Genocide Convention under Article 63 of the Statute; in addition notification was sent to the Secretary-General of the United Nations under Article 34, paragraph 3, of the Statute.

As for ITLOS, Annex VI, Article 32, of the Law of the Sea Convention is similar, but so far as is known, has not been applied, since in no case of

[25] ICJ Rep. 1979, 9 (para. 5). For the notification under Art. 63 of the Statute, *see* Pleadings 498 (doc. 14).

[26] Paragraph 35 of the Order of 10 May 1984 refers to a number of communications from different Governments laid before the Court by the United States, but no attempt at formal intervention under either Article 62 or 63 of the Statute of the ICJ. ICJ Rep. 1984 at 184.

[27] ICJ Rep. 1991, at 13 and 14 (paras. 4, 5, and 9). The Pleadings in this case have not yet been published, and it is not clear from the Order whether the request for the indication of provisional measures was circulated in accordance with Art. 40 of the Statute. For the Copenhagen Convention, *see* 116 CTS 357. It would be difficult today to establish what States are bound by that Convention.

[28] ICJ Rep. 2001, 466, 469 (para. 4); ibid. 2004, 31 March (para. 4).

[29] ICJ Rep. 1992, at 8 (para. 14) and 119 (para. 15).

provisional measures in ITLOS has the request for provisional measures concerned the construction of any treaty other than the Law of the Sea Convention itself.

By Article 74, paragraph 1, of the ICJ Rules and Article 90, paragraph 1, of the ITLOS Rules, a request for the indication of provisional measures has priority over all other cases. Article 54, paragraph 2, of the ICJ Rules clarifies that this refers to priority for the hearings on provisional measures over other hearings and Article 69, paragraph 2 (*b*), of the ITLOS Rules, is to similar effect. Pending hearings in another case will, if necessary, be interrupted to enable the Court to deal fully with a request for provisional measures.[30] Likewise, pending deliberations are interrupted until the proceedings on the request for provisional measures are completed. The request for provisional measures in the *Frontier Dispute* (Burkina Faso/Mali) (Provisional Measures) case before an ad hoc Chamber of the Court was filed on 2 January 1986. The hearings took place on 9 January and the Order was published on 10 January. This was partly during a period when the Court would normally be on vacation, and during a break in its deliberations in an ad hoc Chamber in the merits phase of the *Delimitation of the Maritime Boundary in the Gulf of Maine Area* case. In both the ICJ and ITLOS the decision, in the form of an order, is usually read in open court, due notice having been given to the agents.

The discontinuance or withdrawal of provisional measures proceedings follow the normal practice. Where no action has been taken by the adverse party, the Court will not require it to state its views on the withdrawal.[31]

7.3. THE BENCH

The ICJ normally sits in its full complement of available judges. If the President of the Court is a national of one of the parties or for any other reason is unable to sit in the case, his powers in respect of that case are transferred to the Vice-President or to the next senior judge as president of the bench, with the title Acting President.[32] If the request relates to a case which is paired or linked with another case and the President is a national of

[30] This occurred during 1973, while the Court was deliberating on its advisory opinion in connection with *Review of UNAT Judgment No. 158*. On 9 and 14 May two requests for the indication of provisional measures were filed in the *Nuclear Tests* cases. Hearings took place from 21 to 25 May, and the Orders were published on 22 June. On 11 May a request was filed in the *Trial of Pakistani Prisoners of War* case. Hearings—postponed at the request of the parties—were held on 4, 5, and 26 June, and the Order was published on 13 July. A similar situation occurred during the hearings of the *Gulf of Maine* case, which were interrupted after the first round of oral pleadings to enable the Court to dispose of the request for provisional measures in the *Military and Paramilitary Activities in and against Nicaragua* case.

[31] *Border and Transborder Armed Actions* (Provisional Measures) case, ICJ Rep. 1988, 9.

[32] ICJ Rules, Art. 32, para. 1; ITLOS Rules, Art. 16, para. 1.

one of the parties in that other case, the Acting President will assume the presidency of the bench for all those cases.

ITLOS too will normally sit in its full complement of available judges, with the proviso, however, of Annex VI, Article 25, that if a sufficient number of members is not available—that is eleven elected members—the Chamber of Summary Procedure may take action, subject to review and revision by the Tribunal.[33]

With regard to judges ad hoc, since the ruling of the Permanent Court in the *South-Eastern Greenland* case, no question has been raised of the entitlement of a party concerned to appoint a judge ad hoc in provisional measures proceedings.[34] There is no mention of this in the Rules of either the ICJ or ITLOS. However, it frequently occurs that because of the pressures of time, a State, even an applicant State, is not always in a position to appoint a judge ad hoc at that stage. That does not prevent the Court from dealing with the case. If a judge ad hoc has been appointed, that person is entitled to take part in all provisional measures proceedings but the hearing will not be delayed simply to give the party concerned an opportunity to choose a judge ad hoc—a practice which might put an unwilling and unsuspecting respondent at a disadvantage.

7.4. THE FUNCTIONS OF THE PRESIDENT

In addition to the President's duties regarding the fixing of the date for the hearing, Article 74, paragraph 4, of the ICJ Rules and Article 90, paragraph 4, of the ITLOS Rules confer a special power which can only be exercised by the President of the Bench, pending the meeting of the Court or Tribunal, to call upon the parties to act in such a way as will enable any order that the Court or Tribunal may make on the request for provisional measures to have its appropriate effects. There have been several instances of this. In the *Prince von Pless* case, the President of the Permanent Court (Adatci), after the filing of the request for interim measures had made a direct appeal to the respondent State to suspend certain action pending the meeting of the Court—an appeal which produced the desired results.[35] In the *Anglo-Iranian Oil Co.* (Interim Protection) case, the President (Basdevant) sent an appropriate message to the respondent Government, which however, rejected the appeal.[36] In the *U.S. Diplomatic and Consular Staff in Tehran* (Provisional

[33] On the power of the President of ITLOS to convene the Chamber for Summary Procedure if he ascertains that there would not be a quorum of members of ITLOS on the date fixed for the hearing, and the subsequent control by the Tribunal itself, *see* Annex VI, Art. 25, para. 2, in Ch. 2.

[34] PCIJ Ser. A/B No. 48 (1932) 277, 280. *And see* Ch. 5 text to n. 4.

[35] PCIJ Ser. C (1952) 70, 429, 431.

[36] ICJ Rep. 1950, 89, 91; Pleadings 707 (doc. 20).

Measures) case, the President (Sir Humphrey Waldock) called to the attention of both parties the fact that the matter was *sub judice* before the Court and the need to act in such a way as would enable any order the Court might make to have its appropriate effect.[37] That call was ignored.

In the two *Lockerbie* cases the Acting President (Oda) refused to exercise his powers under paragraph 4; after the most careful consideration of all the circumstances then known to him, he had come to the conclusion that it would not be appropriate for him to exercise what he termed 'the discretionary power' conferred on the President by that provision of the Rules.[38] In the *Application of the Genocide Convention* (Further Provisional Measures) case, the President (Sir Robert Jennings) exercised his power under Article 74, paragraph 4, and addressed an appropriate call to both parties, stressing that the earlier Order still applied.[39] In the *Request for an Examination of the Situation in accordance with paragraph 63 of the Court's Judgment of 20 December 1974 in the Nuclear Tests case*, the President (Bedjaoui) declined to exercise that power before determination of the pre-judicatory issue of whether the Court had a case before it.[40] The President (Bedjaoui) does not seem to have taken any such action on receipt of the request in the *Land and Maritime Boundary between Cameroon and Nigeria* case.[41]

In the *Vienna Convention on Consular Relations* (Breard) case, the Acting President (Weeramantry) immediately on receipt of the request drew the attention of the parties to the need to act in such a way as to enable any order the Court might make on the request to have its appropriate effect.[42] In the *LaGrand* (Provisional Measures) case the Acting President (Weeramantry) sent an urgent request to the United States drawing its attention to the need to act in such a way as to enable any order the Court might make to have its appropriate effects. The Court's Order was made the next day.[43] Although addressed to both parties, the implication in those two cases was that the respondent, the United States, was requested not to proceed with scheduled executions, the dates for which had already been set, so long as the provisional measures proceedings were pending. In the *LaGrand* case the

[37] ICJ Rep. 1979, 7, 10 (para. 6); Pleadings 405 (doc. 6).

[38] *Interpretation and Application of the 1971 Montreal Convention arising from the Aerial Incident at Lockerbie* cases, ICJ Rep. 1992, 3, 8, 9 (paras. 16, 17) and 114, 120 (paras. 17, 18).

[39] ICJ Rep. 1993, 325, 333, 334 (paras. 8, 9, 13). In the previous Order the Court had fixed a very short time-limit for the hearing and refused a request by the respondent for an extension. Ibid. 3, 9 (para. 7). In that Order the Court recalled that under Art. 75, para. 2, it had the power to indicate provisional measures that are in whole or in part other than those requested, or that ought to be taken or complied with by the party which had itself made the request, and proceeded so to act. Ibid. 22 (para. 46).

[40] ICJ Rep. 1995, 296 (para. 29). The President felt that 'it would ... have been difficult for him to accede to those Requests without necessarily prejudging the issues submitted to the Court'.

[41] ICJ Rep. 1996 (I), 13.

[42] ICJ Rep. 1998, 248, 252 (para. 12).

[43] ICJ Rep. 1999 (I), 9, 13 (para. 11).

execution was scheduled to take place eight time zones to the west of The Hague on the day following the request for provisional measures. On the other hand he took no such action in any of the *Legality of Use of Force* cases of 1999. In the *Armed Activities on the Territory of the Congo* (Uganda) (Provisional Measures) case the President (Guillaume) sent similar letters to both parties,[44] but not in the *Arrest Warrant of 11 April 2000* (Provisional Measures) case later in the same year.[45] Likewise he sent no such letter after receiving the request on the *Armed Activities in the Territory of the Congo (New Application: 2000) (Rwanda)* (Provisional Measures) case,[46] or in the *Avena and other Mexican Nationals* (Provisional Measures) case (which was not encumbered by that element of urgency characteristic of the other capital punishment cases).[47] In the *Certain Criminal Proceedings in France* (Provisional Measures) case the President (Shi) also sent no such letters.[48]

No similar appeals were made by the President of ITLOS in the four provisional measures cases in that Tribunal.

These instances are sufficient illustration of the delicate nature of this discretionary power given to the President. It may be noted that in the cases in which no such letters were sent (except the *Avena and other Mexican Nationals* case), the Court subsequently declined to indicate provisional measures.

7.5. FRESH REQUEST

Article 75, paragraph 3, of the ICJ Rules and following it, Article 92 of the ITLOS Rules, provide that the rejection of a request for the indication of provisional measures shall not prevent the party which made it from making a fresh request in the same case based on new facts. There has been no instance of this in either the ICJ or ITLOS. On the other hand, States have developed the practice of making fresh requests for provisional measures if for any reason they are dissatisfied with measures already ordered, or with their implementation by the other party. The ICJ has commented on this as follows:[49]

> whereas an Order indicating, or declining to indicate, provisional measures may be revoked or modified, as stated in Article 76 of the Rules of Court; whereas however according to that text, the Court cannot revoke or modify an Order unless, 'in its opinion, some change in the situation justifies' doing so, and where a request for measures has been rejected, any fresh request must, according to Article 75, paragraph 3, of the Rules of Court, be 'based on new facts'; whereas the same applies when additional provisional measures are requested; whereas it is therefore for the Court to satisfy itself that the second request by Bosnia-Herzegovina, and that of

44 ICJ Rep. 2000, 111, 116 (para. 15).
45 ICJ Rep. 2000, 182.
46 ICJ Rep. 2002, 219.
47 ICJ Rep. 2003, 77.
48 ICJ Rep. 2003, 102.
49 ICJ Rep. 1993, at 337 (para. 22).

Yugoslavia, are based upon new circumstances such as to justify their being examined; whereas, taking into account the development of the situation in Bosnia-Herzegovina in recent months, this condition should be regarded as satisfied[.]

There have been two instances in the ICJ,[50] and one in an Annex VII arbitration,[51] in which a fresh request has been made additional to an earlier order on provisional measures. In the *MOX Plant* arbitration, the Annex VII Arbitral Tribunal had no difficulty in holding that the circumstances as they existed at the time of the ITLOS Order had changed and that it had prima facie jurisdiction over the dispute and accordingly could prescribe provisional measures.[52]

The first instance of this in the ICJ was in the *Military and Paramilitary Activities in and against Nicaragua* case. The fresh request was referred to the Court, but no normal proceedings followed and it has not been fully reported. Nicaragua's fresh request is not included in the volumes of Pleadings in that case, only the reply of President Elias.[53] That gives the gist of Nicaragua's request. The reply reads as follows:

On behalf of the Court I wish to acknowledge the receipt of your communication dated 25 June 1984 addressed to the Registrar of the Court and to give the following reply:

1. The Court recalls that in the *Anglo-Iranian Oil Co.* case Britain asked the Security Council to take certain remedial measures against the Iran Oil Company for failure to carry out certain interim measures ordered by the Court. The complaint was not brought to the Court. The Security Council decided that the new request must await the outcome of the proceedings on jurisdiction which were then pending before the Court.

   The Court sees no reason to take a different position in regard to your present Request and would suggest that you await the outcome of the pending proceedings on jurisdiction.
2. The Court notes paragraph 9 (*c*) of your Request concerning the implementation of the Court's Order of 10 May 1984 in which you stated:

   '(*c*) That, until such time as the United States ceases and desists from all activities that do not comply with the Order of 10 May 1984, the facilities of the Court shall not be available to the United States for the purpose of rendering a decision in its favour in any other pending or future case, and the United

[50] In the Permanent Court Belgium made a request for provisional measures in the *Electricity Company of Sofia* case, and withdrew it. Later, after the preliminary objection phase (and after the Second World War had commenced in Europe), Belgium filed a 'Second Incidental Request ... for the indication of provisional measures of protection'. This was granted. PCIJ Ser. A/B 79 (1939). *See* Ch. 3 nn. 18, 19.

[51] The *MOX Plant* arbitration, Order No. 3; *see* Ch. 3 n. 46.

[52] Ibid.

[53] ICJ Pleadings 382 (doc. 55). There is no mention of this incident in the 1994 Judgment on jurisdiction and admissibility (ICJ Rep. 1984, 392) and the communication of 25 June 1984 is not included in vol. v of the ICJ Pleadings in that case. It is therefore necessary to reproduce above in full the text of the President's letter which is not fully reproduced in the quoted passage from the Judgment on the merits.

States shall not be permitted to invoke the Court's aid in any matter.' [The *Gulf of Maine* case was pending in a Chamber of the Court at that time.]

The Court considers that this somewhat unprecedented request is difficult to contemplate for the following reasons:

(*a*) that the demand 'that the facilities of the Court shall not be available to the United States for the purpose of rendering a decision' is fundamentally unacceptable to the Court since it relates to the rendering of a decision in favour of the United States 'in any other pending or future case' including, one would suppose, the Chamber proceedings in the *Gulf of Maine* case; including also any other proceedings before the Court, not excluding its present Request itself or the pending jurisdictional issue; also, any future case that the United States might wish to bring to the Court.

(*b*) that the United States 'shall not be permitted to invoke the Court's aid in any matter', a request that is considered not only unacceptable but also impermissible in that it unduly restricts the Court in the exercise of its normal function as a court; and

(*c*) that there is no warrant or authority for the request in this paragraph nine (*c*), in neither the Statute of the Court nor the Rules.

3. As regards paragraph nine (*a*) and (*b*), although these demands would seem to come within the ambit of the Order of 10 May 1984, it would seem that they might best be taken along with paragraph 10 of your Request in any further stage of the proceedings dealing with the question of merits of the case, including the issue of compensation.

The Court takes the view that the Government of the United States of America is not unaware that the Court naturally expects it to comply with the Order of 10 May 1984 in strict accordance with its terms.

That was summarized in the judgment on the merits in somewhat pallid terms:[54]

On 25 June 1984, the Government of Nicaragua addressed a communication to the Court referring to the Order indicating provisional measures, informing the Court of what Nicaragua regarded as 'the failure of the United States to comply with that Order', and requesting the indication of further measures. The action by the United States complained of consisted in the fact that the United States was continuing 'to sponsor and carry out military and paramilitary activities in and against Nicaragua'. By a letter of 16 July 1984, the President of the Court informed the Agent of Nicaragua that the Court considered that the request should await the outcome of the proceedings on jurisdiction which were then pending before the Court. The Government of Nicaragua has not reverted to the question.

The second occasion was in the *Application of the Genocide Convention* case between Bosnia-Herzegovina and Yugoslavia [Serbia & Montenegro]. Shortly after the first Order for Provisional Measures was issued on 8 April 1993,[55] Bosnia and Herzegovina, on 27 July 1993, filed a request for additional

[54] ICJ Rep. 1986, 14, 144 (para. 287).

[55] *Case concerning Application of the Convention on the Prevention and Punishment of the Crime of Genocide* (Provisional Measures), ICJ Rep. 1993, 3.

provisional measures.[56] On 10 August Yugoslavia [Serbia & Montenegro] also filed a request for provisional measures to be applied by the applicant State, Bosnia-Herzegovina. Here the Court acted according to its normal procedure for dealing with such requests. After holding hearings as required by the Rules, it reaffirmed one by one the provisional measures indicated in the Order of 8 April 'which should be immediately and effectively implemented'. The significance of this case is in its dealing with the respondent's request. In the first case Yugoslavia, which was consistently denying the Court's jurisdiction, had made some 'recommendations' for provisional measures to be applied by the applicant. The Court had not specifically referred to this and as is customary, two of the three measures indicated were to be undertaken by both parties. In the second case the Court examined more closely whether the doctrine of the *forum prorogatum* was applicable, and whether Yugoslavia, by requesting provisional measures, could be taken to have accepted the Court's principal jurisdiction over the merits. The Court did not accept this argument:

> 34. . . . whereas . . . the provisional measure requested by Yugoslavia in a subsequent request . . . was directed solely to protection of asserted rights under the Genocide Convention; whereas moreover the Respondent has consistently denied that the Court has jurisdiction to entertain the dispute, on the basis of that Convention or on any other basis; whereas in the circumstances the communication from Yugoslavia cannot, even prima facie, be interpreted as 'an unequivocal indication' or a 'voluntary and indisputable' acceptance of the Court's jurisdiction . . .[.]

The Court placed on the applicant the duty of showing that further measures were necessary for the protection of its rights under the Genocide Convention alleged to have been breached (paragraph 39), and found that 'the present perilous situation' demanded not an indication of further provisional measures but immediate and effective implementation of those indicated in the first Order of April (paragraph 59).

Neither the ICJ nor ITLOS has had occasion to consider the meaning of 'new facts' in those Rules. A similar expression, 'new fact' appears in Article 61 of the Statute of the ICJ relating to the revision of a judgment and in the parallel Article 127 of the ITLOS Rules. The expression cannot have the same meaning in those two different contexts. The ICJ has held that the 'new fact' for the purposes of the admissibility of a request for revision of a judgment under Article 61 must be a fact that was in existence when the judgment in question was delivered but was unknown to the party claiming revision, and its later discovery was not due to the negligence of that party.[57]

[56] ICJ Rep. 1993, 325.

[57] *Application for Revision of the Judgment of 11 July 1996 in the case concerning Application of the Convention on the Prevention and Punishment of the Crime of Genocide (Bosnia and Herzegovina* v *Yugoslavia [Serbia & Montenegro]), Preliminary Objections* case, ICJ Rep. 2003, 7, 30 para. 67 of that Judgment.

But when dealing with provisional measures, obviously what is in mind is some event which changes the circumstances on the basis of which the original order for provisional measures was made. That could include a fact which was in existence when the provisional measures were ordered, provided that it was not deliberately suppressed by either of the parties. This was brought out by the Arbitral Tribunal in the *MOX Plant* arbitration which, in its examination of Ireland's request, did not think that there were any new facts that would justify the prescription of further provisional measures.[58] It can also be a new fact altogether that can justify the modification or the revocation of provisional measures previously ordered.

7.6. ACTION BY THE COURT OR TRIBUNAL *PROPRIO MOTU*

Although at the time neither the Statute nor the Rules of the Permanent Court of International Justice contained any provision on the matter, the Permanent Court first raised the issue of its power to act *proprio motu* when dealing with provisional measures in the *South-Eastern Greenland* case in 1932. That case was instituted by the simultaneous filing by Denmark and by Norway of applications, each basing the jurisdiction on the so-called optional clause, now Article 36, paragraph 2, of the Statute. The Court joined the two suits. Norway's application also included a request for provisional measures. In its interpretation of Article 41 of the Statute, the Permanent Court included the following statement:

> Whereas... the Court is satisfied that it may proceed to indicate interim measures of protection both at the request of the Parties (or of one of them) and *proprio motu*; but as the Norwegian request for interim measures of protection must first be examined, leaving the question whether measures should if necessary be indicated *proprio motu* to be determined subsequently[.][59]

After examination, the Court found that in the circumstances mentioned in the Norwegian request and in subsequent oral statements, provisional measures were not required. It then turned to the indication of interim measures by the Court *proprio motu*. It found that in the circumstances, the safeguarding of the alleged rights in question did not 'at present' require that the Court should, *proprio motu*, indicate any provisional measures of protection. Accordingly, in the operative clause of the Order, after dismissing the Norwegian request, the Court reserved the right subsequently to consider whether circumstances have arisen requiring the indication of provisional measures in accordance with Article 41 of the Statute.[60]

[58] *MOX Plant arbitration*, Order No. 3, *see* n.13.
[59] PCIJ Ser. A/B 48 (1932) 277, 284. For the Order joining the two cases, *see* ibid. 268.
[60] Ibid., at 287. The case was subsequently discontinued. Ser. A/B 55 (1933).

Following this, the Permanent Court clarified the position in two separate provisions of the Rules of 1936. In Article 61, paragraph 4, it laid down that it may indicate interim measures other than those proposed in the request. More directly, in paragraph 6 it provided:

6. The Court may indicate interim measures of protection *proprio motu*. If the Court is not sitting, the President may convene the members in order to submit to the Court the question whether it is expedient to indicate such measures.

No cases were heard under that Rule.

In 1946 the International Court of Justice retained both those provisions without change. One relevant case was heard under that Rule, the *Anglo-Iranian Oil Co.* case.[61] The Court gave the following interpretation of its power:

> Whereas the object of interim measures of protection provided for in the Statute is to preserve the respective rights of the Parties pending the decision of the Court, and whereas from the general terms of Article 41 of the Statute and from the power recognized by Article 61, paragraph 6, of the Rules of Court, to indicate interim measures of protection *proprio motu*, it follows that the Court must be concerned to preserve by such measures the rights which may be subsequently adjudged by the Court to belong either to the Applicant or to the Respondent[.]

The broad discretionary power which paragraph 6 gave to the President, so far as is known never used, was severely cut down in the revision of 1978, currently in force. By Article 75, paragraphs 1 and 2, of the 1978 Rules:

1. The Court may at any time decide to examine *proprio motu* whether the circumstances of the case require the indication of provisional measures which ought to be taken or complied with by any or all of the parties.
2. When a request for provisional measures has been made, the Court may indicate measures that are in whole or in part other than those requested, or that ought to be taken or complied with by the party which has itself made the request.

The first instance of the invocation of those provisions was the *Frontier Dispute* (Burkina Faso/Mali) (Provisional Measures) case.[62] The Chamber formed to deal with the case cited Article 75 of the Rules in the *qualités* of its Order, but no further mention was made of that provision. The next instance of this was the *Application of the Genocide Convention* case, but the Court only 'ha[d] regard' to that provision in the *qualités* of each Order.[63] In the second request for provisional measures, the Court cited Article 75, paragraph 2, of the Rules as authority for its indicating measures that were in whole or in part other than those requested.[64] In the *Land and Maritime Boundary between Cameroon and Nigeria* (Provisional Measures) case, the Court merely recited that Article 75, paragraph 2, of the Rules conferred

[61] ICJ Rep. 1951, 89, 93. [62] ICJ Rep. 1986, 3. [63] ICJ Rep. 1993, 3.
[64] Ibid. 325, 347 (para. 47).

upon it the power to indicate measures that are in whole or in part other than those requested, which it proceeded to do.[65]

This case-law does not clarify the relationship between paragraphs 1 and 2 of Article 75. Paragraph 1 allows the Court at any time to decide to examine *proprio motu* whether the circumstances require the indication of provisional measures. *LaGrand* (Provisional Measures) suggests that this empowers the Court, if it decides that an indication of provisional measures is required very urgently, to act without regard for the formal procedure laid down in the Rules, and in particular to act *ex parte*.[66] In that case it reached its decision without holding any hearing as required by Article 74, paragraph 3, of the Rules. In this respect, the Court followed the Applicant's request in a meeting of the President with representatives of the two parties early in the morning of the day in which the Order was issued. The Court gave a long explanation of how it understood that provision in the Rules:

> 21. Whereas, under Article 75, paragraph 1, of the Rules of Court, the latter 'may at any time decide to examine *proprio motu* whether the circumstances of the case require the indication of provisional measures which ought to be taken or complied with by any or all of the parties'; whereas a provision of this kind has substantially featured in the Rules of Court since 1936, and whereas the Court has not, to date, made use of the power conferred upon it by this provision, the latter appears nonetheless to be clearly established; whereas the Court may make use of this power, irrespective of whether or not it has been seised by the parties of a request for the indication of provisional measures; whereas in such a case it may, in the event of extreme urgency, proceed without holding oral hearings; and whereas it is for the Court to decide in each case if, in the circumstances of the case, it should make use of the said power[.]

The Court went on to find that the circumstances required it, as a matter of the greatest urgency and without any other proceedings, to indicate provisional measures in accordance with Article 41 of the Statute and Article 75, paragraph 1, of the Rules.

Most requests for provisional measures are one-sided, asking for the measures to be imposed on the other party. Paragraph 2 gives the Court two options if it decides to indicate provisional measures. One is to indicate measures that are in whole or in part different from those requested. The Court frequently does that, since it is never bound to limit any decision to the precise submissions of one side or the other. The Court uses this provision of the Rules to impose provisional measures on both parties. The second option

[65] ICJ Rep. 1996 (I), 13, 24 (para. 48). This was criticized by Judge ad hoc Ajibola, who explained that the Order was made 'irrespective of the request of Cameroon'. Ibid. 36.

[66] ICJ Rep. 1999 (I), 9, 14 (para. 21) and 15 (para. 26). Criticized by Judge Oda, who stated that he voted in favour of the Order solely for humanitarian reasons (ibid. 20) and by President Schwebel, who thought that it was open to question whether the Court had acted in correct application of Art. 75, para. 1, of the Rules (ibid. 21). He did not oppose the substance of the Order and accordingly did not vote against it.

is that it may also indicate other measures that the party making the request should observe. It is striking that the Court regularly indicates measures that are applicable to both parties, and that part of paragraph 2, retained from previous versions of the Rules, confirms that practice. In fact it is normal for an order indicating provisional measures to contain an element of mutuality and require action (or inaction) by each party, except when the request refers to a particular act by the respondent claimed by the applicant to be in breach of international law or of the obligations of the respondent State.

Despite what the Court said in *LaGrand* about the extent of its power to act *proprio motu*, there has been no instance yet of the Court's taking the initiative in instituting proceedings for provisional measures. That statement was made when the binding force of orders indicating provisional measures was still a matter of controversy—decided only in the merits phase of that case. It is therefore an open question whether the Court would continue to adopt that position should circumstances require in a future case, unless it had assured itself that the parties would accept such an initiative on its part and comply with any obligations imposed by the Court.

The Rules of ITLOS contain nothing corresponding to Article 75, paragraph 1, of the Rules of the ICJ. Article 89, paragraph 5, parallels Article 75, paragraph 2. It reads:

> 5. When a request for provisional measures has been made, the Tribunal may prescribe measures different in whole or in part from those requested and indicate the parties which are to take or comply with each measure.

The ITLOS Order in the *MOX Plant* (Provisional Measures) case furnishes an example of this. As seen, the Tribunal, in the circumstances, did not find that the urgency of the situation required the prescription of the provisional measures requested by Ireland, in the short period before the constitution of the Annex VII arbitral tribunal (paragraph 81).[67] However it continued, citing Article 89, paragraph 5, of the Rules, to prescribe measures which both parties were to take to prevent the pollution of the marine environment (paragraphs 82 to 87).[68] In the *Land Reclamation by Singapore in and around the Straits of Johor* (Provisional Measures) case, the Tribunal simply cited Article 89, paragraph 5, of its Rules as allowing it to prescribe measures different in whole or in part from those requested.[69]

[67] *See* § 5.4.

[68] ITLOS Rep. 2001, 95. The Annex VII arbitral tribunal, in its Order No. 3 of 24 June 2003 suspending the proceedings on jurisdiction and merits, and request for further provisional measures, referred to both Art. 75, para. 2, of the ICJ Rules and Art. 89, para. 5, of the ITLOS Rules, which it drew to the attention of the parties without comment from either, considered that it was also competent to prescribe provisional measures other than those sought by any party, which it did in instructions addressed to both parties in the operative clause of the Order. *See* text to n. 58.

[69] ITLOS Rep. 2003, 8 October (para. 101).

7.7. THE REQUIREMENT OF REPORTING

Article 78 is, as seen (§ 3.6), new. Going beyond anything in the Statute, it appears as another attempt to strengthen the authority of an indication of provisional measures, following the two *Fisheries Jurisdiction* (Interim Protection) cases.[70] Here the Court requested the applicants to furnish the respondent and the Registry with all relevant information, orders, and arrangements made concerning the control and regulation of fish catches in the area concerned.[71] The necessary information was contained in each applicant's memorial, and in each of the Judgments on the merits the Court noted the observance of that requirement. In the *U.S. Diplomatic and Consular Staff in Tehran* (Provisional Measures) case, the ICJ included in the operative clause of its Order a statement that until it delivers its final judgment, 'it will keep the matters covered by this Order continuously under review'.[72] There is no formal machinery at the Court's disposal enabling it to perform this function, and the implications of a clause such as this are not clear. Its inclusion suggests that the Court regards itself as remaining seised of the request for provisional measures, which can be reactivated as required. In the *Frontier Dispute* (Burkina Faso/Mali) (Provisional Measures) case, the Chamber which heard that case required the Agents to inform the Registrar without delay of any agreement between their Governments regarding troop withdrawals as ordered by the Chamber.[73] In the *Application of the Genocide Convention* case, Bosnia invoked Article 78 in each of the provisional measures phases, but the Court made no response to that.[74] In the *Vienna Convention on Consular Relations* (Provisional Measures) case, the Court in its Order indicated that 'the United States should inform the Court of all the measures which it has taken in implementation of this Order'.[75] A similar provision was included in the Order in the *LaGrand* (Provisional Measures) case.[76] After the Court had

[70] *See* on this Ch. 3 n. 33.

[71] ICJ Rep. 1972, at 18 and 35; 1974, at 16 and 138.

[72] ICJ Rep. 1979, at 21 (para. 47 (2)). Followed in the *Military and Paramilitary Activities in and against Nicaragua* (Provisional Measures) case, ICJ Rep. 1984, at 187 (para. 41 (4D)). This was picked up in the merits phase. ICJ Rep. 1986, at 144 (paras. 288 ff.). In the *Frontier Dispute* (Burkina Faso/Mali) (Provisional Measures) case, the Chamber used a slightly different formula: 'Decides that, pending its final judgment, and without prejudice to the application of Article 76 of the Rules, the Chamber will remain seised of the questions covered by the present Order.' ICJ Rep. 1986, at 12 (para. 32 (3)).

[73] ICJ Rep. 1986, 3, 12 (para. 32 (2)).

[74] ICJ Rep. 1993, 7 (para. 3), 329 (para. 4).

[75] ICJ Rep. 1998, 248, 258 (para. 41 (I)). For communications by the United States in implementation of that, *see* the Pleadings in that case, at 194 (docs. 2, 3). Simultaneously with the filing of the memorial the applicant filed an amended application adding new claims to the original application, based on alleged non-compliance with the Order. Ibid. 73. However, the case was discontinued and no counter-memorial was filed. ICJ Rep. 1998, 426.

[76] ICJ Rep. 1999 -(I), 9, 16 (para. 26). For the United States action, *see* counter-memorial, para. 127.

determined that the Order indicating provisional measures imposed obligations on the United States (*see* § 2.5) the Court examined the question whether the report showed compliance with the obligations imposed by the Order. In the view of the Court, notwithstanding the controversy that existed at the time over the binding force of an order indicating provisional measures, the

> mere transmission of the Order to the Governor of Arizona without any comment, particularly without even so much as a plea for a temporary stay and an explanation that there is no general agreement on the position of the United States that orders of the International Court of Justice on provisional measures are not binding

was certainly less than could have been done even in the short time available (paragraph 112). The Court found that the United States had not fully discharged its obligation under the Order and therefore had not complied with the Order.[77]

However, those cases occurred at a time when there was still controversy over whether an order indicating provisional measures had any binding force. That question has now been answered in the affirmative (§ 2.5). One of the consequences could be that failure to comply with such an order would be an internationally wrongful act under the draft articles adopted by the International Law Commission in 2001, but also bringing into play the provisions of those draft articles on circumstances precluding responsibility.[78] This can give the Court a measure of control over the implementation of an order indicating provisional measures, and it could even allow the respondent to such an order some leeway in giving effect to it, should circumstances require, to the satisfaction of the Court. It is doubtful, however, if the Court could impose any sanction for failure to comply with any request made under Article 78.[79]

In the *Avena and other Mexican Nationals* (Provisional Measures) case the Court included a similar direction, but without indicating when the report was to be made. In the covering letter to its memorial the United States informed the Court that it had taken no action of the kind mentioned in the Order calling for a report to the Court.

This aspect has been changed fundamentally in the ITLOS Rules of the Tribunal. Rule 95 requires each party to inform the Tribunal as soon as possible as to its compliance with any provisional measures that the Tribunal

[77] ICJ Rep. 2001, 466, 508 (para. 115). Germany made no other request regarding following from its submission regarding non-compliance with the Order.

[78] Report of the International Law Commission on the work of its 53rd session, UN GAOR Sup. 10 (A/57/10) Ch. IV (2001); reproduced in J. Crawford, *The International Law Commission's Articles on State Responsibility: Introduction, Text and Commentaries* (Cambridge: Cambridge University Press, 2002).

[79] Art. 78 was invoked by Bosnia in its applications for provisional measures in the *Application of the Genocide Convention* case, but the Court made no response to that. ICJ Rep. 1993, at 7 (para. 3) and 329 (para. 3).

has prescribed. In particular, each party shall submit an initial report upon the steps it has taken or proposes to take in order to ensure prompt compliance with the measures prescribed.[80] The emphasis on *compliance* is to be noted.

In ITLOS, Article 95 of the Rules includes a formal requirement of reporting on compliance with an order prescribing provisional measures:

1. Each party shall inform the Tribunal as soon as possible as to its compliance with any provisional measures the Tribunal has prescribed. In particular, each party shall submit an initial report upon the steps it has taken or proposes to take in order to ensure prompt compliance with the measures prescribed.
2. The Tribunal may request further information from the parties on any matter connected with the implementation of any provisional measures it has prescribed.

The practice of ITLOS has been to include in the order prescribing provisional measures the date by which the initial report is to be submitted. Although not specified in the Rules, in cases brought under Article 290, paragraph 5, of the Convention, this obligation to report to ITLOS subsists only until the constitution of the arbitral tribunal. In the *Land Reclamation by Singapore in and around the Straits of Johor* (Provisional Measures) case, the Tribunal went further. It thought that it was consistent with the purpose of proceedings under Article 290, paragraph 5, that the parties submit reports to the Annex VII arbitral tribunal, unless the arbitral tribunal decided otherwise, and it included an appropriate provision in the operative clause of its Order.[81] This may signal an intent on the part of the Tribunal to find a way to integrate itself more closely with an Annex VII tribunal. One of its members (Judge Mensah) is at the same time serving as President of the MOX Plant Annex VII arbitral tribunal.

7.8. PROVISIONAL MEASURES IN ADVISORY CASES

In principle, provisional measures are only relevant to contentious proceedings. This follows from the nature of advisory proceedings in which technically there are no parties, and from the language of Article 41 of the Statute of

[80] This provision was of the Tribunal's initiative. For the Tribunal's Rules, *see* § 3.8. In the *Land Reclamation by Singapore in and around the Straits of Johor* (Provisional Measures) case, ITLOS extended the duty to report to include reporting to the Annex VII arbitral tribunal, unless the arbitral tribunal should decide otherwise. ITLOS Rep. 2003, Order of 8 October (para. 104). To the extent that the reporting is in implementation of Art. 290, para. 6, of the Law of the Sea Convention, requiring prompt compliance with provisional measures prescribed by any competent court or tribunal, it is not a matter for comment here. To the extent that aspects relating to compliance with an indication of provisional measures by the ICJ remain open despite the ruling in *LaGrand*, the question arises whether the International Court could not introduce something similar into its Rules.

[81] ITLOS Rep. 2003, 8 October (paras. 104, 106.3).

the International Court of Justice and from Article 290 of the Law of the Sea Convention, stating that the purpose of provisional measures is to preserve the respective rights of the parties to the dispute. Accordingly, provisional measures would not normally be appropriate in advisory proceedings. Furthermore, since in principle and subject to the terms of the constituent instrument permitting an organ of a specialized agency to request an advisory opinion, an advisory opinion itself is not binding in the sense that it imposes obligations on any of the States members of the organization requesting the advisory opinion, it is difficult to see how a binding order indicating provisional measures could be made in such a case, although the reasoning might declare that an action of a State was not in conformity with international law. Such a statement, however, would not by itself impose any binding obligations on any State, and a priori the possibility of such a statement being made does not justify the indication of provisional measures.

In the order fixing the procedure for dealing with the request for an advisory opinion on the *Applicability of the Obligation to Arbitrate under Section 21 of the United Nations Headquarters Agreement of 26 June 1947*, the International Court recited some of the paragraphs of the resolution of the General Assembly requesting the advisory opinion, which stressed the time constraints leading to that request and even asked the Court to take account of the provisions of the Statute, 'in particular Articles 41 and 68 thereof'. The Court refused to see in that a formal request for the indication of provisional measures and continued:

> Whereas it is not appropriate, in the circumstances of the case, for the Court to consider whether or not provisional measures may be indicated in proceedings on a request for advisory opinion[.][82]

That cautious statement leaves the question open, because sometimes it is possible to employ the advisory procedure to settle a dispute, the parties to the dispute agreeing in advance to accept the advisory opinion as binding. In the *Legal Consequences of the Construction of a Wall in the Occupied Palestinian Territory* advisory opinion, where the Court was requested to give an urgent advisory opinion, the General Assembly made no reference to Article 41 of the Statute, and the Court limited itself to adopting an accelerated procedure.[83]

[82] ICJ Rep. 1988, 3, 4. *And see* the separate opinion of Judge Schwebel at p. 6. This was not followed in the Order of 19 December 2003 in the advisory case relating to Israel's security fence, where too the General Assembly requested the Court to render the opinion urgently. Instead, short time-limits were prescribed.

[83] ICJ Rep. 2003, 428.

7.9. THE ROLE OF THE SECURITY COUNCIL

Before discussing the implication of the requirement of Article 41 of the Statute that when the ICJ indicates provisional measures, notice of the measures suggested is to be given to the Security Council, it is necessary to recall Article 94, paragraph 1, of the Charter: '1. Each Member of the United Nations undertakes to comply with the decision of the International Court of Justice in any case to which it is a party.' Paragraph 2 of that Article imposes a specific obligation on a party to a case to comply with the obligations incumbent on it under a judgment rendered by the Court. It is sometimes suggested that in this context, the word *decision* in paragraph 1 means also *judgment* but the Court has not followed that approach.[84] The Court has considered whether Article 94 precludes attributing binding effect to any order indicating provisional measures. It pointed out that the words 'the decision' in that paragraph could be understood as referring not merely to the Court's judgments but to any decision rendered by it, including orders indicating provisional measures. It could also be interpreted to mean only judgments. The Court found that this second interpretation would in no way preclude orders indicating provisional measures being accorded binding force under Article 41 of the Statute.[85]

As seen, Article 41, paragraph 2, of the Statute of the ICJ requires notice of the indication of provisional measures to be given to the Security Council. That was originally proposed by the Advisory Committee of Jurists of 1920 explaining that its suggestion to inform the League Council of any interim measures was in order that the Council, as the body most competent to take such action, might suggest that the measures calculated to ensure the effect of judgments be carried out.[86] It has been explained that the Court's function is limited to indicating the provisional measures and notifying them to the Council [of the League] and to the parties, and that the Council was responsible for the follow-up of the decision and for compliance with its obligations if necessary.[87] There is no reason to suppose that the San Francisco Conference had any other conception in mind when it adopted Article 41 of the Statute unchanged in this respect, save for specifying the reference to the Security Council. On the other hand, the competent organ of that Conference dealing with the Security Council did not consider the implications of

[84] For this suggestion, *see* the contribution of H. Mosler with K. Oellers-Frahm in B. Simma (ed.), *The Charter of the United Nations: A Commentary*, 2nd edn, vol. II, 1174 (Oxford: Oxford University Press, 2002).

[85] *LaGrand* case, ICJ Rep. 2001, 466, 505 (para. 108). For criticism of the whole of the Court's reasoning on this issue, *see* the dissenting opinion of Judge Oda, 525 at 537 (paras. 29 to 35).

[86] *See* Ch. 2 nn. 1, 11. The original of that awkwardly translated passage reads: 'pour proposer au regard des sentences . . . les mesures qui doivent en assurer l'effect [sic]'.

[87] B. von Stauffenberg (ed.), *Statut et Règlement de la Cour internationale de Justice: Eléments d'interprétation* 317 (Berlin: Carl Heymans, 1934).

that revision of Article 41 of the Statute. However, to follow unquestioningly the practice of the Permanent Court, the League Council, and its Secretary-General does not take account of the major differences in the functions of the Security Council and of the Secretary-General of the United Nations in comparison with their predecessors of the League. There is no obvious reason why, when the Secretary-General transmits a communication from the Court to the Security Council about an order indicating provisional measures, the Secretary-General should not add observations in so far as they would come within the wide competence of the Secretary-General, not only as regards the affairs of the organization of which the Court is one of the principal organs. The Secretary-General's specific power under Article 99 of the Charter, to bring to the attention of the Security Council any matter which in his or her opinion may threaten the maintenance of international peace or security, is also relevant. Some of the provisional measures ordered since the establishment of the United Nations have been made in circumstances threatening the maintenance of international peace and security.

For the ICJ that provision of the Statute is supplemented by Article 77 of the 1978 Rules, by which any measure indicated by the Court under Article 73 and 75 of the Rules, and any decision under Article 76, paragraph 1, is to be communicated forthwith to the Secretary-General for transmission to the Security Council.[88] In the case of ITLOS, Article 94 of the Rules provides that any provisional measures prescribed by the Tribunal or any modification or revocation be notified to the parties and to such other States Parties as the Tribunal considers appropriate in each case.[89]

The transmission of the ICJ order to the Security Council does not imply that the Security Council will automatically take the matter on its agenda or how it will designate it. That is a separate aspect, governed by the Security Council's practice and its provisional Rules of Procedure.[90] Until now, the Security Council has only once taken on its agenda a question of compliance with an order indicating provisional measures, and it did so without acting under Article 94. That was in 1951, when the United Kingdom submitted a

[88] Under current practice, the Registrar makes this communication to the Secretary-General who in turn transmits it to the Security Council. Cf. Rules of Court, Art. 26, para. 1 (*a*).

[89] By Article 20 of the Instructions for the Registry (Ch. 6 n. 6) unless otherwise directed by the Tribunal the Registrar is to communicate orders in the same manner. This means that unless the Tribunal directs otherwise, its orders prescribing provisional measures are also communicated automatically to the Secretary-General of the United Nations. In turn, this is supplemented by Article 4, paragraph 1 (*b*) (ii), of the Agreement on Cooperation and Relationship between the United Nations and the International Tribunal for the Law of the Sea (*see ITLOS Yearbook 1996–97* 178 and Ch. 4 n. 93). If the Seabed Disputes Chamber was dealing with the case and had prescribed provisional measures, its decision would come within the scope of Annex VI, Art. 39, by which the 'decisions' of that Chamber shall be enforceable in the territories of States Parties in the same manner as judgments or orders of the highest court of the State Party in whose territory the enforcement is sought.

[90] S/96/Rev.7.

complaint at the failure of the Iranian Government to comply with the provisional measures indicated by the Court in the *Anglo-Iranian Oil Co.* case.[91] This has since been to some extent formalized in Article 77 of the Rules which provides in an impersonal way that any measures indicated under Articles 73 and 74 of the Rules, and any decision taken under Article 76 (a decision to revoke or modify any decision concerning provisional measures), 'shall forthwith be communicated to the Secretary-General of the United Nations for transmission to the Security Council in pursuance of Article 41, paragraph 2, of the Statute'.[92]

The Order indicating provisional measures in the *Land and Maritime Boundary between Cameroon and Nigeria* case was the first to omit the transmission phrase.[93] This unexplained omission is all the more extraordinary, as one of the measures indicated was that both parties should lend every assistance to the fact-finding mission which the Secretary-General of the United Nations was proposing to send to the Bakassi Peninsula, the scene of the incidents that led to the request for provisional measures.

The Court's practice regarding the transmission to the Security Council of orders declining to indicate provisional measures is mixed. In the *Interhandel*, *Aegean Sea Continental Shelf*, and *Passage through the Great Belt* cases this was not done. In the *Trial of Pakistani Prisoners of War* it was. There is no provision in the Statute or in the Rules for formally notifying the Security Council that provisional measures have lapsed.[94] ITLOS has never yet included in an order prescribing provisional measures a specific instruction regarding its transmission to the Security Council.

While, then, the general principles governing the power of the Court to indicate provisional measures are clear, and it is beyond dispute, having regard to the language of the constituent documents and to the judicial practice of the Court that the Court can act on the basis of provisional findings of fact and a prima facie finding of jurisdiction over the merits, there is room for hesitation how far the competence of the Security Council may or can usefully be invoked in face of the refusal of a State to comply with the obligations that an order indicating or prescribing provisional measures may impose upon it, or where the jurisdiction of the Court is contested. If a permanent member of the Security Council is an 'unwilling respondent' in the Court proceedings, the mere existence of its right of veto in the Security Council could prevent any persuasive action by that body to give effect to

[91] On that action in the Security Council, *see Law and Practice*, vol. I at 260. For provisional measures in disputes that are also simultaneously before the Security Council, *see* § 8.3.

[92] Under Art. 26 of the Rules, the Registrar's functions include to effect all communications, notifications and the transmission of documents required by the Statute or by the Rules, and to ensure that the date of despatch and receipt thereof may be readily verified.

[93] ICJ Rep. 1996, 13.

[94] For notifications to the Security Council that provisional measures had lapsed, *see Anglo-Iranian Oil Co.* case, Pleadings 764 (doc. 158); *Nuclear Tests* cases, II Pleadings 443 (doc. 211).

any indication of provisional measures against it made by the Court. In other cases, the political fragmentation repeatedly demonstrated in the proceedings of the Security Council is likewise likely to make it difficult to obtain the required majority of nine members of the Security Council in favour of any effective majority. Experience to date may support the view that, under the present wording of the Charter and the practice of the Security Council, political expediency and not any considerations of law carries more weight in that body, although the Court's standing in the matter has not been overlooked. If that is so, then the effectiveness of any provisional measures indicated by the Court will depend upon the extent of the real consent by the parties that the Court should settle the dispute, or at least contribute to its settlement. Having regard to the exceptional power which this jurisdiction involves, it may be arguable that it ought to be more closely integrated with the principal jurisdiction to deal with the case on the merits than it sometimes appears to be.

For courts or tribunals competent under the Convention on the Law of the Sea, Article 290, paragraph 4, of the Convention provides that the court or tribunal shall forthwith give notice to the parties to the dispute, and to such other States parties as it considers appropriate, of the prescription, modification, or revocation of provisional measures. For ITLOS, those documents would also be transmitted to the Secretary-General of the United Nations, whose action on receipt of the necessary information would have to conform to the general powers of the Secretary-General under the Charter.[95]

7.10. THE ROLE OF OTHER ORGANS

The fact that the Court is a principal organ of the United Nations and its principal judicial organ would require the other principal organs, indeed all organs of the United Nations, to exert every effort to frame their decisions on a matter which has formed the object of an indication of provisional measures—when asked to do so by an interested party—in a way that is compatible with the pronouncement of the Court. This has not always been the case since 1946, largely due to the fact that these organs have allowed themselves to be misused as arenas for confrontation rather than for diplomacy or reconciliation. That is not conducive to the creation of a propitious atmosphere in which the Court can operate.

Despite the fact that the Charter refers specifically to the role of the Security Council for securing compliance with a judgment, it does not follow that the competence of that organ is exclusive. There is no reason why the General Assembly, subject to Article 12 of the Charter, should not discuss

[95] *See further* in Ch. 6 text to n. 16.

such a matter under Articles 10 or 11, or why the Economic and Social Council should not do likewise if the matter comes within its limited competence. Indeed the very fact that the post-adjudication phase is political, using the word *political* in antithesis to *legal*, leads to the view that it is not necessarily within the exclusive competence of any one organ. That principle has in fact long been recognized, in so far as concerns the International Labour Organization, in Article 33 of its Constitution. Here, in the event of any member failing to carry out within the time specified the decision of the Court, the Governing Body may recommend to the Conference such action as it may deem wise and expedient to secure compliance with it. In addition, the power of these organs as well as of the specialized agencies to take measures to give effect to certain decisions of the Court is the necessary and implicit consequence of their right to request advisory opinions. The general tendency which found expression in the Uniting for Peace resolution 377 (V), 3 November 1950 (with its amendments to the Rules of Procedure of the General Assembly) to attempt to create a stronger parallelism between the powers and functions of the General Assembly and those of the Security Council, implies as a natural consequence recognition that organs other than the Security Council can deal with problems concerning compliance with decisions of the Court.[96]

The general principles applicable to define the permissible attitude of the Security Council towards decisions of the Court are equally applicable to delimit the permissible attitude of the other organs. The legitimate focus of attention can never be the order or the judgment but its consequences, and the recommendations (normally those organs do not have power to take binding decisions) can at the most have a suspensive or moratory effect on the order or judgment. The practice of the General Assembly in so far as concerns the cognate problem of its reception of advisory opinions gives ground for believing that it is conscious of its general responsibilities for sustaining the authority of international law of which the Court is the organ.

It may be noted that Article 98 of the Charter, which requires the Secretary-General to act in that capacity in all meetings of the General Assembly,

[96] This need not be limited to organs of the United Nations. Thus, Art. 50 of the American Treaty of Pacific Settlement (the Pact of Bogotá) provides that if one of the parties should fail to carry out the obligations imposed upon it by a decision of the International Court of Justice or by an arbitral award, the other party or parties concerned shall, before resorting to the Security Council, propose a Meeting of Consultation of the Ministers of Foreign Affairs to agree upon appropriate measures to ensure the fulfilment of the judicial decision or arbitral award. For the Meeting of Consultation of the Foreign Ministers, *see* Ch. XI of the Charter of the Organization of American States. This may also be extended in appropriate circumstances to the autonomous bodies of the United Nations such as the United Nations Conference on Trade and Development (UNCTAD) and the United Nations Environment Programme (UNEP), to mention two. For further discussion of the differential between political and legal action in a United Nations context, *see* Sh. Rosenne, *The Perplexities of Modern International Law*, revd edn, 454 (Leiden: Martinus Nijhoff, 2004).

of the Security Council, of the Economic and Social Council, and of the [now defunct] Trusteeship Council, four of the six principal organs established by Article 7, does not include any reference to the International Court of Justice, also a principal organ established by that Article. On the other hand, the Statute imposes a number of functions on the Secretary-General as on other organs of the United Nations, notably the General Assembly and the Security Council. This serves to emphasize the functional autonomy of the Court in relation to the other organs, principal and subsidiary, of the United Nations. Yet this has not deterred the Secretary-General from action in connection with the judicial work of the Court if he felt that action on his part was necessary for the maintenance of international peace and security. One of the most significant instances of this was Mr Kofi Annan's attempt, even before judgment was given, to ensure that whatever the decision in the *Land and Maritime Frontier between Cameroon and Nigeria* case, both parties would comply with it; and when difficulties arose on that score, to take further diplomatic action to that end.[97] In this connection it is noted that orders indicating provisional measures do not contain anything in their operative clauses about transmitting the order to the Security Council. This has always been left to the testimonium, which at one time would indicate in how many signed and sealed copies the order were made, which text is authoritative, and the destination of the copies, one being the Secretary-General of the United Nations 'for transmission to the Security Council'. That phrase has been dropped since 1996, without any explanation being offered, so modern orders contain no specific reference to their being transmitted to the Security Council.

[97] *See* text to Ch. 8 n. 26. *See also* General Assembly resolution 58/294, 18 June 2004.

8

A Survey of the Decisions

8.1. MEASURES REQUESTED AND PRINCIPAL CLAIM

The Permanent Court of International Justice, in the twenty years of its effective existence, received seven requests and made two orders indicating provisional measures.[1] The present Court, in the period 1947 to the end of April 2004, has received forty-one such requests (one in a case heard by an ad hoc Chamber specially formed to deal with the case)[2] and the International Tribunal for the Law of the Sea four in the period commencing in 1997 to June 2004. The International Court of Justice has acceded to eighteen of these requests (one in a Chamber), and ITLOS to all four of its cases. This makes it possible to show the different sets of circumstances in which requests for provisional measures have come to be made, and when not.

Most of the requests for provisional measures were filed together with or close to the instrument instituting the proceedings, normally an application. They fall into two classes. One is where at the time the request falls to be considered the respondent (to the request, usually also the respondent to the application) has not indicated any challenge to the jurisdiction over the merits as invoked in the instrument instituting the proceedings. That automatically allows the court or tribunal to deal with any request for provisional

[1] The Appendix lists all the cases to date, in the PCIJ and the ICJ (together the 'International Court') and in ITLOS in which provisional measures were requested. It also shows where they were granted and where denied, and relevant dates.

[2] The formal statistics are misleading. Six cases with requests for provisional measures in the International Court of Justice related to three single disputes. Two of those disputes involved two applicants against a single respondent, and one a single applicant against two respondents. All those cases were formulated in six separate but 'paired' or linked cases, the *Fisheries Jurisdiction* cases of the Federal Republic of Germany and the United Kingdom against Iceland and the *Nuclear Tests* cases of Australia and New Zealand against France, and the *Interpretation and Application of the Montreal Convention of 1971 arising out of the Aerial Incident at Lockerbie* cases of Libya against the United Kingdom and the United States. In addition, ten requests related to the same dispute, the action of the NATO armed forces against Serbia in 1999 in the first Kosovo crisis. On technical grounds relating to the Court's jurisdiction over the merits and to the composition of the Court (appointment of judges ad hoc), all these sixteen cases are listed and treated separately, but from the point of view of the provisional measures procedure they should be regarded as four cases since the relevant Orders were identical *mutatis mutandis* (except in two of the Orders in the Kosovo cases where the absence of jurisdiction over the merits was manifest and the Court ordered those two cases to be removed from the General List). These technical differences are not of direct concern here, but they are noted elsewhere where relevant, notably in connection with the Court's jurisdiction to deal with the requests for provisional measures. Likewise, two cases introduced separately in ITLOS, the *Southern Bluefin Tuna* cases brought by Australia and by New Zealand against Japan, were formally joined and are to be treated as one case.

measures. Jurisdiction to decide the principal case includes jurisdiction to decide all incidental questions that might arise in the course of the proceedings, including requests for provisional measures. But each type of incidental jurisdiction has its own requirements for its exercise, and in previous chapters the distinguishing features of requests for provisional measures, especially the concept of prima facie jurisdiction and the relationship of urgency to the apprehended damage, have been demonstrated.

The other situation is where the respondent—frequently an 'unwilling respondent'—is politically unwilling to submit the dispute to adjudication and consistently denies the jurisdiction of the court or tribunal over the merits of the claim, sometimes without waiting for preliminary objection proceedings. In this respect, the ICJ has been faced with a new situation (in comparison with the experience of the PCIJ). That is where immediately on receipt of the notification of the institution of the proceedings, the respondent's reaction has been either to challenge the title of jurisdiction invoked, or to exercise its right under Article 53 of the Statute and not take part in the proceedings.[3] The first and major example of this is the *Anglo-Iranian Oil Co.* case in 1951. That led to the concept of prima facie jurisdiction over the merits as the basis for the Court's ability to deal with a request for provisional measures (discussed in Chapter 4). If the proceedings on the request for provisional measures bring out that it is manifest that the respondent has not in any way consented to the exercise of jurisdiction over that dispute, the Court can order the case to be removed from the General List (*see* § 4.7). In this context, the Court has made it clear that issues of the principal jurisdiction over the dispute cannot be decided in proceedings for provisional measures. In the *Interhandel* (Interim Protection) case, the Court refused to deal with a question of jurisdiction over the principal claim, leaving that for formal preliminary objection proceedings.[4]

An important question arises when the claim in the request for provisional measures corresponds very closely if not entirely to the main *petitum* in the merits of the case. Early in its existence the Permanent Court refused to give effect to a request by Germany as applicant, made in reliance on Article 41 of the Statute, that Poland should pay to it a sum of money as a provisional measure, following an earlier judgment awarding compensation to Germany subject to further proceedings to determine the amount of that compensation. The Permanent Court did not regard the German request as relating to the indication of measures of protection, but as designed to obtain an interim judgment in favour of part of Germany's claim. Consequently that request was not covered by the terms of the provisions of the Statute and of

[3] *See* on this Ch. 3 n. 29.
[4] *Interhandel* (Interim Protection) case, ICJ Rep. 1957, 105, 111, *and see* Ch. 4 n. 9.

the Rules cited in the request.[5] The present Court has given the following explanation for this:[6]

There is no provision in the Statute of the Court either specifically empowering the Court to make an interim award of this kind [an interim payment of compensation], or indeed debarring it from doing so. In view of the final and binding character of the Court's judgments, under Articles 59 and 60 of the Statute, it would however only be appropriate to make an award of this kind, assuming that the Court possesses the power to do so, in exceptional circumstances and where the entitlement of the State making the claim was already established with certainty and precision. Furthermore, in a case in which the respondent State is not appearing, so that its views on the matter are not known to the Court, the Court should refrain from any unnecessary act which might prove an obstacle to a negotiated settlement.

More should not be read into the Permanent Court's decision than it says. The dictum refers in terms to an interim decision regarding the payment by the respondent of a defined sum of money on account of a final judgment to be delivered by the Court determining the amount of compensation due. As has recently been written, The Permanent Court did not decide that the mere fact that the Applicant State seeks the same remedy in the interim measures phase as it seeks on the merits precludes the indication of provisional measures.[7]

It has been left to the present Court to indicate provisional measures which in substance coincide with the main claim advanced by the applicant. The outstanding instance of this is the *U.S. Diplomatic and Consular Staff in Tehran* case. Here in its application the United States asked for the release of the hostages held in the American Embassy at Tehran, and in the request for provisional measures of protection it also asked for their release. The Court granted that request, despite Iran's absence from the proceedings.[8] Referring to the *Chorzów Factory* case and the question of an interim judgment, the Court said:

whereas, however, the circumstances of that case were entirely different from those of the present one, and the request there sought to obtain from the Court a final judgment on part of a claim for a sum of money; whereas, moreover, a request for provisional measures must by its very nature relate to the substance of the case since, as Article 41 expressly states, their object is to preserve the respective rights of either party; and whereas in the present case the purpose of the United States request

[5] *Factory at Chorzów*, PCIJ Ser. A 12 (1927).

[6] *Military and Paramilitary Activities in and against Nicaragua* (Merits) case, ICJ Rep. 1986, 24, 143 (para. 285).

[7] L. Collins, 'Provisional and Protective Measures in International Litigation', 231 *Recueil* 9, 229 (1992-II).

[8] *United States Diplomatic and Consular Staff in Tehran* (Provisional Measures) case, ICJ Rep. 1979, 7, 16 (para. 28).

appears to be not to obtain a judgment, interim or final, on the merits of its claims but to preserve the substance of the rights which it claims *pendente lite*[.]

The *Arrest Warrant of 11 April 2000* (Provisional Measures) case raised similar problems. In the application instituting the proceedings the Congo asked the Court to declare that Belgium should annul the international arrest warrant issued on 11 April 2000, and in the request for provisional measures, Congo sought an order for the immediate discharge of the disputed arrest warrant. In the course of the proceedings Belgium argued that the relief sought by the Congo by way of provisional measures was identical to the relief sought in the merits of the claim, and in that context referred to the Order in the *Chorzów Factory* case. In its decision on the request for provisional measures the Court found that the need for provisional measures had not been established, rendering it unnecessary for it to consider further Belgian arguments, 'in particular the argument that the measure relating to the discharge of the arrest warrant . . . is identical to that sought by it [the Congo] on the merits'.[9] Since that Order was made, the Court has clarified the question of the binding force of an order indicating provisional measures (*see* § 2.5). It therefore remains to be seen how in the future the Court will deal with a request for provisional measures in an order which would have an effect virtually indistinguishable from that of an interim judgment.

Another issue that has faced the present Court is where the request for provisional measures required action by one or more third states or entities that are not party to the proceedings. The second provisional measures requested by Bosnia-Herzegovina in the *Application of the Genocide Convention* case raised this issue in an acute form.[10] Among the ten measures requested were three (Nos. 5, 7, and 9) addressed to all the parties to the Genocide Convention, one (No. 10) addressed to the United Nations Peace-keeping forces in Bosnia (UNPROFOR), three (Nos. 4, 6, and 7) requesting that Bosnia-Herzegovina be provided with the means necessary for its self-defence, and two (Nos. 2 and 6) concerning the possibility of the dismemberment of Bosnia-Herzegovina. The Court was painstaking in its discussion of

[9] ICJ Rep. 2000, 182, 201 (para. 73). In its Judgment on the merits the Court found in favour of the Congo and held that Belgium must, by means of its own choosing, cancel the arrest warrant and so inform the authorities to whom the warrant was circulated. ICJ Rep. 2002, 3. It appears from para. 14 at p. 9 of that Judgment that Interpol was included among the authorities to whom the warrant was circulated.

[10] *Application of the Convention on the Prevention and Punishment of the Crime of Genocide* (Further Provisional Measures) case, ICJ Rep. 1993, 325, 344 (para. 40). At the Meeting of Experts convened at The Hague in May 1999 in honour of the centenary of the Peace Conference of 1899, under the rubric of the International Court of Justice the Experts drew attention to the need to solve existing problems of requesting interim measures of protection, including due regard for abuse of the system of the compulsory jurisdiction of the Court under Art. 36, para. 2 of the Statute. UN doc. A/54/381, para. 93. Reproduced in F. Kalshoven (ed.), *The Centennial of the First International Peace Conference: Reports and Conclusions* 457 (The Hague: Kluwer Law International, 2000).

these requests, keeping in mind all the time that in the earlier Order it had limited the extent of its prima facie jurisdiction to matters covered by the jurisdictional clause (Article IX) of the Genocide Convention:

40. Whereas the list of measures which the Applicant now requests the Court to indicate ... includes certain measures, (and in particular those numbered 5, 7, 9 and 10 on that list) which would be addressed to States or entities not parties to the proceedings; whereas the Applicant has explained that it is not asking for an Order binding upon any State other than the Parties, but for a clarification of the Applicant's rights 'which can be used in the Security Council and the General Assembly and elsewhere'; whereas the judgment in a particular case by which disputed rights may be adjudged by the Court to belong to the Applicant or to the Respondent has, in accordance with Article 59 of the Statute of the Court, 'no binding force except between the parties'; whereas accordingly the Court may, for the preservation of those rights, indicate provisional measures to be taken by the parties, but not by third States or other entities who would not be bound by the eventual judgment to recognize and respect those rights; whereas consequently the Court cannot, in the exercise of its power to indicate provisional measures, indicate by way of 'clarification' that those States or entities should take, or refrain from, specific action in relation to the acts of genocide which the Applicant alleges are being committed in Bosnia-Herzegovina;

41. Whereas three of the measures requested by the Applicant (those numbered 4, 6 and 8 on the list ...), provide that the Government of Bosnia-Herzegovina 'must have the means' to prevent the commission of genocide, and to defend its people against genocide, and 'must have the ability to obtain military weapons, equipment, and supplies' from the other parties to the Genocide Convention; whereas the Applicant has made it clear ... that it bases these proposed measures on the Genocide Convention and on the right of self-defence referred to in Article 51 of the United Nations Charter, and on its claim that because of the arms embargo laid down by the Security Council by resolution 713 (1991), the Applicant is unable to protect its people from genocide; whereas a similar claim was before the Court when it examined the first request for provisional measures, when some of the requested measures were directed to the question of self-defence, but were not regarded by the Court as within the scope of the jurisdiction under Article IX of the Genocide Convention; whereas Article 41 of the Statute empowers the Court to indicate measures 'which ought to be taken to preserve the respective rights of either party', and ... this means measures which ought to be taken by one or both parties to the case; whereas however it is clear that the intention of the Applicant in requesting these measures is not that the Court indicate that the Respondent ought to take certain steps for the preservation of the Applicant's rights, but rather that the Court make a declaration of what those rights are, which 'would clarify the legal situation for the entire international community', in particular the members of the United Nations Security Council; whereas accordingly this request must be regarded as outside the scope of Article 41 of the Statute;

42. Whereas two of the measures requested ... (those numbered 2 and 3 on the list ...) relate to the possibility of 'partition and dismemberment', annexation or incorporation of the sovereign territory of Bosnia and Herzegovina ... ;

whereas it appears to the Court, from the definition of genocide in Article II of the Genocide Convention... that its essential characteristic is the intended destruction of 'a national, ethnical, racial or religious group', and not the disappearance of a State as a subject of international law or a change in its constitution or its territory; whereas, accordingly, the Court is unable to accept, for the purposes of the present request for the indication of provisional measures, that a 'partition and dismemberment', or annexation of a sovereign State, or its incorporation into another State, could in itself constitute an act of genocide and thus a matter falling within the jurisdiction of the Court under Article IX of the Genocide Convention; whereas, on the other hand, in so far as it is the Applicant's contention that such 'partition and dismemberment', annexation or incorporation will result from genocide, the Court, in its Order of 8 April 1993 has already indicated that Yugoslavia should 'take all measures within its power to prevent commission of the crime of genocide', whatever might be its consequences;

43. Whereas the remaining measure requested... (that numbered 1 in the list...), which does not refer to the Genocide Convention, is almost identical in wording with the second measure requested in [the] first request for provisional measures... save that it is wider in scope... [.]

8.2. PROVISIONAL MEASURES IN TERRITORIAL DISPUTES

In territorial disputes, where hostile incidents have occurred or are feared in disputed areas, the provisional measures procedure has been invoked to restore the peace, to protect the legal interests of the injured party (including the security of evidence), and to restore the element of serenity essential for the successful conduct of the judicial process. The first case of this nature was the *South-Eastern Greenland* case in 1932. Here, however, both parties gave appropriate assurances to the Court which found that in the circumstances the safeguarding of the alleged rights of the parties did not 'at present' require that the Court should *proprio motu* indicate any provisional measures of protection.[11]

In the present Court, this type of issue first arose in the *Frontier Dispute* (Burkina Faso/Mali) (Provisional Measures) case, a rare instance of a request for provisional measures in a case submitted by a special agreement to an ad hoc Chamber of the Court.[12] That was the first in a chain of cases on territorial disputes in which the nature of the rights claimed was extended to cover the eligibility of actual or potential injury to human beings for protection through the indication of provisional measures, later extended to disputes over the interpretation or application of a treaty. While the written proceedings on the merits were in progress, grave incidents took place between the armed forces of the two parties in the disputed border regions

[11] *Legal Status of the South-Eastern Territory of Greenland* case, PCIJ Ser. A/B 48 (1932).

[12] *Frontier Dispute* (Burkina Faso/Mali) (Provisional Measures) case, ICJ Rep. 1986, 3.

between them, settled by a cease-fire agreement after mediation efforts by different States and regional organizations. Following that, both parties indicated to the Chamber that they would be requesting provisional measures. The Chamber interpreted Article 41 of the Statute as empowering it to indicate provisional measures with a view to preventing the aggravation or extension of the dispute whenever it considered that circumstances so required (paragraph 18). In the Chamber's words:

> 19. Whereas, in particular, when two States jointly decide to have recourse to a chamber of the Court, the principal judicial organ of the United Nations, with a view to the peaceful settlement of a dispute, in accordance with Article 2, paragraph 3, and Article 33 of the Charter of the United Nations, and incidents subsequently occur which not merely are likely to extend or aggravate the dispute but comprise a resort to force which is irreconcilable with the principle of the peaceful settlement of international disputes, there can be no doubt of the Chamber's power and duty to indicate, if need be, such provisional measures as may conduce to the due administration of justice[.]

In an important innovation regarding provisional measures in a territorial dispute, the Chamber took into consideration that the facts that gave rise to the mutual requests for the indication of provisional measures 'expose the persons and property in the disputed area, as well as the interests of both States within that area, to serious risk of irreparable damage'.[13] It accordingly indicated a series of provisional measures including observance of the cease-fire instituted by agreement between the parties and the withdrawal of armed forces of both parties to a line to be agreed between them or, failing agreement, to be determined by the Chamber itself. It required the parties to inform the Registrar without delay of any agreement concluded between them and decided that pending the final judgment, the chamber would remain seised of the questions covered by the Order.[14]

The Court carried this further in the case between Cameroon and Nigeria, an unwilling respondent, instituted unilaterally by Cameroon on the basis of the mutual acceptances of the jurisdiction under Article 36, paragraph 2, of the Statute.[15] Instead of filing a counter-memorial, Nigeria filed preliminary objections to the jurisdiction and admissibility of the case, thereby suspending the proceedings on the merits. Shortly after the filing of those objections, an armed incident occurred in the principal disputed part of the frontier, the Bakassi Peninsula, following which the parties were in contact to ensure that peace prevailed in the region pending the Court's judgment. However, armed

[13] *Frontier Dispute* (Burkina Faso/Mali) (Provisional Measures) case, ICJ Rep. 1986, para. 21.

[14] For the implementation of this Order, which is similar to a resolution of the Security Council under Ch. VII of the Charter, *see* the Judgment on the merits, ICJ Rep. 1986, 554, 559 (para. 10).

[15] *The Land and Maritime Boundary between Cameroon and Nigeria* (Provisional Measures) case, ICJ Rep. 1996 (I), 15. And *see Yearbook of the United Nations*, vol. 50 (1996), 146.

incidents continued and Cameroon invoked Article 41 of the Statute, submitting a request for provisional measures. In the proceedings on that request the Court found that it prima facie had jurisdiction and that prima facie the application did not appear to be inadmissible (paragraphs 31, 33). The Court took into consideration that the rights at issue in those proceedings were sovereign rights claimed by the parties over territory, those rights also concerning persons. The Court followed the *South-Eastern Greenland* and *Frontier Dispute* (Burkina Faso/Mali) cases to justify the indication of provisional measures to prevent aggravation or extension of the dispute (paragraph 40). It included the following paragraph in its Order, in that way clarifying and emphasizing that the saving of human life is an element to be taken into consideration in considering requests for provisional measures in a territorial dispute, even if that is not directly the subject of the claim itself:

> 39. Whereas the rights at issue in these proceedings are sovereign rights which the Parties claim over territory, and whereas these rights also concern persons; and whereas armed actions have regrettably occurred on territory which is the subject of proceedings before the Court[.][16]
>
> [. . .]
>
> 42. Whereas the events that have given rise to the request, and more especially the killing of persons, have caused irreparable damage to the rights that the Parties may have over the Peninsula; whereas persons in the disputed area and, as a consequence, the rights of the Parties within that area are exposed to serious risk of further irreparable damage; and whereas armed actions within the territory in dispute could jeopardize the existence of evidence relevant to the present case; and whereas, from the elements of information available to it, the Court takes the view that there is a risk that events likely to aggravate or extend the dispute may occur again, thus rendering the settlement of that dispute more difficult[.]

Both the Secretary-General of the United Nations and the Security Council, already seised of the dispute more generally than the Court, intervened in this situation. The Secretary-General sent a fact-finding mission to the region to find ways to dissipate the tension between the parties. In its Order of 15 March 1996 the Court indicated various measures that both parties should take, including observing a cease-fire agreement reached earlier and lending every assistance to the proposed fact-finding mission. No more incidents of this character interfered with the conduct of the proceedings, which continued until the Judgment on the merits.[17]

That Order is also significant in demonstrating that the suspension of proceedings on the merits following the filing of preliminary objections does not impair the Court's prima facie jurisdiction to indicate provisional

[16] ICJ Rep. 1996, at 22 (para. 39). The use of provisional measures to protect human life is foreseen in the *Application of the Genocide Convention* (Further Provisional Measures) case, *passim*. That, however, was a direct consequence of the claim of breach of that Convention.

[17] ICJ Rep. 2002, 303. *See further* in text to nn. 25 to 27.

measures which by their very nature can refer only to the merits. In the merits, Cameroon included a claim based upon Nigeria's alleged non-compliance with that Order. The Court found that Cameroon had not established the facts and accordingly rejected its submissions on that point (Judgment, paragraph 322).

8.3. DISPUTES ALSO BEFORE THE SECURITY COUNCIL

The first case to be simultaneously before the Court and the Security Council was the *Aegean Sea Continental Shelf* case. On 10 August 1976 Greece filed an application introducing proceedings in the Court, at the same time requesting provisional measures. Later (Hague time) Greece in New York brought the matter before the Security Council, which adopted resolution 395 (1976), 25 August 1976. In that resolution the Security Council

> 4. *Invites* the Governments of Greece and Turkey . . . to take into account the contribution that appropriate judicial means, in particular the International Court of Justice, are qualified to make to the settlement of any remaining legal differences which they may identify in connexion with their present dispute.

For its part, the Court, in its Order of 11 September 1986 declining to indicate provisional measures recalled the proceedings in the Security Council and continued:

> 41. Whereas both Greece and Turkey, as Members of the United Nations, have expressly recognized the responsibility of the Security Council for the maintenance of international peace and security; whereas in the . . . resolution, the Security Council has recalled to them their obligations under the United Nations Charter with regard to the peaceful settlement of disputes . . . ; whereas, furthermore, as the Court has already stated these obligations are clearly imperative in regard to their present dispute concerning the continental shelf in the Aegean; and whereas it is not to be presumed that either State will fail to heed its obligations under the Charter of the United Nations or fail to heed the recommendations of the Security Council addressed to them with respect to their present dispute[.][18]

That was the first contentious dispute simultaneously on the active agenda of both the Court and the Security Council in which the Court was asked to indicate provisional measures of protection. It is also the starting point of the movement—for the moment mostly confined to the academic world although references to it are found in opinions in the Court—to introduce some sort of judicial review of the actions of the Security Council, especially those taken under Chapter VII of the Charter. That aspect is not our concern here. The handling by both organs of this dispute is also the starting point of a new

[18] ICJ Rep. 1976, 3, 13 (para. 41).

political process deliberately designed to implicate both those organs. We will trace the development of that new process in the next set of cases to be examined.

The Court has also been faced with disputes with which the Security Council had been dealing and before the Court was seised of the dispute had adopted resolutions, under either Chapter VI or Chapter VII of the Charter. The general principle governing this type of case was established in the combined action of the Security Council and the Court in connection with the U.S. diplomatic staff held hostage in the American Embassy in Tehran. Although the United States had informed the Security Council of the problem as far back as 9 November 1979, on 25 November the Secretary-General first requested a meeting of the Security Council, which adopted its initial resolution 457 (1979) on 4 December 1979. On 29 November, the United States filed an application instituting the proceedings in the ICJ at the same time requesting provisional measures. In that resolution the Security Council did not mention the proceedings in the Court. However, in the Order indicating provisional measures of 13 December 1979, the Court included the following sentence:

> whereas the Court notes in this regard that the Secretary-General of the United Nations has indeed referred to these occurrences as 'a grave situation' posing 'a serious threat to international peace and security' and that the Security Council in resolution 457 (1979) expressed itself as deeply concerned at the dangerous level of tension between the two States, which could have grave consequences for international peace and security[.][19]

That was followed by a further meeting of the Security Council on 31 December 1979, which adopted resolution 461 (1979). Here the Security Council took note of the Court's order indicating provisional measures, and went on to deplore the continued detention of the hostages contrary to its earlier resolution 'and the Order of the International Court of Justice of 15 December 1979'.

The Court expounded the legal side of this incident in the two phases of the *U.S. Diplomatic and Consular Staff in Tehran* case. In the Order indicating provisional measures, the Court stated that there is no provision of the Statute or Rules contemplating that it should decline to take cognizance of one aspect of a dispute merely because that dispute had other aspects, however important.[20] In its Judgment on the merits the Court referred to later proceedings in the Security Council and went on:

> and it does not seem to have occurred to any member of the Council that there was or could be anything irregular in the simultaneous exercise of their respective functions

[19] ICJ Rep. 1979, 3, 15 (para. 23). For a fuller account of this incident in the Security Council, *see* 33 *Yearbook of the United Nations* 1979 307 (New York: United Nations Sales No. E. 82.1.1.).

[20] ICJ Rep. 1979, at 15 (para. 24).

> by the Court and the Security Council. Nor is there in this any cause for surprise. Whereas Article 12 of the Charter expressly forbids the General Assembly to make any recommendation with regard to a dispute or situation while the Security Council is exercising its functions in respect of that dispute or situation, no such restriction is placed on the functioning of the Court by any provision of either the Charter or the Statute of the Court. The reasons are clear. It is for the Court, the principal judicial organ of the United Nations, to resolve any legal questions that may be in issue between parties to a dispute; and the resolution of such legal questions by the Court may be an important, and sometimes decisive, factor in promoting the peaceful settlement of the dispute. This is indeed recognized by Article 36 of the Charter . . . [.][21]

This has been complemented by the following major statement of principle in the *Military and Paramilitary Activities in and against Nicaragua* (Jurisdiction and Admissibility) case:

> The Charter . . . does not confer *exclusive* responsibility upon the Security Council for this purpose [the Court had referred to Article 24 of the Charter which confers on the Security Council *primary* responsibility for the maintenance of international peace and security]. While in Article 12 there is a provision for a clear demarcation of functions between the General Assembly and the Security Council, in respect of any dispute or situation, that the former should not make any recommendation with regard to that dispute or situation unless the Security Council so requires, there is no similar provision anywhere in the Charter with respect to the Security Council and the Court. The Council has functions of a political nature assigned to it, whereas the Court exercises purely judicial functions. Both organs can therefore perform their separate but complementary functions with respect to the same events[.][22]

The Court reached its logical conclusion in that case, when it said:

> The [Security] Council has functions of a political nature assigned to it, whereas the Court exercises purely judicial functions. Both organs can therefore perform their separate but complementary functions with respect to the same events[.][23]

Something similar occurred in the 3199th meeting of the Security Council on 16 April 1993, when the Security Council was dealing with items relating to the situation in the former Yugoslavia. Here, on the initiative of the applicant in the Court proceedings, the Security Council adopted resolution 819 (1993), 16 April 1993, which picked out one of the three operative clauses

[21] ICJ Rep. 1980, at 21 (para. 40); *Military and Paramilitary Activities in and against Nicaragua* (Jurisdiction and Admissibility) case, ICJ Rep. 1984, 433 (para. 93).

[22] *Military and Paramilitary Activities in and against Nicaragua* (Jurisdiction and Admissibility) case, ICJ Rep. 1984, 397, 434 (para. 95); *Application of the Genocide Convention* (Provisional Measures) case, ICJ Rep. 1993, 3, 19 (para. 33); *Armed Activities on the Territory of the Congo* (Uganda) (Provisional Measures) case, ICJ Rep. 2000, 111, 126 (para. 36). *See also* Ch. 7 n. 85.

[23] ICJ Rep. 1984 at 435 (para. 95).

of the first order indicating provisional measures in the *Application of the Genocide Convention* case.[24]

In connection with the tension between Cameroon and Nigeria which preceded Nigeria's request for the indication of provisional measures, both parties had brought the matter before the Security Council. The Security Council welcomed the fact that the dispute had been referred to the Court and adopted some other decisions aiming at reducing the tension. After the Court had issued its Order, the Security Council requested the Secretary-General to continue to keep it informed of the measures he was able to take to monitor the situation in the disputed area, 'bearing in mind the Court's Order on provisional measures on the matter issued on 15 March 1996'.[25] Shortly before the Judgment on the merits was delivered the Secretary-General invited the two Presidents to meet him. Following that meeting both Presidents agreed to respect and implement the anticipated decision of the Court and to establish an implementation mechanism, with the support of the United Nations.[26] In a statement to the press after delivery of that Judgment, the President (Guillaume) concluded with the following:

9. I would add that the Court was happy to learn that the Heads of State of Cameroon and Nigeria had met on 3 September last in the presence of the United Nations Secretary-General. It welcomes the result of that meeting and hopes that the Judgment which it has delivered today will contribute to friendly relations between the two brother countries.[27]

This is an important illustration of co-operation between three principal organs of the United Nations—the Security Council, the International

[24] The original request of Bosnia and Herzegovina invoked both Art. 94 and Ch. VII of the Charter. The matter was settled in informal consultations, and there is no explanation on the record why the Security Council did not refer to the whole of the Order. The Security Council's resolution 819 (1993) is based on Ch. VII only. 48 SCOR S/PV.3199, 16 April 1993 and doc. S/25616, 48 SCOR Sup. April, May, June 1993 70. That followed on a communication from Bosnia and Herzegovina. For the official transmission of the Order to the Security Council, *see* doc. S/25686, 29 April 1996 (mimeo). There is no record of any discussion in the Security Council of the second Order of 1993 in that case.

[25] *See Land and Maritime Frontier between Cameroon and Nigeria* (Provisional Measures) case, ICJ Rep. 1996, 13, 23 (para. 45). For the initial approach to and decision of the Security Council, *see* in the dissenting opinion of Judge ad hoc Ajibola at 42. For the later statements of the Security Council, *see* docs. S/1996/150, 29 February 1996 and S/1996/391, 29 May 1996, *Resolutions and Decisions of the Security Council 1996*, 51 SCOR (S/INF/52) 91 (1996). Following the Judgment, further meetings took place and on 15 November 2003 the parties asked the Secretary-General to establish a Mixed Commission of Cameroon, Nigeria, and the United Nations, to consider ways of following up the Court's decision and moving the process forward. The Secretary-General appointed his Special Representative for West Africa to chair this commission, which at the time of writing has not completed its work.

[26] UN Press Release SECRETARY-GENERAL/SM/8638—AFR/476, 5 September 2002. For further details *see* the Report of the Secretary-General on the work of the Organization, 58 GAOR Sup. No. 1, para. 29 and above, Ch. 7 n. 97.

[27] ICJ, Statement of the President of the Court, 10 October 2002, available on the Court's website.

Court of Justice, and the Secretary-General—for the maintenance of international peace. At the same time it indicates recognition by the Court of the relativity of its judgments, compliance with which is obligatory on the parties. It is well established that the parties are free to negotiate how a judgment will be implemented. It remains to be seen whether the same flexibility will develop in relation to an order indicating provisional measures, which like a judgment imposes obligations on the parties.

All this notwithstanding, the provisions of Article 27 of the Charter regarding the majority required for any decision of the Security Council and the composition of that majority, meaning that none of the Permanent Members of the Council has cast a negative vote, introduces a major political element into the working of the Security Council and in a specific case may prevent it from taking effective action to secure compliance with an order indicating or prescribing provisional measures.

The *Armed Activities in the Territory of the Congo* (Uganda) (Provisional Measures) case is of no less importance.[28] This case, one of three filed in 1999 by the Congo against its neighbours Burundi, Rwanda, and Uganda, was connected with the disturbed situation in that part of Africa.[29] That situation had engaged the attention of the Security Council which adopted resolution 1304 (2000), 16 June 2000, under Chapter VII of the Charter. In its Order of 1 July 2000 the Court noted Uganda's contention that the request for provisional measures concerned essentially the same issues as the resolution and was accordingly inadmissible and moot. However, the Court found that neither the resolution nor the measures taken in its implementation precluded the Court from acting in accordance with its Statute and Rules (paragraph 36). The Court also stated that it was not precluded from indicating provisional measures in a case merely because a State which has simultaneously brought a number of similar cases before the Court seeks provisional measures in only one of them (paragraph 38). The Court in stronger terms refined its approach to the rights entitled to protection in a case of this character:

> 40. Whereas the rights which, according to the Congo's Application, are the subject of the dispute are essentially its rights to sovereignty and territorial integrity and to the integrity of its assets and natural resources, and its rights to respect for the rules of international humanitarian law and for the instruments relating to the protection of human rights; and whereas it is upon the rights thus claimed that the Court must focus its attention in its consideration of this request for the indication of provisional measures[.][30]

[28] *Armed Activities on the Territory of the Congo* (Provisional Measures) case, ICJ Rep. 2000, 111. *See further* on this aspect in § 5.2 n. 13.

[29] ICJ Rep. 1999 (II), 1018 (Burundi); ibid. 1023 (Uganda); ibid. 1025 (Rwanda). The cases against Burundi and Rwanda were discontinued. ICJ Rep. 2001, 3, 6. A new application was filed against Rwanda in 2002. ICJ Rep. 2002, 299. *See further* Ch. 4 n. 117.

[30] ICJ Rep. 2000, 111, 127.

The Court found that fighting had taken place and had caused a large number of civilian casualties in addition to substantial material damage, that the humanitarian situation remained of profound concern, and that repeated violations of human rights and international humanitarian law, including massacres and other atrocities, had been committed on Congolese territory. The Court went on to express its opinion that persons, assets, and resources present on Congolese territory, particularly in the area of conflict, 'remain extremely vulnerable', that there was a serious risk that the rights at issue as noted in paragraph 40 might suffer irreparable damage and that provisional measures must be indicated as a matter of urgency to protect those rights.[31] It accordingly indicated a series of measures, including compliance with Security Council resolution 1304, which both parties 'must' [*doivent*] take—the first occasion in which the Court has used the word 'must' in the English text of an order indicating provisional measures. The Order contains more than the resolution of the Security Council, the additions relating to the requirements of Article 41 of the Statute concerning the litigation pending in the Court. However, following precedents, the Court also included a general provision requiring the parties to take all measures to ensure full respect within the zone of conflict for fundamental human rights and for the applicable provisions of humanitarian law.

The incidents described here show that the two organs can perform their functions simultaneously without either trespassing on the prerogatives and functions of the other.

8.4. PROVISIONAL MEASURES, HUMAN RIGHTS, AND HUMANITARIAN LAW

In addition to the legal considerations addressing directly the substance of the request for provisional measures, the Court devoted paragraphs 38 to 44 of its Order in the *U.S. Diplomatic and Consular Staff in Tehran* case to a series of general pronouncements on the significance of personal inviolability in diplomatic and consular relations between States. While no State is under any obligation to maintain diplomatic or consular relations with another, yet a State cannot fail to recognize the imperative obligations inherent in those relations, codified in the Vienna Conventions of 1961 and 1963. The Court also expressed concern at the exposure of human beings to privation, hardship, anguish and even danger to life and health, and it referred to the 1973 Convention on the Prevention and Punishment of Crimes against

[31] Ibid. 128 (para. 43). For the refusal of the Court to follow those two cases, on the ground that in the circumstances of the case there was no need for the indication of provisional measures, see *Certain Criminal Proceedings in France* (Provisional Measures) case, ICJ Rep. 2003, 102, 111 (para. 39).

Internationally Protected Persons including diplomatic agents.[32] That was the first time that the Court had used an order indicating provisional measures as the vehicle for a general pronouncement about basic legal issues raised in the case and to demonstrate direct concern with the welfare of human beings. The inclusion of the protection of human life in an order indicating provisional measures in this type of case is an important and timely innovation. It reflects the importance that the Charter gives to the promotion and protection of human rights, and in so acting the Court appears not merely as the principal judicial organ of the United Nations but also as one of its principal organs established in Article 7 of the Charter.

The Court demonstrated its concern with observance of human rights in one case in which it did not have prima facie jurisdiction to indicate any provisional measures, the *Armed Activities on the Territory of the Congo (New Application: 2000)* (Rwanda) (Provisional Measures) case.[33] It concluded its Order rejecting the request for provisional measures with the statement stressing the necessity for the parties to those proceedings to use their influence to prevent the repeated grave violations of human rights and international humanitarian law which had been observed even recently (paragraph 93).

8.5. CAPITAL PUNISHMENT CASES

Cases in the ICJ involving urgent requests for provisional measures to prevent the carrying out of the death penalty on convicted persons are in a class of their own—these are the cases brought by Paraguay (*Breard*), Germany (*LaGrand*), and Mexico *(Avena and other Mexican Nationals*) against the United States.[34] Technically, all those cases were disputes concerning the interpretation or application of Article 36 of the Vienna Convention on Consular Relations of 1963, the provision dealing with the detaining State's obligations to inform the detainee of his/her right to consular assistance and to inform the consular official of a foreign State in the event of the detention of a national of that State.[35] The dispute over

[32] 1035 UNTS 167.

[33] ICJ Rep. 2002, 219.

[34] *Vienna Convention on Consular Relations*, ICJ Rep. 1998, 248 (Provisional Measures), ibid. 526 (Discontinuance); *LaGrand*, ICJ Rep. 1999, 9 (Provisional Measures), ibid. 2001, 466 (Merits); *Avena and other Mexican Nationals*, ICJ Rep. 2003, 77 (Provisional Measures), ibid. 2004, 31 March (Merits).

[35] For the Vienna Convention, *see* 596 UNTS 261. In each of these cases jurisdiction was based on the Optional Protocol concerning the compulsory settlement of disputes, ibid. 487. The issue had also been the subject of an advisory opinion of the Inter-American Court of Human Rights, *The Right to Information on Consular Assistance in the Framework of Guarantees of the Due Process of Law*, OC.16/99, Ser. A No. 16 (1 October 1999). For my critical views on that advisory opinion, *see* Sh. Rosenne, *The Perplexities of Modern International Law* 103 (Leiden:

the interpretation of the Consular Convention was a peg on which to hang an attempt to have the ICJ pronounce itself on the legality of the death sentence in modern international law, and this introduced into the cases an important non-juridical factor which the Court was able to resist.

The *Vienna Convention on Consular Relations* (Provisional Measures) case (otherwise known as the *Breard* case) was the first of this series. Breard, a Paraguayan national, had been convicted and sentenced to death by a Virginia court and his execution was fixed for 14 April 1998. On 3 April Paraguay filed an application alleging breach of Article 36 of the Vienna Convention on Consular Relations. At the same time Paraguay filed a request for provisional measures, the most important of which was for a stay of execution pending the disposition of the case. Hearings were held on 7 April and on 9 April the Court issued its Order in which it indicated as provisional measures that the United States should take all measures at its disposal to ensure that Breard was not executed pending the final decision in the case, and should inform the Court of all measures which it has taken in implementation of the Order. The Court also decided to remain seised of the matters which formed the subject-matter of the Order. In the Order, the Court cited Article 75 of the Rules among the provisions on which it based its action, but without drawing any conclusions relating to any of the three paragraphs of that Article.[36] Despite the intervention of the Federal Government, the Governor of Virginia refused to grant a stay. Later Paraguay discontinued the proceedings. Although the dispute as presented to the Court concerned the interpretation and application of a treaty and the appropriate remedies should breach of the treaty be established, a human life was at stake, and Article 75 could justify the very speedy action by the Court in the circumstances.

In the *LaGrand* (Provisional Measures) case, the execution of a convicted German national in the state of Arizona was set for 3 March 1999. At 7:30 p.m. (Hague time) on 2 March, Germany filed an application instituting proceedings and a request for provisional measures. The case raised the same legal issues of the interpretation and application of the Consular Relations Convention, and the appropriate remedies should a breach be established. The principal provisional measure requested was, as in *Breard,* that the United States should take all measures at its disposal to ensure that LaGrand not be executed pending the final decision, and should inform the Court of all measures which it has taken in implementation of the Order. Germany asked the Court to treat its request as a matter of the greatest urgency, relying on various provisions, including Article 75 of the Rules. This

Martinus Nijhoff, 2004). The abolition of the death penalty is the subject of the second optional protocol to the International Covenant on Civil and Political Rights of 13 December 1985, UNTS No. 14668.

[36] ICJ Rep. 1998, 248.

presented the Court with the opportunity to give its interpretation of Article 75, paragraph 1, of the Rules.[37] In paragraph 26 of the Order the Court found that the circumstances required it to indicate as a matter of the greatest urgency, and without any other proceedings, provisional measures in accordance with Article 41 of the Statute and with Article 75, paragraph 1, of the Rules.[38] As in the previous case, although the suit concerned a number of technical legal questions, a human life was at stake, and that was the justification for the invocation of Article 75, paragraph 1, of the Rules. Here the Court tried to extend the reach of the Order, by requiring the Federal Government of the United States to 'transmit the Order to the Governor of the State of Arizona'. The Federal Government did this, but the Governor of Arizona declined to grant a stay.[39]

In the *Avena and other Mexican Nationals* (Provisional Measures) case, the application filed on 9 January 2003 referred to fifty-four convicted Mexican nationals (later amended to fifty-two persons), all sentenced to death in ten different states of the Union. In this case the principal claim related not so much to the interpretation and application of Article 36 of the Convention on Consular Relations as to the appropriate remedy, Mexico considering that *LaGrand* and the undertakings given by the United States in connection with that case not to be sufficient. The request for provisional measures in terms referred generally to all those persons except for three whose sentences the Governor of Louisiana had meanwhile commuted. It also referred specifically to three persons, whose execution was imminent, the earliest being set for 14 February 2003, and the others anticipated for various dates during that year. The principal provisional measure requested was that the United States should take all measures necessary to ensure that no Mexican national be executed pending final judgment in the case. The request cited Article 75 of the Rules.

The Court's examination of the facts led it to the conclusion that three of the persons named in the application were in danger of execution in the coming months or even weeks, and it limited its Order to those three persons.[40] At the same time it indicated that it might, if appropriate, indicate provisional measures under Article 41 of the Statute in respect of those other individuals before it rendered final judgment in the case. The operative clause of the Order consequently referred by name to those three individuals, and otherwise followed the previous cases. Here too, the Court gave no interpretation of Article 75 of the Rules, but the Order seems to imply that the Court has reserved the right to act *proprio motu* should it find that the circumstances so warrant.

[37] *LaGrand* (Provisional Measures) case, ICJ Rep. 1999, 9, 14 (para. 21) *and see* Ch. 7 at n. 66.
[38] Ibid. at 15 (para. 26)
[39] For the Court's views on this, *see* Ch. 7 text to n. 77.
[40] ICJ Rep. 2003, 77. For the time-limits on the merits, *see* ibid. 96, 99.

8.6. PROVISIONAL MEASURES FOR THE PROTECTION OF RIGHTS

We should now try and see if the established jurisprudence of the International Court makes it possible to systematize the types of case in which the Court would be inclined to indicate provisional measures, on the assumption that the conditions of jurisdiction and urgency are met, and those in which it is not so inclined.

A basic principle on this issue was laid down in the first provisional measures case to come before the Permanent Court—the *Denunciation of the Treaty of November 2nd, 1895, between China and Belgium* case.[41] In his first Order of 8 January 1927 the President of the Court (Huber), acting alone on the basis of Article 57 of the Rules of Court then in force, after stating the principle that the object of the interim protection contemplated by the Statute is to preserve the respective rights of the parties pending the Court's decision, proceeded to analyse the rights in question in that case. He found that the rights were those reserved to Belgium and to Belgian nationals in China by the Treaty. He went on to explain that as, in the event of an infraction of certain of the rights which Belgium or Belgian nationals would possess in China if the Treaty were recognized as still operative, 'such infraction could not be made good simply by the payment of an indemnity or by compensation or restitution in some other material form'. The President accordingly indicated

> provisionally, pending the final decision of the Court . . . by which decision the Court will either declare itself to have no jurisdiction or give judgment on the merits—and subject to any modification which it may subsequently be considered desirable to make in the present Order . . . .[42]

The Order went on to indicate a series of provisional measures, applicable as regards Belgian nationals, as regards property and shipping, and as regards judicial safeguards. On 15 February 1927 the President, following an agreement between the parties, declared that the previous Order ceased to be operative.[43] He found that the new agreement between the parties would provisionally take the place of the 1865 Treaty which would cease to be operative as regards the rights set out in the provisional measures Order,

> which could not, therefore, no matter what the tenor of the Court's final judgment may be, serve as a basis for any claim enforceable at law and put forward on the ground of some violation of these rights during the period for which the new régime agreed upon between the Parties might be applicable.

[41] PCIJ Ser. A 8 (1927), also Ser. A 9, 12 (1927). For that Treaty, *see* 131 CTS 373.
[42] Ser. A 8 (1927) at 7.
[43] Ibid. at 10.

The Order continued that a unilateral declaration by the Belgian Government to the same effect, which should be regarded as a modification of Belgium's original submissions, would suffice, if it were accepted by the Court, to produce the same result. The new fact brought to the knowledge of the Court had removed the circumstances which required the indication of provisional measures in the previous Order. There were no other circumstances independent of the legal situation created by the parties resulting either from agreements concluded between them or from unilateral declarations in regard to matters concerning which they might use their discretion, which would point to the indication of provisional measures 'in the interests of the procedure alone'. Then comes another major statement of principle:

> measures of protection, indicated by the Court as being for purely legal reasons rendered necessary by circumstances, cannot be dependent, as regards their applicability, upon the position of negotiations that may be in progress between the Parties; that, consequently, the Order of January 8th, 1927 indicating provisional measures can, if revoked, only be so finally and in its entirety[.][44]

The only instance since 1927 of the request for provisional measures being withdrawn to facilitate negotiations between the parties was the *Border and Transborder Armed Actions* (Provisional Measures) (Nicaragua *v* Honduras) case, where the request was withdrawn before any proceedings on it had taken place.[45]

The two *Fisheries Jurisdiction* cases brought in 1972 by the Federal Republic of Germany and by the United Kingdom against Iceland furnish another instance in a dispute which concerned a country's natural resources (the *Anglo-Iranian Oil Co.* case was the first in this category). Iceland took no part in these proceedings. For the two Judgments, on the jurisdiction of the Court and on the merits, this brought Article 53 of the Statute into play, but not for the phases of provisional measures. These cases, following the *Anglo-Iranian Oil Co.*, are important for developing the concept of prima facie jurisdiction in the absence of an appearance by the respondent. As to their substance, the timing of these cases was important. They came at a critical moment in the development of the law of the sea, and at the commencement of the serious decline in the cod fisheries of the northern hemisphere. Preparations for the Third United Nations Conference on the Law of the Sea were nearly completed, and it was clear that one of the principal and controversial issues for that Conference would be coastal State rights to the living resources of the sea beyond the outer limits of the territorial sea. The object of the applications was to test the legality of Icelandic fisheries regulations said to contradict undertakings given to each of the applicant Governments.

[44] Ibid. 11.
[45] ICJ Rep. 1988, 9.

The Court had no difficulty in finding that the immediate application by Iceland of its regulations would, by anticipating the Court's judgment, prejudice the rights claimed by the applicants and affect the possibility of their full restoration in the event of a judgment in their favour. At the same time it was necessary to bear in mind Iceland's exceptional dependency upon coastal fisheries for its livelihood and economic development and that from this point of view account must be taken of the need for the conservation of fish stocks in the Iceland area.

The provisional measures in these cases were complicated. To achieve the balance that the Court had indicated they were partly addressed to both parties and partly to one or other of the parties only. All parties were to ensure that no action of any kind was to be taken which might aggravate or extend the dispute and should ensure that no action was taken which might prejudice the rights of the other party in respect of the carrying out of whatever decision on the merits that the Court might render. Iceland was to refrain from taking any measures to enforce its regulations against vessels registered in the applicant States and engaged in fishing activities in the waters around Iceland outside the 12-mile fishery zone, and should also refrain from applying administrative, judicial, or other measures against ships registered in the applicant States, their crews or other related persons, because of their having engaged in fishing activities in the waters around Iceland outside the 12-mile fishery zone. The applicants, for their part, were to ensure that vessels of their registry would not take an annual catch of more than a defined quantity from the Sea Area of Iceland as defined by the International Council for the Exploration of the Sea and were to furnish Iceland and the Registry of the Court with all relevant information, orders issued, and arrangements made concerning the control and regulation of fish catches in the area. Unless the Court in the meantime should have delivered its final judgment, it should, at an appropriate time before one year from the date of the Order, review the matter at the request of either party in order to decide whether those measures should continue or need to be modified or revoked.[46] The Court upheld its jurisdiction to deal with the merits in judgments of 2 February 1973, and had no difficulty, at the request of the applicants, in confirming the provisional measures which should remain operative until the Court had given final judgment in the case.[47] In 1974 the Court gave its final Judgments, holding that the impugned Icelandic

[46] ICJ Rep. 1972, 12 (U.K.) and 30 (FRG). Iceland did not participate in these proceedings, but sent several communications to the Court. Somewhat inconsistently, however, the Court immediately decided that in the circumstances it was necessary to resolve first of all the question of the Court's jurisdiction, and it fixed time-limits for the written proceedings addressed to that question, the applicants to plead first. Ibid., 181 and 188. These cases were heard under the Rules of 1946.

[47] ICJ Rep. 1972, 3 and 49 (jurisdiction); 302 and 313 (continuance of provisional measures).

regulations were not opposable to the applicant, but not otherwise deciding on their compatibility with international law.[48]

In the two *Nuclear Tests* cases against France, Australia asked the Court to declare that the carrying out of further atmospheric nuclear weapons tests in the South Pacific Ocean was not consistent with the applicable rules of international law, and to order France not to carry out any further such tests. New Zealand requested the Court to declare that the conduct by the French Government of nuclear tests in the South Pacific region that gave rise to radioactive fallout constituted a violation of New Zealand's rights under international law, and that those rights would be violated by any further such tests. France completely rejected the jurisdiction of the Court. It did not regard itself as a party to the cases at that stage and did not appear in any of the proceedings. Both the essential elements of the claims together with the attitude of France, a permanent member of the Security Council, posed delicate problems for the Court.[49]

After establishing its prima facie jurisdiction in each case, the Court proceeded to examine the requests for provisional measures. The Court once again interpreted Article 41 of the Statute as having as its object to preserve the respective rights of the Parties pending the decision of the Court, and as presupposing that irreparable prejudice should not be caused to rights which were the subject of dispute in judicial proceedings and that the Court's judgment should not be anticipated by reason of any initiative regarding the matters in issue before the Court.[50] The Court went on to explain that by the terms of Article 41 it may indicate interim measures 'only when it considers that circumstances so require in order to preserve the rights of either party'. From that point of departure the Court found in the applicants' allegations substance to the contention that there was an immediate possibility of a further atmospheric nuclear test being carried out by France in the Pacific, and that for the purpose of the present proceedings the information submitted to the Court did not exclude the possibility that damage to each applicant might be shown to be caused by the deposit on their territory of radioactive fallout resulting from such tests and to be irreparable. In light of those considerations 'the Court was satisfied that it should indicate interim measures of protection in order to preserve the right claimed by Australia/New

[48] ICJ Rep. 1974, 3, 175. This litigation was a major factor in the negotiations regarding the exclusive economic zone in the Third UN Conference on the Law of the Sea.

[49] ICJ Rep. 1973, 99 at 105 (para. 31) and 135 at 141 (para. 31). In 1974, following some unilateral undertakings by France *dehors* the Court, the Court found that the cases had become moot and that the claims no longer had any object, so that it was not called upon to give any decision on them. At the same time it declared that the provisional measures ceased to be operative and lapsed. Ibid. 1974, 253, 457. For an unsuccessful attempt by New Zealand to reopen the case in respect of other nuclear tests in the area, *see* the *Request for an Examination of the Situation in accordance with paragraph 63 of the Court's Judgment of 20 December 1974 in the* Nuclear Tests case, ICJ Rep. 1995, 288. These cases were all heard under the Rules of 1972.

[50] ICJ Rep. 1973, 99 at 103 (para. 20), 135 at 139 (para. 21).

Zealand in the present litigation in respect of the deposit of radioactive fallout on their territory but not in respect of other rights claimed by the applicants'.[51]

Here the purpose of the provisional measures was not to preserve any *status quo* or a specific object, but the applicants' claimed rights, concerning which at the time international law had no clear rule. This is an important extension of the purpose for which provisional measures can be claimed.

8.7. REFUSALS TO GRANT PROVISIONAL MEASURES

The refusal of the Permanent Court to indicate provisional measures when the request was interpreted as designed to obtain an interim judgment in favour of part of a claim for financial compensation on which the Court had not yet adjudicated is mentioned above.[52]

In the *Prince von Pless Administration* (Provisional Measures) case, after some preliminary objections had been joined to the merits a request for the indication of provisional measures was filed. On receipt of the notification from the Registry, the respondent (Poland) announced the annulment of the impugned action, and that was accepted by Germany. The Court then found that the grounds for Germany's request for provisional measures no longer existed. Since the request ceased to have any object, it was unnecessary for the Court to consider whether it would have been competent to adjudicate upon it or whether the request was admissible. This was without prejudice to the question of the Court's jurisdiction over the application instituting the proceedings or the admissibility of that application. The Court accordingly took note of the various declarations and declared that the request for the indication of provisional measures had ceased to have any object.[53]

The *Polish Agrarian Reform and the German Minority* (Provisional Measures) case, the last of the cases between Germany and Poland arising out of the 1919 Peace Settlement and the situation of the German Minority that remained in the new Poland (a series of disputes that occupied a prominent place on the agenda of the Permanent Court), the subject of the dispute as expressed in the application instituting the proceedings was in somewhat general terms, the claim being for a declaration that 'violations of the Treaty of June 28th, 1919, have been committed to the detriment of Polish nationals of German race and to order reparation to be made'. The provisional measures were requested in order to preserve the *status quo* until the Court has delivered final judgment in the case. The Court found after the hearing

[51] Ibid. 105 (para. 30), 141 (para. 31).

[52] *See* text to n. 5.

[53] PCIJ Ser. A/B 54 (1933). Later in the year the case was withdrawn. PCIJ Ser. A/B 59 (1933). This coincided with nazi Germany's withdrawal from the League of Nations.

that while the original application instituting the proceedings referred to named individuals, the requested provisional measures would result in a general suspension of the impugned actions as far as concerns Polish nationals of German race, 'and cannot therefore be regarded as solely designed to protect the subject of the dispute and the actual object of the principal claim as submitted to the Court by the Application instituting proceedings'. The Court explained that according to Article 41,

> the essential condition which must necessarily be fulfilled in order to justify a request for the indication of interim measures should circumstances require them, is that such measures should have the effect of protecting the rights forming the subject of the dispute submitted to the Court[.]

In the circumstances the Court, without considering the scope of the treaty provision that had been invoked and irrespective of the question whether it might be expedient for the Court in other cases to exercise its power to act *proprio motu*, and without in any way prejudging the question of its own jurisdiction to adjudicate upon the application or its admissibility, 'confines itself to the statement that the request for interim measures is not in conformity with the provisions of Article 41 of its Statute'. It accordingly dismissed the request.[54]

Those decisions of the Permanent Court formed the jurisprudential basis for the more developed activities of the International Court of Justice in connection with provisional measures.

The *Interhandel* (Interim Protection) case was the first in which the ICJ declined to indicate provisional measures. Switzerland included three points in its request, but the Court found that only one was formulated in terms fulfilling the requirement of Article 41, 'and which relates to the concern of the Court to preserve the rights which may subsequently be adjudged by the Court to belong either to the Applicant or to the Respondent'. Accordingly, the Court had to direct its attention to that one point, which related to a request by the Government of the United States to sell some shares claimed to be property of Swiss nationals so long as the proceedings in the dispute were pending. On that issue, the Court found, in the light of information furnished to it, that such sale could only be effected after termination of a judicial proceeding which was pending in the American courts, and that the U.S. Government was not taking action at the present time to fix a schedule for the sale of the shares. In the premises it did not appear to the Court that the circumstances required the indication of the requested provisional

[54] PCIJ Ser. A/B 58 (1933). There were dissenting opinions by Judges Baron Rolin-Jacquemyns and Anzilotti, and jointly by Schücking and van Eysinga—the first instance of dissenting opinions in an Order on provisional measures. As in the previous case, Germany withdrew the case later in the year. PCIJ Ser. A/B 60 (1933).

measures, and it accordingly found that there was no need to indicate any interim measures of protection.[55]

The *Aegean Sea Continental Shelf* (Provisional Measures) case, in which the respondent chose not to appear, also concerned rights.[56] Turkey's grant of permits to the Turkish State Petroleum Company for exploration for petroleum in areas in the Aegean claimed by Greece, in particular seismic research activities, were claimed to be an infringement of Greece's sovereign rights in the areas concerned. There was no claim that this form of seismic research involved any risk of physical damage to the seabed or subsoil or to their natural resources. The contemporary proceedings in the Security Council produced a complicated situation for the Court. The dispute submitted to the Court concerned the delimitation of the continental shelf between Greece and Turkey in the Aegean Sea. The request for provisional measures asked the Court to direct each Government unless with the consent of the other to refrain from all exploration activity or any scientific research, with respect to the continental shelf areas within which Turkey had granted such licences or permits or adjacent to the Islands, or otherwise in dispute in the present case, and to refrain from further military measures or actions which might endanger the peaceful relations between the two countries. The Court's finding from the evidence on this part of the case has been set out above.[57]

On the second part of the request, relating to further military measures or actions, the Court explained that before it could entertain that request it would have to determine whether, under Article 41 of the Statute, it had such an independent power to indicate interim measures having that object (paragraph 36). However, in light of the simultaneous proceedings in the Security Council and resolution 395 (1976), the Court did not find it necessary to examine whether Article 41 confers upon it the power to indicate interim measures for the sole purpose of preventing the aggravation or extension of the dispute (paragraph 42). The Court recalled to the parties their obligations under the Charter and found that the circumstances as they then presented themselves were not such as to require the exercise of the power under Article 41 to indicate interim measures of protection.

The application in the *Arbitral Award of 31 July 1989* (Provisional Measures) case related to a dispute concerning the existence and validity of the arbitral award of that date by the Arbitral Tribunal for the Determination of the Maritime Boundary between the two States.[58] Guinea-Bissau challenged

[55] ICJ Rep. 1957, 105. The Court later found that the claim was inadmissible. Ibid. 1959, 6.

[56] ICJ Rep. 1976, 3. Later the Court decided that it was without jurisdiction to entertain the application in this case. Ibid. 1978, 3. For the parallel proceedings in the Security Council, *see* text to n. 18.

[57] *See* Ch. 4 text to n. 4.

[58] ICJ Rep. 1990, 64. The Judgment on the merits of this case found that the Arbitral Award was final and binding for the two parties, which have the obligation to apply it. Ibid. 1991, 53. For the Arbitral Award, *see* 19 UNRIAA 149.

the validity of the Award for reasons not relevant here, and requested provisional measures in order to safeguard the rights of each of the parties that they should abstain in the disputed area from any act or action of any kind whatever, during the whole duration of the proceedings until the decision was given by the Court. Senegal participated in the proceedings in both phases of this case. In its Order the Court explained that the purpose of exercising its power to protect rights which are the subject of a dispute before it is such that they would no longer be required once the dispute over those rights was resolved by the Judgment on the merits (paragraph 24). Guinea-Bissau recognized in its application that the dispute of which it had seised the Court was not the dispute over maritime delimitation that had been brought before the Arbitral Tribunal, but a new dispute. The Court explained that the application asked it to pass upon the existence and validity of the Award but not on the respective rights of the parties in the maritime areas in question, so that the alleged rights sought to be made the subject of provisional measures were not the subject of the proceedings on the merits of the case, and no such measures could be subsumed by the Judgment on the merits (paragraph 26). Furthermore,

> 27. Whereas moreover a decision of the Court that the award is inexistent or null and void would in no way entail any decision that the Applicant's claims in respect of the disputed maritime delimitation are well founded, in whole or in part; and whereas the dispute over those claims will therefore not be resolved by the Court's judgment[.][59]

The Court accordingly dismissed the request for the indication of provisional measures.

The application in the *Passage through the Great Belt* (Provisional Measures) case related to a dispute between Finland and Denmark arising out of a Danish project to construct a fixed traffic connection for both road and rail traffic across the strait of the Great Belt (Storebælt) which, it was alleged, would close the Baltic for deep-draught vessels of more than 65 metres in height.[60] The provisional measures requested were that Denmark should, pending the decision of the Court, refrain from continuing or otherwise proceeding with those construction works as would impede the passage of ships, including drill ships and oil rigs to and from Finnish ports and shipyards and should refrain from any other action that might prejudice the outcome of the proceedings. The Court noted that Finland's right of passage was not challenged, the dispute being over the nature and extent of that right: 'such a dispute may be protected by the indication of provisional measures under Article 41 of the Statute if the Court "considers that

[59] ICJ Rep. 1990 at 70.

[60] ICJ Rep. 1991, 12. Following the directions given in the Order the parties were able to settle this dispute and the case was later withdrawn. Ibid. 1992, 348.

circumstances so require"'. The Court could not at that interlocutory stage suppose that interference with the right claimed by Finland might be justified on the grounds that the passage to and from the Baltic of drill ships and oil rigs might be achieved by other means, which might be less convenient or more costly. Accordingly, if construction works on the East Channel Bridge which would obstruct the right of passage claimed were expected to be carried out prior to the Court's decision on the merits, that might justify the indication of provisional measures (paragraph 26). However, the Court placed on record assurances given by Denmark that no physical obstruction of the East Channel would occur before the end of 1994, and 'considering that the proceedings on the merits would, in the normal course, be completed before that time', found that it had not been shown that the right claimed would be infringed by the construction work during the pendency of the proceedings (paragraph 27). On the evidence the Court also found that it had not been shown that a decline in orders to Finnish shipyards was attributable to the existence of the Great Belt project. Referring to other Finnish arguments, the Court recalled the *South-Eastern Greenland* (Provisional Measures) case[61] and decided that the circumstances as they then presented themselves were not such as to require the Court to exercise its power under Article 41 of the Statute. At the same time the Court tendered some advice to each party, which assisted them in reaching an agreed solution of the dispute.

It is sometimes said that in giving advice of this nature or in making general statements 'at large' about the legal position in orders on provisional measures the Court is exceeding its functions, which are limited to declaring the law. There is an element of attraction in this idea, although opposition to this has been expressed in the Court.[62] However, the Court is a principal organ of the United Nations and although it has so far never made any pronouncement about that element of its new constitution since 1945, it may undertake any action which furthers the maintenance of international peace and security, the primary purpose of the United Nations. These are not *obiter dicta* in the strict common law sense, but what have been called 'judicial dicta', not part of the *ratio* but relevant to a collateral matter.[63] If its pronouncements lead to the settlement of the dispute outside the Court, the Court has achieved its primary function which, under the revised version of Article 38 of the Statute, is to 'decide in accordance with international law

[61] PCIJ Ser. A/B 48 (1932) at 287.

[62] Note the hesitations of Judge Oda in that case in his separate opinion, at p. 25.

[63] D. M. Walker, *The Oxford Companion to Law* 897 (Oxford: Clarendon Press, 1980). It should not be overlooked that the concept of *obiter dictum* is a common law concept related to the common law doctrine of *stare decisis*, the binding force of a decision of a court of record. That concept is unknown to international law, and there is no clear conception of what the term *obiter dictum* means or can mean in international law, where a judicial pronouncement, whether a judgment, an award, or an order, is a collegial production of the majority of the members of the court or tribunal making the pronouncement.

such disputes as are submitted to it'. ITLOS, whose power to prescribe provisional measures has never been in question, early in its existence decided that this did not preclude it from making recommendations to the parties in an Order prescribing provisional measures. There too opposition was expressed by some members of the Tribunal.[64]

The final case in this series to date is *Certain Criminal Proceedings in France* (Provisional Measures).[65] After finding that there was no urgency in this case, the Court took the opportunity to nail down once and for all a question that had not been fully clarified in its earlier case-law:

> 39. Whereas, independently of the requests for the indication of provisional measures submitted by the parties to preserve specific rights, the Court possesses by virtue of Article 41 of the Statute the power to indicate provisional measures with a view to preventing the aggravation or extension of the dispute whenever it considers that circumstances so require[.]

This is another indication that the Court is integrating itself into the general peace-keeping functions of the United Nations, in its capacity of a principal organ.

8.8. THE INTERNATIONAL TRIBUNAL FOR THE LAW OF THE SEA

All the disputes in ITLOS in which provisional measures were requested were disputes related to the interpretation of the UN Convention on the Law of the Sea—the constituent instrument of ITLOS. They were all initiated in the special circumstance of Article 290, paragraph 5, where the merits were to be decided by arbitration, but the arbitral tribunal had not been constituted when the request for the provisional measures was filed. Only in the first of these cases, the *Saiga No. 2* (Provisional Measures) case, did the parties during the proceedings in ITLOS on that request agree that ITLOS should determine the merits, and the provisional measures proceedings were accordingly redesignated as proceedings under Article 290, paragraph 1.[66] The Tribunal applied the rule of prima facie jurisdiction to establish its jurisdiction to prescribe provisional measures. It prescribed a series of provisional measures, one directed to the respondent in this case, Guinea, and the others addressed to both parties, a common form of an order indicating provisional measures in the International Court of Justice, as well as a recommendation addressed to both parties.[67]

[64] On recommendations in ITLOS, *see* Ch. 2 text to n. 48.

[65] ICJ Rep. 2003, 102. On urgency in this case, *see* Ch. 5 text to n. 16.

[66] ITLOS Rep. 1998, 10 (redesignation), 24 (provisional measures), ibid. 1999, 10 (merits). And *see* R. Wolfrum, 'Provisional Measures of the International Tribunal for the Law of the Sea', P. Chandrasekhara Rao and Rahmatullah Khan (eds.), *The International Tribunal for the Law of the Sea; Law and Practice* 173 (The Hague: Kluwer Law International, 2001).

[67] ITLOS Rep. 1998, at 41.

The next case, which proceeded to an Annex VII arbitration, was *Southern Bluefin Tuna*. Originally two cases, initiated separately by Australia and by New Zealand through notifications submitted to Japan on 15 July 1999 and requests for provisional measures filed in ITLOS on 30 July 1999, ITLOS joined the proceedings and after the required hearings the Order was issued on 27 August. In its submissions, Japan also suggested provisional measures that should be applied by Australia and New Zealand. After a survey of the diplomatic history of the dispute as presented to it and of the proceedings in the Tribunal, ITLOS found that the Annex VII tribunal might have jurisdiction to determine the dispute. Accordingly it prescribed a series of measures to be observed by both parties, pending a decision of the arbitral tribunal. One of those measures required the parties each to ensure that no action was taken which might prejudice the carrying out of any decision on the merits which the arbitral tribunal might render. The Arbitral Tribunal did not interfere with the provisional measures which remained in force until the award was rendered on 4 August 2000, nearly one year later, when they ceased to have further effect. However (as seen in § 6.3 note 25), the Arbitral Tribunal made some important remarks about the long-term consequences of those measures and of the parties' compliance with them, and that laid the basis for renewed negotiations and the final settlement of the dispute between the parties.

The third case in this series was the *MOX Plant* case between Ireland and the United Kingdom, also an Annex VII arbitration.[68] This case concerned the movement of radioactive materials and the protection of the marine environment of the Irish Sea between the two countries. On 9 November Ireland submitted to ITLOS its request for the prescription of provisional measures. The issue was complicated because Ireland had also submitted a similar dispute to arbitration under the 1993 Convention for the Protection of the Marine Environment of the North-East Atlantic (the OSPAR Convention[69]) and that arbitration at the time was pending. The OSPAR arbitration has been completed, but the Annex VII arbitration is pending together with an action in the European Court of Justice, but not before Ireland submitted to the Arbitral Tribunal a request for the prescription of provisional measures, a request granted in part.

The proceedings in ITLOS were curious and do not seem to be in strict conformity with Article 290, paragraph 5, of the Convention. ITLOS found that the provisions invoked by Ireland appeared to afford a basis on which the jurisdiction of the Annex VII arbitral tribunal might be founded (paragraph 61), but that in the circumstances of the case it did not find that the urgency of the situation required the prescription of provisional measures in

[68] For particulars of this complicated litigation, *see* Ch. 3 n. 46.
[69] On that arbitration and the relevant OSPAR Convention, *see* Ch. 3 n. 46.

the short period before the constitution of the Annex VII tribunal (paragraph 81). Nevertheless ITLOS went on to state that the duty to co-operate is a fundamental principle of the prevention of pollution of the marine environment under Part XII (Articles 192 to 247) of the Convention and it prescribed some provisional measures for that. However, it did not include the measure prescribed in the *Southern Bluefin Tuna* case to the effect that the parties should ensure that no action was taken which might prejudice the carrying out of any decision on the merits which the arbitral tribunal might render. Since the OSPAR arbitration has been completed but the Annex VII arbitration proceedings are pending together with those in the European Court of Justice, nothing more about this case can be said at this time.

The fourth case of this character, between Malaysia and Singapore, concerned land reclamation by Singapore in and around the Straits of Johor.[70] This dispute has its roots in the acute land shortage in Singapore, and had been building up over a long period. On 4 July 2003 Malaysia commenced proceedings under Annex VII of the Law of the Sea Convention, informing Singapore of its Statement of Claim under various articles of that Convention. The Statement of Claim also sought provisional measures under Article 290 and proposed that the parties referred that request to ITLOS in accordance with Article 290, paragraph 5. Some inconclusive meetings and exchanges of notes took place after that, and on 4 September 2003 Malaysia instituted provisional measures proceedings in ITLOS. In response, Singapore accepted the jurisdiction of ITLOS as pleaded, and at the same time raised a series of objections to the admissibility of the request. These were not raised as preliminary objections suspending the proceedings on the merits and to be decided before any further proceedings on the merits could take place, but as pleas in bar to be decided before the Tribunal could deal with the merits of the request.[71] Hearings were duly held between 15 and 27 September and on 8 October ITLOS published its Order.

The Tribunal first decided that it must satisfy itself that prima facie the Annex VII tribunal would have jurisdiction. That required it to dispose of the objections to the admissibility of the request. After examining the objections

[70] ITLOS Rep. 2003, 10. This dispute must be distinguished from the dispute between the same countries concerning *Sovereignty over Pedra Branca/Pulau Batu Puteh, Middle Rocks and South Ledge*, submitted to the ICJ by special agreement. ICJ Rep. 2003, 146.

[71] The distinction between preliminary objections incurring the suspension of the merits, and pleas in bar in which the pleadings take their normal course, was first identified by ITLOS in the *Saiga No. 2* (Merits) case, ITLOS Rep. 1999, 10, 33 (para. 53). It has since been formally adopted by the International Court of Justice in the *Avena and other Mexican Nationals* (Merits) case, ICJ Rep. 2004 (para. 24). It had been applied before that, although there have been cases in which after upholding its jurisdiction in preliminary objection proceedings, the Court has been faced with pleas in bar formulated in subsequent proceedings then termed the 'Second Phase' of that case. The two outstanding examples of this are the *South West Africa* (Second Phase) cases, ICJ Rep. 1966, 6 and the *Barcelona Traction, Light and Power Company, Limited* (Second Phase) case, ICJ Rep. 1970, 3.

(paragraphs 37 to 59), the Tribunal found that the Annex VII tribunal would have prima facie jurisdiction over the dispute. That finding enabled ITLOS to proceed to deal with the request for provisional measures. ITLOS did not include the statement customarily employed by the ICJ in orders of this type, that its decision in no way prejudged the question of the Annex VII tribunal's jurisdiction or the admissibility there of the claim, leaving unaffected the right of each party to submit arguments in respect of those questions (the 'without prejudice' clause). This must be regarded as implicit in any order indicating or prescribing provisional measures, and with added force in the case of an order made under Article 290, paragraph 5, of the Law of the Sea Convention.

Turning to the request, ITLOS relied on Article 89, paragraph 5, of the Rules to prescribe measures different in whole or in part from those requested (paragraph 101). The measures thus prescribed related primarily to the establishment and work of a group of independent experts to determine within a period of one year from the date of the Order the effect of Singapore's land reclamation and to propose appropriate measures to deal with any adverse effects of such reclamation. At the same time the Tribunal directed Singapore 'not to conduct its land reclamation in ways that might cause irreparable prejudice to the rights of Malaysia or serious harm to the marine environment, especially taking into account the reports of the group of independent experts'. These measures were to remain in effect pending a decision by the Annex VII arbitral tribunal.

In its reasoning the Tribunal made several important pronouncements, partly procedural and partly substantive. As a matter of substance, for the Tribunal, the existence of a claim to an area of territorial sea is not per se a sufficient basis for the prescription of provisional measures under Article 290, paragraph 5, and for that reason the Tribunal declined to prescribe provisional measures with respect to one aspect of Singapore's land reclamation (paragraph 73). There followed a series of formal undertakings by Singapore which the Tribunal placed on record.[72] The Tribunal did not exclude that in the particular circumstances of the case the land reclamation works might have adverse effects on the marine environment, and that considering the possible implications of land reclamation on the marine environment, prudence and caution required that the two countries establish mechanisms for exchanging information and assessing the risks or effects of land reclamation works and devising ways to deal with them in the areas concerned. The two countries were also enjoined to ensure that no action would be taken that might prejudice the carrying out of any decision on the merits which the Annex VII arbitral tribunal might render.

[72] Above, § 5.3, text to n. 22. For the related procedural pronouncement of ITLOS, *see* text to Ch. 6 n. 3.

This important Order, compliance with which is obligatory on both parties by virtue of Article 290, paragraph 6, of the Convention, is similar in its implications for the land reclamation works to an interim judgment, although it lacks all the characteristics of a *res judicata* and can be amended by the Annex VII arbitral tribunal at any time at the initiative of either of the parties or on the initiative of the arbitral tribunal. It is an illustration of the potential reach of a binding provisional measures order for the maintenance of international legality.

8.9. PROVISIONAL MEASURES AND INTERNATIONAL CRISIS MANAGEMENT

Aside from the complicated legal technicalities that have evolved around the concept of provisional measures of protection and the globalization of international litigation, the accelerated use of this procedure during the last quarter of the twentieth century has pitchforked the Court into the delicate area of crisis management, consonant with its status of a principal organ of the United Nations.[73]

During the last twenty or so years, requests for provisional measures have gone beyond measures required to protect the rights which the requesting party is claiming. The Court has been cautious when faced with far-reaching claims. For instance, it has strongly asserted that it cannot make an order indicating provisional measures addressed to States or entities not parties to the proceedings, or an order that would 'clarify' action required of third States by virtue of decisions of the Security Council.[74] At the same time, in proper cases the provisional measures procedure can be a factor in maintaining or restoring international peace. There is little doubt that the order in the *Anglo-Iranian Oil Co.* case was a factor in defusing tension. In the same way, the order in the *Nicaragua* case, especially its indication that the mining of Nicaraguan ports should cease, is widely seen as a factor in reducing that instance of international tension. In other cases, orders indicating provisional measures have been used to remedy frontier incidents and their tensions in pending cases and to restore the *status quo*, essential if the judicial proceedings are to continue in an appropriately calm atmosphere, and to ensure the preservation of evidence necessary for the trial on the merits of a case. In such instances the Court has been assisted by, or has itself assisted,

[73] The pages that follow are taken from my *Perplexities in Modern International Law* at 76 (Leiden: Martinus Nijhoff, 2004). *See also* Sh. Rosenne, 'A Role for the International Court of Justice in Crisis Management', G. Kreijen (Editor in Chief), *State, Sovereignty, and International Governance* 195 (Oxford: Oxford University Press, 2002).

[74] Above n. 10.

parallel activities by the Security Council or by the competent regional organization.

The situation following the dissolution of Socialist Federal Republic of Yugoslavia provided significant instances of attempts to invoke Court procedures alongside the Security Council and other judicial and arbitral proceedings in a grave crisis in which major use of armed force was characteristic. This first occurred in 1993 when Bosnia and Herzegovina brought the *Application of the Genocide Convention* case against Yugoslavia and simultaneously requested provisional measures.[75] Bosnia claimed that the Court should reinterpret Security Council resolution 713 (1991), 25 September 1991, which had imposed an arms embargo on all the territories of the former Socialist Federal Republic of Yugoslavia. That the Court refused to do, because had it done this without the consent of the Security Council, it would have immediately thrown itself into direct confrontation with the Security Council with no apparent advantage to anyone.

The best-known, and probably the most controversial, of these cases are the two *Lockerbie* cases brought by Libya against the United Kingdom and the United States.[76] Here the Court accepted that its ability to indicate provisional measures was trumped by a Security Council resolution under Chapter VII of the Charter. To put this in perspective, however, it should be kept in mind that it was widely assumed that the real purpose of that request for provisional measures was to forestall Chapter VII action by the Security Council which was already itself seised of the situation. In its Judgments on preliminary objections, the Court also kept open the issue whether the relevant Security Council resolutions allowed it to deal with the merits of the cases, while at the same time deciding that they did not affect its jurisdiction to deal with the merits.[77] On occasion a carefully worded refusal by the Court to indicate provisional measures has laid a basis for satisfactory negotiations to settle the dispute, or prevent it from growing more serious.[78]

The ten *Legality of Use of Force* cases brought by Yugoslavia in April 1999 against NATO members are the boldest attempt to involve the Court in crisis management. Yugoslavia requested provisional measures to stop the NATO bombing of Serbia, invoking (among others) as a title of jurisdiction the compromissory clause (Article IX) of the Genocide Convention and, where appropriate, declarations accepting the compulsory jurisdiction. Yugoslavia's major difficulty, which it could not overcome, was that the absence of jurisdiction was manifest as regards the principal respondent, the United

[75] Ibid.

[76] *Questions of Interpretation and Application of the 1971 Montreal Convention arising from the Aerial Incident at Lockerbie* (Provisional Measures), ICJ Rep. 1992, 3 (U.K.), 114 (U.S.A.).

[77] (Preliminary Objections), ICJ Rep. 1998, 9, 26 (para. 46) (U.K.); 115, 131 (para. 45) (U.S.A.). And cf. operative paras. 2(a) and 3 of each Judgment.

[78] A classic illustration of this is the *Passage through the Great Belt* case, ICJ Rep. 1991, 12.

States of America (and as it turned out, also as regards Spain). The Court had no choice but to remove those two cases from its list. In the other eight cases, applying the test of prima facie jurisdiction over the merits, the Court found that although it might have jurisdiction, it could not indicate provisional measures (which in the circumstances would have been useless in any event) because it did not find that the circumstances brought to its notice came within the scope of the Genocide Convention or Yugoslavia's acceptance of the compulsory jurisdiction. However, in all those orders, including those in the cases against Spain and the United States, the Court included three paragraphs in which it gave expression to its views on the legal duties of all the parties in the situation.[79] Significantly, there is no mention of the 'essential parties' rule in any of the remaining eight cases, notwithstanding the exclusion of the case against the United States from the Court's docket. This issue was to come up in the preliminary objection phase in 2004.

Those cases show several things. They indicate that a State is prepared in very special circumstances to invoke Court procedures, especially its power to indicate provisional measures of protection, even if it has only a slender chance of establishing prima facie jurisdiction over the merits. On the other hand, the Court, while taking up these cases, has shown itself careful not to trespass on the authority of the Security Council to deal with a crisis situation involving the use of armed force if to do so would exceed the judicial function in the particular case. At the same time the Court will not hesitate to act even if the general situation is on the active agenda of the Security Council, provided that it is satisfied that its action comes within the judicial competence in that case. This is emphasized by the last case in this series, the *Armed Activities on the Territory of the Congo* (*Congo* v *Uganda*) case, where the Court indicated as provisional measures virtually the same measures as had been ordered by the Security Council under Chapter VII of the Charter a few days earlier in its resolution 1304 (2000), 16 June 2000.[80]

At the same time, as Judge Treves (of ITLOS) has observed,

> Sometimes one has the impression that the real objective of the applicant is to bring to the Court a request for provisional measures, rather than institute proceedings in the Court. The previous institution of proceedings is often seen only as a legally necessary prerequisite for requesting provisional measures.[81]

[79] *Legality of Use of Force* cases, *see* Ch. 4 text to n. 65.

[80] ICJ Rep. 2000, 111. It appears that the Congo attempted to obtain from the Court measures that the Security Council had not ordered. *See* the statement of Mr Reichler for Uganda in CR2000/20, 26 June 2000 at 27; and *see* the striking opinion of Judge Oda, who doubted if this was a genuine case.

[81] 'The Political Use of Unilateral Applications and Provisional Measures Proceedings', J. A. Frowein *et al.* (eds.), *Verhandeln für den Frieden/Negotiating for Peace: Lieber Amicorum Tono Eitel* 463, 466 (Berlin: Springer, 2002); Christine Gray, 'The Use and Abuse of the International Court of Justice: Cases concerning the use of force after Nicaragua', 14 *European J. Int'l* L. 867 (2003). While this impression is certainly justified, no concrete examples are given of cases in

The implication of that remark is that the institution of proceedings with the sole intention of making a request for provisional measures, with the political excitement and publicity that such a step can provoke in the news-hungry written and electronic media, is abusive of the Court and an action in bad faith. There is certainly truth in that. In one sense, the relatively low threshold of prima facie direction over the merits as sufficient for the indication of provisional measures is tempting. However, it is matched by a high threshold of urgency in relation to the main claim of the application, and that can protect the Court from this kind of activity, should it be encountered. For its part, the Court has been cautious before attributing to an applicant State bad faith or an abuse of the Court. The *Certain Phosphate Lands in Nauru* (Preliminary Objections) case is a good illustration of this:

> 38. The Court considers that the Application by Nauru has been properly submitted in the framework of the remedies open to it. At the present stage, the Court is not called upon to weigh the possible consequences of the conduct of Nauru with respect to the merits of the case. It need merely note that such conduct does not amount to an abuse of process.[82]

At the same time the Court has shown, for instance in the *Maritime Delimitation and Territorial Questions between Qatar and Bahrain* case, that it is fully capable of devising appropriate procedures in the event of any questionable litigation tactic by any party to litigation before it.[83] Treves has also suggested that what is termed *obiter dicta*, meaning those general statements outlining major legal issues in the case, should be employed with restraint, especially in cases in which provisional measures are not granted for lack of prima facie jurisdiction. Restraint and careful crafting of the judicial pronouncement are certainly necessary. But the real test for the Court in considering whether to include such general statements in any order on provisional measures or in any other judicial pronouncement is whether the statement is likely to contribute to the peaceful settlement of the dispute. In the *Passage through the Great Belt* (Provisional Measures) case, the Court recalled the well-known observation of the Permanent Court that the judicial settlement of international disputes, with a view to which the Court has been established, is simply an alternative to the direct and friendly settlement of such disputes between the parties, and that in consequence it is for the Court to facilitate, so far as is compatible with its Statute, such direct and friendly

which, provisional measures not having been granted, the applicant has discontinued the proceedings. The outstanding instance to the contrary is Yugoslavia's insistence on continuing the eight NATO cases, notwithstanding that in the provisional measures proceedings the Court quite clearly found nothing to suggest that it might have prima facie jurisdiction over the merit. On these cases, *see* Ch 4. n. 69.

[82] ICJ Rep. 1992, 240, 255 (para. 38).

[83] ICJ Rep. 2001, 40, 46 (paras. 14 to 23) and the Orders cited therein.

settlement.[84] That is all the more justification for this type of dictum by one of the principal organs of the United Nations and its principal judicial organ.

Although the requirement of prima facie mainline jurisdiction is a low threshold, the Yugoslavia cases of 1999 demonstrate that even that low threshold must be reached before the Court will entertain the requests. Of the cases in the ICJ examined in this context, the finding of prima facie jurisdiction was later upheld in preliminary objection proceedings except in the *Anglo-Iranian Oil Co.* case. That was the only instance in which the Court was to find that it had no jurisdiction over the merits. Even there, however, it formally stated that the order indicating the provisional measures only ceased to be operative upon the delivery of the Judgment finding that the Court was without jurisdiction in the case.[85]

8.10. SOME CONCLUSIONS

We can now see that the International Court of Justice has mobilized its power to indicate provisional measures in situations of dire emergency to protect human rights and, when there are armed hostilities, the observance of the international humanitarian law and to assist in the restoration of peace. This function, inherent in the establishment of the International Court of Justice as a principal organ of the United Nations (and not merely its principal judicial organ, giving it a hierarchical standing in relation to other courts and tribunals established or to be established by or under the auspices of the United Nations or otherwise), has become more prominent with the end of the tensions provoked by the Cold War. States, especially new States, are showing increasing willingness to establish and if necessary enforce or reinforce their legal rights through judicial procedures, especially through the International Court. It is in this respect that the Court's power to indicate binding provisional measures is slowly bringing the Court into the general context of the international mechanisms for the maintenance and restoration of international peace and security, in cases and situations in which an authoritative resolution of legal issues is accepted as a relevant factor for the resolution of the dispute.

The principal element distinguishing provisional measures proceedings from other incidental proceedings is that the jurisdiction of the competent court, tribunal or arbitral tribunal, whether standing or ad hoc, is relaxed in

[84] ICJ Rep. 1991, 12, 20 (para. 35) quoting the *Free Zones of Upper Savoy and the District of Gex* case, PCIJ Ser. A 22 (1929) 13, and Judgment of the Chamber in the *Frontier Dispute* (Burkina Faso/Mali) case, ICJ Rep. 1986, 554, 577 (para. 46).

[85] In the *Interhandel* case the Court held that it had prima facie jurisdiction to indicate provisional measures but that in the circumstances found that there was no need for it to do so. Later it found that the claim was inadmissible. ICJ Rep. 1957, 157; 1959, 3.

comparison with the jurisdiction to entertain the main case, while being conditioned by other factors. The threshold of prima facie jurisdiction to determine the merits is easily reached, but it must be reached, and if the proceedings for provisional measures bring out that the absence of jurisdiction over the merits is manifest, that will be the end of the matter. The judicial organ seised with a request for provisional measures only has to be satisfied that the jurisdiction to entertain the principal case is established prima facie. This relaxed jurisdiction is matched by a more stringent control over the element of urgency and its relation to the anticipated harm likely to result if provisional measures are not granted. Provisional measures are an exceptional remedy in international litigation, and should only be granted if the court or tribunal seised of the request is satisfied that the urgency of the circumstances justifies the granting of the request. This is a matter of fact and of appreciation by the organ seised of the request and it is not given to any systematic analysis or presentation.

There are two main classes of cases in which provisional measures might be required. The first is the original conception of the early part of the twentieth century, namely measures needed to preserve the *status quo*, to restore appropriated objects the aim of the litigation, and to preserve evidence, and to this is added the restoration of calmness in the relations of the litigating States. The second class is where the claim in the principal litigation relates to the actual or potential rights of the parties, whether to territory or some other right recognized by international law. Here, if the litigation is not directly related to a given incident, whether or not involving the use of armed force, the issue of the nature and extent of the right may well not meet the requirement of urgency and irreparability. In those cases, the International Court has been careful in preserving the issue of principle, namely whether those rights might be the subject of provisional measures, while finding that the circumstances do not justify the indication of provisional measures. This differentiation is consonant with the exceptional character of the provisional protection of rights in international law, and is rendered even more necessary when there is no doubt as to the obligation of the parties to comply with any order granting provisional protection pending the final decision of the competent court or tribunal in the case.

Both the ICJ and ITLOS regularly grant provisional measures that are different from what a party has requested. While express power to do this is included in the respective Rules of Court or of the Tribunal, it is inherent in judicial power that the court or tribunal authorized to deal with a case is free to reach whatever decision commends itself in all the circumstances, provided that in doing so it does not exceed its jurisdiction or go beyond the *ne ultra petitum* rule. In the case of provisional measures of protection, this formal provision has led to the common practice of ordering provisional measures to be observed mutually by both parties. This does not exclude an order addressed to one or other party only, when the claim itself is addressed to action claimed to be due from the respondent. In line with this, the generalized wording of Article 41 of the ICJ Statute and its parallel, Article 290, paragraph 1, of the Law of the Sea Convention, allow a party to the litigation which is contesting the principal jurisdiction itself to make a claim for provisional measures to be observed by its opponent, without it being taken to have accepted the principal jurisdiction of the Court through the doctrine of the *forum prorogatum*. This is another illustration of the completely autonomous nature of provisional measures proceedings in international litigation.

Reviewing the general history of the development of rules regarding provisional measures, Elkind has written:

> What we observe from this history is that provisional measures are regarded as an important part of the international dispute settlement process whether that settlement involves the submission of a dispute to a judicial or to a political organ. Thus we see that interim protection has an additional function in international law, that of helping to keep the peace.[86]

The President of the Court, Judge Shi, in his statement in the fifty-eighth session of the General Assembly at its fiftieth meeting, on 31 October 2003, said this:[87]

> I would like to stress the fact that both Judgments and orders indicting provisional measures made by the Court are binding on the parties. For it is indeed this binding nature of its decisions which lies at the heart of the Court's mission to solve legal disputes between States and is the necessary condition for the successful achievement of that mission. Under Article 94, paragraph 1, of the Charter, each Member of the United Nations undertakes to comply with the decision of the International Court of Justice in any case to which it is a party. Article 60 of the Statute of the Court adds that Judgments of the Court are final and without appeal. The binding effect of orders indicting provisional measures under Article 41 of the Statute of the Court has recently been confirmed by the Judgment rendered by the Court in the *LaGrand* case. The Court has no doubt, therefore, that parties to litigation before it will continue to implement its decisions, as they have one in the past.

He concluded that address with the following words:

> While the International Court of Justice carries out its work in the tranquil setting of The Hague—far from the hustle and bustle of Headquarters in New York—its activities contribute in a very direct way to the overall aims and objectives of the

[86] J. B. Elkind, *Interim Protection: A Functional Approach* 50 (The Hague: Martinus Nijhoff, 1981). I have reservations over placing judicial and political settlement of international disputes on the same footing. They are entirely different processes, governed by entirely different sets of criteria and rules. The concept of *lis pendens* does not and cannot apply as between the two sets of process.

[87] A/58/PV.50, 4. Also on the Court's website.

United Nations. The Court's potential in that regard is apparent in the wide-ranging impact its work already has on the international community. In particular, the role that the Court plays—through the power of justice and international law—in resolving disputes between States is widely recognized and evidenced by the number of cases on the Court's docket. Furthermore, it is not uncommon that these cases deal directly with issues concerning international peace and security.

The Court's work in the sphere of provisional measures of protection, as it has developed from its cautious beginnings at the start of the existence of the Permanent Court in 1927, is probably the most significant of the Court's activities for the settlement of international disputes and the maintenance of international peace and security, the prime objective of the United Nations of which the Court is a principal organ.

Appendix
Orders on Provisional Measures

Cases marked with an asterisk (*) are pending at the time of writing. In cases marked with a degree sign (°), provisional measures were granted

The Permanent Court of International Justice and the International Court of Justice

1927

Denunciation of the Treaty of November 2nd, 1865, between China and Belgium, A 8, 6°
Application including request filed on 25 November 1926, no hearing, Order made on 8 January 1927.
Chorzów Factory (Indemnities) (Germany *v* Poland), A 12
Application filed on 8 February 1927, request filed on 14 October 1927, no hearing, Order made on 21 November 1927.

1932

Legal Status of the South-Eastern Territory of Greenland (Norway *v* Denmark, Denmark *v* Norway), A/B 48, 277
Applications filed on 18 July 1932, Norway's application including request, hearings on 28 July 1932, Order made on 3 August 1932.

1933

Administration of the Prince von Pless (Germany *v* Poland), A/B 54, 150
Application filed on 18 May 1932, request filed on 2 May 1933, no hearing, Order made on 11 May 1933.
Polish Agrarian Reform and the German Minority (Germany *v* Poland), A/B 58, 175
Application and request filed on 3 July 1933, hearings on 11 July 1933, Order made on 29 July 1933.

1939

Electricity Company of Bulgaria and Sofia (Belgium *v* Bulgaria), A/B 79°
Application filed on 26 January 1938, request filed on 4 October 1939, hearings on 4 December 1939, Order made on 5 December 1939.

1951

Anglo-Iranian Oil Co. (U.K. *v* Iran), ICJ Rep. 1951, 89°
Application filed on 26 May 1951, request filed on 22 June 1951, hearings on 30 June 1951, Order made on 5 July 1951.

1957

Interhandel (Switzerland *v* U.S.A.), ICJ Rep. 1957, 105
Application filed on 2 October 1957, request filed on 3 October 1957, hearings on 12–14 October 1957, Order made on 24 October 1957.

1972

Fisheries Jurisdiction (U.K. *v* Iceland), ICJ Rep. 1972, 12° (under the Rules of 1946)
Fisheries Jurisdiction (FRG *v* Iceland), ICJ Rep. 1972, 49° (under the Rules of 1946)
Paired cases. Applications filed on 14 April and 5 June 1972, requests filed on 19 and 21 July 1972, hearings on 1–2 August 1972, Orders made on 17 August 1972.

1973

Nuclear Tests (Australia *v* France), ICJ Rep. 1973, 99°
Nuclear Tests (New Zealand *v* France), ICJ Rep. 1973, 135°
Paired cases. Applications and requests filed on 9 May 1973, hearings on 21–25 May 1973, Orders made on 22 June 1973.
Fisheries Jurisdiction (U.K. *v* Iceland), ICJ Rep. 1973, 302° (under the Rules of 1946)
Fisheries Jurisdiction (FRG *v* Iceland), ICJ Rep. 1973, 313° (under the Rules of 1946)
Paired cases. Requests made on 22 June 1973, no hearings, Orders made on 12 July 1973.
Trial of Pakistani Prisoners of War (Pakistan *v* India), ICJ Rep. 1973, 328
Application and request filed on 11 May 1973, hearings on 4, 5, and 26 June 1973, Order made on 13 July 1973.

1976

Aegean Sea Continental Shelf (Greece *v* Turkey), ICJ Rep. 1976, 3
Application and request filed on 10 August 1976, hearings on 25–27 August 1976, Order made on 11 September 1976.

1979

U.S. Diplomatic and Consular Staff in Tehran (U.S.A. *v* Iran), ICJ Rep. 1979, 7°
Application and request filed on 29 November 1979, hearings on 10 December 1979, Order made on 15 December 1979.

1984

Military and Paramilitary Activities in and against Nicaragua (Nicaragua *v* U.S.A.), ICJ Rep. 1984, 169°
Application and request filed on 9 April 1984, hearings on 25–27 April 1984, Order made on 10 May 1984.
—Second application, see Judgment on the merits, ICJ Rep. 1986, 14, 144 (para. 282).

1986

Frontier Dispute (Burkina Faso/Mali), ICJ Rep. 1986, 3°
Special agreement filed on 20 October 1983, requests by both parties notified to the Chamber on 30 December 1985, hearings on 9 January 1986, Order made on 10 January 1986.

1988

Border and Transborder Armed Actions (Nicaragua *v* Honduras), ICJ Rep. 1988, 9 (withdrawn)

1990

Arbitral Award of 31 July 1989 (Guinea-Bissau *v* Senegal), ICJ Rep. 1990, 64
Application filed on 23 August 1989, request filed on 18 January 1990, hearing on 12 February 1990, Order made on 2 March 1990.

1991

Passage through the Great Belt (Finland *v* Denmark), ICJ Rep. 1991, 12
Application filed on 17 May 1991, request filed on 23 May 1991, hearings on 1–5 July 1991, Order made on 29 July 1991.

1992

Questions of Interpretation and Application of the 1971 Montreal Convention arising from the Aerial Incident at Lockerbie (Libya *v* U.K.), ICJ Rep. 1992, 3°
Questions of Interpretation and Application of the 1971 Montreal Convention arising from the Aerial Incident at Lockerbie (Libya *v* U.S.A.), ICJ Rep. 1992, 114°
Paired cases. Applications and requests filed on 3 March 1992, hearings on 26–28 March 1992, Orders made on 14 April 1992.

1993

Application of the Convention on the Prevention and Punishment of the Crime of Genocide (Bosnia & Herzegovina *v* Yugoslavia), ICJ Rep. 1993, 3*°
Application and request filed on 20 March 1993, hearings on 1–2 April 1993, Order made on 8 April 1993.
—(Further provisional measures), ICJ Rep. 1993, 325*°
Request filed on 27 July 1993, hearings on 25–26 August 1993, Order made on 13 September 1993.

1995

Request for an Examination of the Situation in Accordance with Paragraph 61 of the Court's Judgment of 20 December 1974 in the Nuclear Tests (New Zealand *v* France) case, ICJ Rep. 1995, 288 (under the Rules of 1978)
Proceedings instituted on 21 August 1995, hearings on 11–12 September 1995, Order made on 22 September 1995.

1996

Land and Maritime Boundary between Cameroon and Nigeria, ICJ Rep. 1996 (I), 13°
Application filed on 29 March 1994, request filed on 10 February 1996, hearings on 5–8 March 1996, Order made on 15 March 1996.

1998

Vienna Convention on Consular Relations (Paraguay *v* U.S.A.), ICJ Rep. 1998, 248°
Application and request filed on 3 April 1996, hearings on 7 April 1998, Order made on 9 April 1998.

1999

LaGrand (Germany *v* U.S.A.), ICJ Rep. 1999, 9°
Application and request filed on 2 March 1999, no hearing, Order made on 3 March 1999.

Legality of Use of Force *, ten linked cases by Yugoslavia against the following:
- Belgium, ICJ Rep. 1999, 124*
- Canada, ICJ Rep. 1999, 299*
- France, ICJ Rep. 1999, 363*
- Germany, ICJ Rep. 1999, 422*
- Italy, ICJ Rep. 1999, 481*
- Netherlands, ICJ Rep. 1999, 542*
- Portugal, ICJ Rep. 1999, 656*
- Spain, ICJ Rep. 1999, 761
- U.K., ICJ Rep. 1999, 826*
- U.S.A., ICJ Rep. 1999, 916

Applications and requests filed on 29 April 1999, hearings on 10–12 May 1999, Orders made on 2 June 1999.

2000

Armed Activities on the Territory of the Congo (Congo *v* Uganda), ICJ Rep. 2000, 111*°
Application and request filed on 23 June 2000, hearings on 26–28 June 2000, Order made on 1 July 2000.

Arrest Warrant of 11 April 2000 (Congo *v* Belgium), ICJ Rep. 2000, 182
Application and request filed on 17 October 2000, hearings on 20–23 November 2000, Order made on 8 December 2000.

2002

Armed Activities on the Territory of the Congo (New Application: 2002) (Congo *v* Rwanda), ICJ Rep. 2002, 219*
Application and request filed on 28 May 2002, hearings on 13–14 June 2002, Order made on 10 July 2002.

2003

Avena and other Mexican Nationals (Mexico *v* U.S.A.), ICJ Rep. 2003, 5 February°

Application and request filed on 9 January 2003, hearings on 21 January 2003, Order made on 77 2003.

Certain Criminal Proceedings in France (Congo *v* France), ICJ Rep. 2003, 102*
Application and request filed on 9 December 2002, case entered on General List on 11 April 2003, hearings on 28–29 April 2003, Order made on 17 June 2003.

The International Tribunal for the Law of the Sea

1998

The M.V. Saiga No. 2 Case (St Vincent and the Grenadines *v* Guinea), ITLOS Rep. 1998, 24°
Notification under Annex VII made on 22 December 1997, request to ITLOS filed on 13 January 1998, case transferred to ITLOS on 20 February 1998, hearings on 23–24 February 1998, Order made on 11 March 1998.

1999

Southern Bluefin Tuna (Australia & New Zealand *v* Japan), ITLOS Rep. 1999, 280°
Joined cases. Notifications under Annex VII made on 15 July 1999, requests to ITLOS filed on 30 June 1999, hearings on 18–20 August 1999, Order made on 27 August 1999.

2001

MOX Plant Case (Ireland *v* U.K.), ITLOS Rep. 2001, 95°
Notification under Annex VII made on 25 October 2001, request to ITLOS filed on 9 November 2001, hearings on 19–20 November 2001, Order made on 3 December 2001.

2003

Land Reclamation by Singapore in and around the Straits of Johor (Malaysia *v* Singapore), 8 October 2003°
Notification under Annex VII made on 4 July 2003, request to ITLOS made on 5 September 2003, hearings on 25–27 September 2003, Order made on 8 October 2003.

Subject Index